AN AMERICAN BIBLE

Edited by

ALICE HUBBARD

Published by

THE ROYCROFTERS

EAST AURORA
NEW YORK

AN AMERICAN BIBLE

Edited by

ALICE HUBBARD

Published by

THE ROYCROFTERS

EAST AURORA
NEW YORK

ISBN 978-1-4341-0466-3

Published by Waking Lion Press, an imprint of the Editorium.
Originally published in 1911 by the Roycrofters in Aurora, New York.

Waking Lion Press™ and Editorium™ are trademarks of:

The Editorium, LLC
West Jordan, UT 84081-6132
www.editorium.com

Contents

FOREWORD

Foreword

I N courts of law, the phrase " I believe " has no standing. Never a witness gives testimony but that he is cautioned thus, " Tell us what you know, not what you believe."

In theology, belief has always been regarded as more important than that which your senses say is so.

Almost without exception, " belief " is a legacy, an importation—something borrowed, an echo, and often an echo of an echo.

The Creed of the Future will begin, " I know," not, " I believe." And this creed will not be forced upon the people.

It will carry with it no coercion, no blackmail, no promise of an eternal life of idleness and ease if you accept it, and no threat of hell if you don't.

It will have no paid, professional priesthood, claiming honors, rebates and exemptions, nor will it hold estates free from taxation. It will not organize itself into a system, marry itself to the State, and call on the police for support. It will be so reasonable, so in the line of self-preservation, that no sane man or woman will reject it, and when we really begin to live it we will cease to talk about it.

As a suggestion and first rough draft, we submit this.

I KNOW:

That I am here

In a world where nothing is permanent but change,

❡ And that in degree I, myself, can change the form of things

❡ And influence a few people;

❡ And that I am influenced by these and other people;

❡ That I am influenced by the example and by the work of men who are no longer alive,

❡ And that the work I now do will in degree influence people who may live after my life has changed into other forms;

❡ That a certain attitude of mind and habit of action on my part will add to the peace, happiness and well-being of other people,

❡ And that a different thought and action on my part will bring pain and discord to others;

❡ That if I would secure reasonable happiness for myself, I must give out good-will to others;

❡ That to better my own condition I must practise mutuality;

❡ That bodily health is necessary to continued and effective work;

❡ That I am ruled largely by habit;

❡ That habit is a form of exercise;

❡ That up to a certain point, exercise means increased strength or ease in effort;

❡ That all life is the expression of spirit;

❡ That my spirit influences my body,

❡ And my body influences my spirit;

❡ That the universe to me is very beautiful, and everything and everybody in it good and beautiful, when my body and my spirit are in harmonious mood;

❡ That my thoughts are hopeful and helpful unless I am filled with fear,

❡ And that to eliminate fear my life must be dedicated to useful work—work in which I forget myself;

❡ That fresh air in abundance, and moderate, systematic exercise in the open air are the part of wisdom;

❡ That I can not afford, for my own sake, to be resentful nor quick to take offense;

❡ That happiness is a great power for good,

❡ And that happiness is not possible without moderation and equanimity;

❡ That time turns all discords into harmony if men will but be kind and patient,

❡ And that the reward which life holds out for work is not idleness nor rest, nor immunity from work, but increased capacity, GREATER DIFFICULTIES, MORE WORK

—*ELBERT HUBBARD*

INTRODUCTION

As the years go by, there will be constructed other bibles and better bibles.—*Alice Hubbard.*

Introduction

HE word *bible* means "book." Once the world had, practically, but one book. Until a century ago books were few and they were costly

Only wealthy people could own them. Not many people could read and write.

Books were written painstakingly by learned men; and any man who could read and write was looked upon as educated.

Naturally, when a book was made, there was a desire to put into it all the wisdom the writer could gather together. Long years were required to make one copy of the Old and the New Testament, and the book was very precious. The men who worked upon it were set apart for this sacred task. Reverence for the man and his work increased as he continued to give his life for it

Then, too, he who could read possessed secrets which ordinary men could not know. In England, a few hundred years ago, a man was exempt from punishment if he could read and write. Often the judges who tried the prisoner could do neither.

Superstition has ever been a strong factor in influencing the actions of people. It has been the strongest force in attracting man to a particular religious belief. The book which was accepted by people in authority as containing the most wisdom was the most holy book and became The Book, or the Bible. A king appointed a committee to decide upon what was holy in it. The Bible of the Hebrews and of the Christians is now only one of many books that contain wisdom and good counsel.

American people who live on the fortieth parallel, in the Twentieth Century, need a book—many books —of truth, for truth is relative, not fixed or static. This book, which we call *An American Bible*, is for people on this continent. '

❡ This American Bible is fitted to the needs of men and women now on earth, and the hope is that it will help them to live—we can die without assistance. Any one may accept or reject it, may add to it or subtract from it

As the years go by, there will be constructed other bibles and better bibles

---

MERICAN people have distinct needs. They think, and have a thinking, unfolding world with which to deal

There have been no new religions since religions were new; but in Seventeen Hundred Seventy-six there began to grow an American religion —not a religion of gods, but a religion for men And in Eighteen Hundred Seventy-six there began to grow the religion which is for all women and all men. Americans need a practical bible which will inspire them for their day's work. We need a bible that shall give us facts concerning business principles, acceptable and honorable—principles that apply to new methods, new morals, new needs. We need a bible that shall teach us to be well, and how to keep well; that will inspire us to obey the common laws of health; that will teach us how to exercise, work, play, think; how to breathe and to eat. We need instruction in the democracy of man's own self, the family, the town, the State, the general government. Europeans say that America has no poor. Americans want to make this literally true. America demands that man shall be economically free, and she gives the opportunity. So the American Bible must treat of Economics —the highest science man has yet discovered This bible must teach the philosophy of business and show how it benefits man.

❡ It must show, too, the beauty and poetry of business, as well as that it is the means by which man has evolved. The American Bible must show us that

life is very simple, and that all the beauty and luxury
we can use, all of anything and everything we can use,
is right at hand. It must be a book that does not
require a priesthood to explain and expound. It must
be a book that appeals to commonsense, and one
that requires neither apology nor defense

It will teach us that to eat more than the body uses
brings disease and then death—also, that to read and
study and not use the knowledge brings auto-intoxi-
cation or ankylosis. This American Bible will teach
us that every energy of man was made to use, and
that death follows disuse and misuse.

It will teach the practical application of the Golden
Rule; that women were born free and equal with men
in every and all natural right; that woman has every
right, as has man, to life, liberty and happiness

This American Bible must be simple and practical,
in order to meet the needs of Americans, who are
essentially a plain, practical, upright, progressive,
evolving people, intent on obeying the divine law of
self-preservation. For these reasons, we have selected
practical truth concerning every-day life, from the
writings of eight Americans

BENJAMIN FRANKLIN was the man of
energy, the typical American, one of the
few educated men of all history

He was the youngest son of Josiah and Abiah
Franklin, and one of a family of seventeen children.
His father was a poor candlemaker and soap-boiler of
Boston

Benjamin Franklin became a businessman, a financier,
an inventor, a philosopher, a statesman, a diplomat—
a man of affairs.

He lived obedient to the simple rules that bring to
man the best results in liberty and happiness. He
made his own opportunities!

He started with the capital of health, good-will,

determination to win success, and an energy which never flagged. And be it said to his credit as a teacher, he kept this capital to the end of his life. In business he laid well the foundation for every man's success —economic independence. When he had all the experience he wanted in business, and had money besides, he gave his time and energy to public interests. He founded the first public library in America. While he was Postmaster-General for the Colonies, he founded our postal system. He established the University of Pennsylvania. It was he who first demonstrated that lightning and electricity are the same

America needed him to represent her in Europe, and he went. He was statesman, diplomat, financier, for a new nation and a people in trouble. He was always a philosopher, and he was ever a student. He had the " four habits " which are necessary to develop Americans : the health habit, the work habit, the study habit, the play habit. He was a cultured gentleman, at home with any class of people. His society was sought in the court of France, and he was welcomed in the most popular salons of Paris.

So great was he in personality that he could set the fashion of homespun, Deborah-made clothes

Franklin indeed was always the honest, simple, democratic, American gentleman, who loved truth above all else

He believed that for man to develop his body, his brain, his sense of beauty and refinement, was the best use to which he could give his life.

He knew various countries, all peoples, all types of men and women, therefore he knew Americans as few Americans could

He knew the principles upon which this country is founded. Deep in his heart he held noble ideals. The intent of his writings is to teach and to inspire us to live with these sentiments clearly before us

HOMAS JEFFERSON, democrat—framer of the Declaration of Independence—lawyer, educator, diplomat, stands side by side with Franklin. Jefferson taught a nation to love to govern itself. He showed that the purpose of government is to benefit the people. Our government was instituted for the people, by the people, and those who hold office are to be of the people.

The young Republic made this man President of the United States. He rode to the Capitol building alone, on horseback; tied his horse; went in and took the oath of office as a private citizen assuming a great and grave responsibility

Thomas Jefferson established no court at Washington. He did not ape and imitate nobility. There was only one nobility he recognized, and that was the nobility of character. He lived his simple life there, and his business was to work for the people.

Thomas Jefferson was a Democrat, and he believed in political and natural equality as opposed to aristocracy

He had prescience. He was so great that he saw that the days of conquest were passing, and he took the initial step in modern business when he made the Louisiana Purchase. This is the greatest act of his entire life

He saw that the day would dawn when the religion of our mothers would not be good enough for us, because he knew we are an evolving race; that freedom of thought is necessary to freedom of action. So he laid the foundation for separation of Church and School, Church and State. We have not yet recognized that one structure is independent of the other. There is an underground connection between Church and School—a sort of subway. And the country still feels a little safer if a candidate for political office " goes to church."

Yet there is no wall nor roof holding them together.

They are fundamentally free, because Thomas Jefferson knew that they must be free

The man who wrote the Declaration of Independence put the thought of human rights forever before the world. In Seventeen Hundred Seventy-six it made all tyrants tremble; today they know that death to tyranny is near, even at the door.

The Declaration of Independence was the announcement of the new birth of the world. Thomas Jefferson laid a foundation for Democracy for all nations Democracy amalgamates the classes of master and slave, rich and poor, patrician and plebeian, for Democracy is a recognition of monism—" ye are all brethren."

Thomas Jefferson, the man of culture of refinement, the lover, the husband, the father, lived the life he taught. This country would do well to catch up with Thomas Jefferson

HOMAS PAINE, the patriot, lover of liberty, American in spirit, taught the world that liberty is the natural right of every human being. He loved freedom for himself, but he could not enjoy what was not within the reach of all. " Where liberty is, there is my home," said Jefferson. " Where liberty is not, there is my home," said Paine. His work was to make all men long for their birthright

He came to America when this country needed a great brain to formulate into an argument a divine feeling which American men and women could not express for themselves. He wrote his thoughts in clear, limpid English which he who read could understand. He printed and distributed at his own expense many thousands of pamphlets because he wanted the people to know that in Seventeen Hundred Seventy-six there was an opportunity to give to mankind its birthright—freedom. He knew it would take many years for man to be born free, because man is entangled and enmeshed in a network of bondage. Superstitions, fears, barbaric instincts are still man's inheritance. A free man—the superman—is as yet only a hope and a beautiful dream. But it is a dream which shall yet come true

Thomas Paine was a great factor in giving to us thoughts which are growing. The result must be a nation where men may be born with their divine birthright of Liberty.

England, France and America were made more noble, more intelligent, more civilized by the work he did for each country and for all countries. No nation of the world has forgotten Paine, and certainly no religious sect has. He wrote of the rights of man when men believed that only gods had rights. At best, men had only privileges. Today we dare to affirm that women as well as men have rights. Paine was the pioneer of this thought. The " Rights of Man " will never die so long as men have rights.

He believed that even in his time man was passing from the age when man's actions were the result of his passions; that man was leaving the confines of the dominion of animals, and that the age of reason was here, even at the door

Paine was a Quaker by birth and a friend by nature. The world was his home, mankind were his friends, to do good was his religion

⌐⌐

ABRAHAM LINCOLN, liberator of men, man of the people ! He was so wise that he knew there was no freedom for any man while any man was a slave

There is no one in history with whom to compare Lincoln. He was a unique figure. His work was unique and individual. He saved the people from themselves. America was in great peril. When the North hated the South and the South hated the North—bitter foes—Lincoln was counselor for the whole country. He was neither Confederate nor Federal. He was foe to no man. He was the friend to all and to each—the savior of his country.

No man then knew better than did Lincoln the worth to civilization of this Republic. He knew how precious was the life of this form of government, and his whole desire was to preserve it.

❡ It is easy to act when judgment says, " This side is right and that side wrong." Lincoln knew that both the North and the South were right and wrong. He had to deal with that hydra-headed monster, the people. The multitude must be educated, made to see that others had rights, even when these others were wrong.

❡ But Lincoln's work was not to teach. He must act. Preachers, teachers, lecturers, even private citizens, harangued, stormed, became embittered. It was a time when feeling, not judgment, was in the saddle and riding mankind.

Editors of newspapers and magazines praised, blamed and denounced this great executive. He stopped for none of this. He had no personal griefs, although invectives were hurled at him. Out of this chaos and turmoil, he created, set in order, brought peace, and saved the country from the ruin which threatened.

❡ No man today doubts the honesty of the heart of this great man, and few doubt the wisdom of his acts. Time has vindicated his deeds.

❡ He charmed men by his integrity and his nobility of soul.

He believed in the common people, and knew that eventually they would see the right. He was willing to wait for them to see for themselves, and to let time adjust men to conditions inevitable.

Lincoln was a child of Nature, so close to the source of wisdom that he did not need to call upon books nor educators from schools, for his brain and heart

divined the wisdom of the ages. His will and courage
overcame the opposition of friend and foe, so that
the Ship of State weathered the most fearful storm
any nation could endure.

¶ Lincoln was the man of heart and will and brain;
the man who worked for all of the people all of the
time ⚹ ⚹

He loved humanity. His life was spent in serving
humanity ⚹ ⚹

WALT WHITMAN, of whom Thoreau said,
" He is Democracy," expressed for America
the spirit of liberty. This man was born free,
and he was never in bonds to traditions. He
kept his body and brain unshackled, and he lived,
loved and worked unconventionally in a conventional
world ⚹ ⚹

He lived his own life of thought, and he expressed his
thoughts in his own way. To him man was greater
than the laws man had made, or the gods man had
made, and he said so—easily, naturally and frankly.
Whitman knew that he, himself, typified humanity,
and so he sang the " Song of Myself," believing that
this song was the honest thought of honest minds.

¶ Patriotism is a positive quality—it is love of country, and does not involve hatred of other countries.
A patriot is one who loves his country, supports it,
and works for its good. His individual interests are
absorbed into the interest for the whole. He spends
his time and energy for the people. Only a free man
could be a patriot. He must have perspective and
genuine faith. Such men are few ⚹ ⚹

Whitman was a genuine patriot who loved his country
because his country, he believed, would afford opportunity for the development of men and women who
would be children of liberty.

¶ He loved Nature. He believed that the Great
Power manifests Itself through all phenomena and

every form of life; that there is in Nature no high and low, no good and bad : that all is high and good.

¶ Things petty and small did not interest him. He had a perspective of life, and saw as many seers have not yet seen

He loved men as individuals, as types, and as principles personified. He mourned the death of Lincoln as one incarnate for another. And who can forget the words of Lincoln when he first saw Whitman, " There goes a man ! "

¶ Whitman could lose himself in the universal. Egotists such as he can do this. He did not feel as the dying soldier—" I am that man," said Whitman.

¶ Walt Whitman had the dramatic perception, lived the life of all things, and he taught others the beauty of such living. Whatever is, is good, was his attitude toward the world of Nature

He taught these: Live your own life. Be free. Be honest. Dare to sing the song of " Myself."

ROBERT INGERSOLL was humorist, iconoclast, and lover of humanity

It is said that the difference between man and the lower animals is that man has the ability to laugh.

¶ When you laugh you relax, and when you relax you give freedom to muscles, nerves and brain-cells. Man seldom has use of his reason when his brain is tense. The sense of humor makes a condition where reason can act

Ingersoll knew that he must make his appeal to man's brain. Paine knew this, too, and so did Voltaire, and Rousseau. But it is a winding way to reach the reason of most people. The unenlightened mind is in serious, solemn darkness.

¶ Ingersoll let the light of human sympathy penetrate first, and from the good-nature which followed, he added good humor, then sent shafts of wit

He showed that not God, but man's conception of a god, was preposterous, ridiculous, childish, unjust, impossible. For those who would listen he showed the way to get a perspective and see mythology as mythology, no matter where its record was found.

❦ He caused men and women to use the same reasoning faculties when contemplating the character of a god as of a man, of history in one book as in another. He knew their conclusions would then be sensible and bring a degree of peace and happiness unknown before to the world ❦ ❦

Ingersoll taught that what was wrong for men ought to be wrong for gods and saints; that what was considered not good, sin, for man on earth, should not be considered as fit for reward in heaven; that there was no justice in eternal punishment for temporal or temporary sins.

❦ Ingersoll asked men to be men—gentlemen in their religion, as they were in their politics and in their relations with their neighbors and families ❦ Especially did he ask justice, plain common justice, for women and children, and for all those who were not physically able to enforce their right to life, liberty and the pursuit of happiness.

❦ He asked consideration for criminals, those who had actually done wrong to their fellow-men ❦ ❦ He pleaded for Christians and Infidels alike to follow the Golden Rule, and do unto others as they would have these others do unto them ❦ ❦

Robert Ingersoll preferred to every political and social honor the privilege of freeing humanity from the shackles of bondage and fear. He knew no holier thing than truth. He preferred using his own reason to receiving popular applause or approbation. His keen wit, clear brain and merciless sarcasm uncrowned the King of Superstition and made him a puppet in the court of reason ❦ ❦

He dethroned for us the God of Wrath, and proved

himself to be more noble, more lovable, more godlike, than the Jehovah of the Jews. No god today is so well loved as is this man

R ALPH WALDO EMERSON was our modern Plato. He brought from Asia and the East all that was applicable to Americans. The best of the philosophy of India, Egypt, Assyria, Greece and Rome was his.

He was " the culminating flower " of a long line of New England clergymen, and he inherited not only the tendency to study but to think. " Beware when Nature sets loose a thinker in the land," he said. And Emerson himself had to beware, for his thinking caused men to fear for their theology

Unitarians were supposed to be liberal. Emerson found that no denomination more surely than they has the god Terminus erected as limits beyond which no man may think with safety

But no one could mark the boundary and confines for Emerson's thought. He was master of his own mind.

No man had ever lived before Emerson who thought with less restraint. Had he lived in the time of Servetus he would doubtless have had a tragic death.

Had he spoken in terms such as Ingersoll used, he would have been denounced as infidel—dangerous to mankind

But Emerson used always the scholarly expression, the chaste form, and the classic allusion. His heresy was cultured and gentle. His appeal was to the student mind, to men and women who lived in the realm of thought more than in the world of feeling.

So Emerson was not feared by the common people —they did not know of him. The "Divinity Address" was nothing to them. The symbols of Greek and Roman mythology meant nothing to the churchgoing people of America

But when Ingersoll talked frankly of the " Mistakes

of Moses," the veil of the temple was rent in twain,
and fathers and mothers clasped their children in
their arms to keep them from impending, imminent
danger ⋙ ⋙

Ingersoll was denounced by preachers, teachers and
school boards.

❦ Emerson's philosophy stole softly into homes of
conservative culture and remained as one of the
household, because he made heresy, pantheism and
reason so beautiful and necessary that no one wanted
to turn them away. Father Taylor said that if Emerson were sent to Hell he would change the climate
and start immigration in that direction. Literally he
did these things for New England. Concord, Massachusetts, proudly claims him as her First Citizen.
The city of Boston boasts of him as her most learned
Native Son ⋙ ⋙

America is proud to call him her great thinker,
scholar and teacher, also poet and philosopher. We
return again and again to his teaching for mental
stimulant and soul tonic.

❦ He has made for Americans a philosophy that
applies to the conduct of life, and in it is the wisdom
of the ages ⋙ ⋙

ALBERT HUBBARD, the most positive
human force of his time, is a man of genius
in business, in art, in literature, in philosophy.
He is an idealist, dreamer, orator, scientist.
In his knowledge of the fundamental, practical affairs
of living, in business, in human interests, in education,
politics and law he seems without a competitor ⋙ ⋙

He is like Jefferson in his democracy, in teaching a
nation to love to govern itself and to simplify all
living.

❦ He is like Paine in his love for liberty and in his
desire that all shall be free to act in freedom and to
think in freedom ⋙ ⋙

He is like Lincoln in that he would free all mankind. He, too, knows that there can be no free man on the earth so long as there is one slave.

¶ Elbert Hubbard sees, too, that just so long as there is one woman who is denied any right that man claims for himself, there is no free man ; that no man can be a superior, true American so long as one woman is denied her birthright of life, liberty and happiness.

¶ He knows that freedom to think and act, without withholding that right from any other, evolves humanity. Therefore he gives his best energy to inspiring men and women to think and to act, each for himself. He pleads for the rights of children, for so-called criminals, for the insane, the weak, and all those who having failed to be a friend to themselves, need friendship most. The Golden Rule is his rule of life

His work is to emancipate American men and women from being slaves to useless customs, outgrown mental habits, outgrown religion, outgrown laws, outgrown superstitions. He would make each human being rely upon himself for health, wealth and happiness

Elbert Hubbard is like Emerson in seizing upon truth, embalmed and laid in pyramids of disuse. Into these truths he has breathed the breath of life and they have become for many of us living souls. From the thoughts of Moses, Socrates, Solomon, Pythagoras, Loyola, Jesus, Buddha, Mohammed, he has brought to us wisdom that applies to the art of living today

Elbert Hubbard is a unique figure in history. The strength of his individuality comes from his having lived much and intensely. He lives his philosophy before he writes it, proves his theory before he announces it. Like Shakespeare he has access to universal knowledge, and from this storehouse he draws the vital fact whenever he needs it. Without effort, his mind seizes upon the important part of any subject, scene or situation, and he presents the few parts which will suggest the whole. He knows psychology, the needs of humanity at large, the needs of races, the needs of classes in races, and individuals in a class. He knows men and women, American men and women, their hopes, their fears, their strength, their weakness, their possibilities, and he deals with them, having ever before him the ideal. He, too, is looking for a Hapi, a Messiah, a Superman

He is never discouraged, never tired, never depressed. Eternal hope is in his heart, so every morning brings to him a New Day, and ushers in a New Year of the Better Day. Work, laugh, play, think, be kind, is the day's program he lives and recommends.

Economic freedom is the first necessity in human happiness. So Elbert Hubbard's first lesson is industry, producing wealth, using it wisely, distributing it. He knows, too, that food, shelter, clothing, fuel, are not enough to fill man's needs. Man has a soul to be fed and evolved as well. Love, beauty, music, art, are necessities, too. Had he but two loaves of bread he would sell one and buy white hyacinths with which to feed his soul. He loves all animal life, and believes that man should spend a part of every day in the garden, on the farm, with horses and animals, which are the civilizers of man

Elbert Hubbard is a businessman and a philosopher. He is a wise man in the use of his time, his energy. The law of his life is action. He knows that to focus his mind on the development of man is to degenerate into something less than a man. Man is developed, quite incidentally, through his work. Work is the exercise which develops brain, nerve, muscle. Work is the means which man uses to accomplish the end, the superman who shall understand Nature. He knows that greed is the subjugation of the individual, so his desire is to give every person about him equal opportunity with himself. He loves humanity. He believes in man, in the ultimate triumph of the noblest qualities in man. He is brother to all mankind and kindred to every living thing. He lives as a nobleman, every day without fear. All days are holy days. All natural phases of human life are sacred, and he respects them all. Through the power of his imagination he has lived all lives, and he condemns no man. Content to live in one world at a time, he has the genuine faith which does not peep into the Unknown, but lives to the full today, assured that "the power which cares for us here will not desert us there."

So this, then, is the book we offer—a book written by Americans, for Americans. It is a book without myth, miracle, mystery or metaphysics—a commonsense book for people who prize commonsense as a divine heritage. The book that will benefit most is not the one that imparts the most facts, but the one that inspires men to think and to act for themselves. The world can only be redeemed through action—movement—motion. Uncoerced, unbribed and unbought, humanity will move toward the light

—ALICE HUBBARD

THE GOSPEL ACCORDING TO
BENJAMIN FRANKLIN

Sin is not hurtful because it is forbidden,
but it is forbidden because it is hurtful.

Franklin

ROM a child I was fond of reading, and all the little money that came into my hands was ever laid out in books. Pleased with the " Pilgrim's Progress," my first collection was of John Bunyan's works in separate little volumes. I afterwards sold them to enable me to buy R. Burton's Historical Collections; they were small chapman's books, and cheap, forty or fifty in all. My father's little library consisted chiefly of books in polemic divinity, most of which I read, and have since often regretted that, at a time when I had such a thirst for knowledge, more proper books had not fallen in my way. Plutarch's " Lives " there was, in which I read abundantly, and I still think that time spent to great advantage. There was also a book of De Foe's, called " An Essay on Projects," and another of Doctor Mather's, called " Essays to Do Good," which perhaps gave me a turn of thinking that had an influence on some of the principal future events of my life This bookish inclination at length determined my father to make me a printer, though he had already one son (James) of that profession. In Seventeen Hundred Seventeen my brother James returned from England with a press and letters to set up his business in Boston. I liked it much better than that of my father, but still had a hankering for the sea. To prevent the apprehended effect of such an inclination, my father was impatient to have me bound to my brother. I stood out for some time, but at last was persuaded, and signed the indentures when I was yet but twelve years old. I was to serve as an apprentice until I was twenty-one years of age, only I was to be allowed journeyman's wages during the last year. In a little time I made great proficiency in the business, and became a useful hand to my brother.

I now had access to better books. An acquaintance with the apprentices of booksellers enabled me sometimes to borrow a small one, which I was careful to return soon and clean. Often I sat up in my room reading the greatest part of the night, when the book was borrowed in the evening and to be returned early in the morning, lest it should be missed or wanted

ABOUT this time I met with an odd volume of the " Spectator." It was the third. I had never before seen any of them. I bought it, read it over and over, and was much delighted with it. I thought the writing excellent, and wished if possible to imitate it. With this in view I took some of the papers, and, making short hints of the sentiment in each sentence, laid them by a few days, and then, without looking at the book, tried to complete the papers again, by expressing each hinted sentiment at length, and as fully as it had been expressed before, in any suitable words that should come to hand.

Then I compared my Spectator with the original, discovered some of my faults, and corrected them. But I found I wanted a stock of words, or a readiness in recollecting and using them, which I thought I should have acquired before that time if I had gone on making verses; since the continual occasion for words of the same import, but of different length to suit the measure, or of different sound for the rhyme, would have laid me under a constant necessity of searching for variety, and also have tended to fix that variety in my mind, and make me master of it.

Therefore I took some of the tales and turned them into verse; and, after a time, when I had pretty well forgotten the prose, turned them back again. I also sometimes jumbled my collection of hints into confusion, and after some weeks endeavored to reduce them into the best order, before I began to form the full sentences and complete the paper

This was to teach me method in the arrangement of

my thoughts. By comparing my work afterwards with
the original, I discovered many faults and amended
them; but I sometimes had the pleasure of fancying
that, in certain particulars of small import, I had been
lucky enough to improve the method or the language,
and this encouraged me to think I might possibly in
time come to be a tolerable English writer, of which I
was extremely ambitious.

My time for these exercises and for reading was at
night, after work or before it began in the morning.
or on Sundays, when I contrived to be in the Printing-
House alone, evading as much as I could the common
attendance on public worship which my father used
to exact of me when I was under his care, and which
indeed I still thought a duty, though I could not,
as it seemed to me, afford time to practise it

HEN about sixteen years of age I happened to
meet with a book, written by one Tryon, recom-
mending a vegetable diet. I determined to go into it.
My brother, being yet unmarried, did not keep house,
but boarded himself and his apprentices in another
family

My refusing to eat flesh occasioned an inconveniency,
and I was frequently chid for my singularity. I made
myself acquainted with Tryon's manner of preparing
some of his dishes, such as boiling potatoes or rice,
making hasty pudding, and a few others, and then
proposed to my brother, that if he would give me,
weekly, half the money he paid for my board, I would
board myself. He instantly agreed to it, and I presently found that I could save half what he paid me.

This was an additional fund for buying books.
But I had another advantage in it. My brother and
the rest going from the printing-house to their meals,
I remained there alone, and despatching presently
my light repast, which often was no more than a
biscuit or a slice of bread, a handful of raisins or a
tart from the pastry cook's, and a glass of water,

had the rest of the time until their return for study, in which I made the greater progress, from that greater quickness of head and quicker apprehension which usually attend temperance in eating and drinking

AND now it was that, being on some occasion made ashamed of my ignorance in figures, which I had twice failed in learning when at school, I took Cocker's book of Arithmetic, and went through the whole with great ease.

I also read Seller's and Shermy's books of Navigation, and became acquainted with the little Geometry they contain, but never got far in that science.

And I read about this time Locke on the Human Understanding, and the Art of Thinking, by Messrs. du Port Royal

While I was intent on improving my language, I met with an English Grammar (I think it was Greenwood's), at the end of which there were two little sketches of the arts of rhetoric and logic, the latter finishing with a specimen of a dispute in the Socratic method; and soon after I procured Xenophon's "Memorable Things of Socrates," wherein there are many instances of the same method. I was charmed with it, adopted it, dropped my abrupt contradiction and positive argumentation, and put on the humble inquirer and doubter. And being then, from reading Shaftesbury and Collins, become a real doubter in many points of our religious doctrine, I found this method safest for myself and very embarrassing to those against whom I used it; therefore I took a delight in it, practised it continually, and grew very artful and expert in drawing people, even of superior knowledge, into concessions, the consequences of which they did not foresee, entangling them in difficulties out of which they could not extricate themselves, and so obtaining victories that neither myself nor my cause always deserved

I continued this method some few years, but gradually left it, retaining only the habit of expressing myself in terms of modest diffidence; never using, when I advanced anything which possibly may be disputed, the words certainly, undoubtedly or any other that give the air of positiveness to an opinion; but rather say, I conceive or apprehend a thing to be so and so; it appears to me; or I should think it so and so, for such and such reasons; or I imagine it to be so; or it is so if I am not mistaken.

This habit, I believe, has been of great advantage to me when I have had occasions to inculcate my opinions, and persuade men into measures that I have been from time to time engaged in promoting; and, as the chief ends of conversation are to inform or to be informed, to please or to persuade, I wish well-meaning, sensible men would not lessen their power of doing good by a positive, assuming manner, that seldom fails to disgust, tends to create opposition, and to defeat every one of those purposes for which speech was given to us, to wit: giving or receiving information or pleasure.

For, if you would inform, a positive and dogmatical manner in advancing your sentiments may provoke contradiction and prevent a candid attention. If you wish information and improvement from the knowledge of others, and yet at the same time express yourself as firmly fixed in your present opinions, modest, sensible men, who do not love disputation, will probably leave you undisturbed in the possession of your error. And by such a manner, you can seldom hope to recommend yourself in pleasing your hearers, or to persuade those whose concurrence you desire

I SHOULD have mentioned before that, in the Autumn of the preceding year, I had formed most of my ingenious acquaintance into a club of mutual improvement, which we called the Junto; we met on Friday evenings. The rules that I drew up required that every member, in his turn, should produce one or more queries on any point of Morals, Politics or Natural Philosophy, to be discussed by the company; and once in three months produce and read an essay in his own writing, on any subject he pleased. Our debates were to be under the direction of a president, and to be conducted in the sincere spirit of inquiry after truth, without fondness for dispute or desire for victory; and, to prevent warmth, all expressions of positiveness in opinions, or direct contradiction, were after some time made contraband, and prohibited under small pecuniary penalties

RULES of Health and Long Life, and to Preserve From Malignant Fevers, and Sickness in General

Eat and drink such an exact quantity as the constitution of thy body allows of, in reference to the Services of the Mind.

They that study much, ought not to eat so much as those that work hard, their digestion being not so good.

The exact quantity and quality being found out, is to be kept to constantly

Excess in all other things whatever, as well as in meat and drink, is also to be avoided.

Youth, age and sick require a different quantity. And so do those of contrary complexions; for that which is too much for a Phlegmatic Man is not sufficient for a Choleric.

The measure of food ought to be (as much as possibly may be) exactly proportionate to the Quality and Condition of the Stomach, because the Stomach digests it

That quantity that is sufficient, the Stomach can perfectly concoct and digest, and it sufficeth the due Nourishment of the Body.

A greater quantity of some things may be eaten

than of others, some being of lighter digestion
The difficulty lies in finding out an exact measure;
but eat for Necessity, not Pleasure, for Lust knows
not where Necessity ends
Would'st thou enjoy a long life, a healthy body and
a vigorous mind, and be acquainted also with the
wonderful works of God? Labor in the first place to
bring thy appetite into subjection to reason

RULES to Find Out a Fit Measure of Meat and
Drink:

If thou eatest so much as makes thee unfit for
business, thou exceedest the due measure
If thou art dull and heavy after meat, it's a sign
thou hast exceeded the due measure; for meat and
drink ought to refresh the body, and make it cheerful,
and not to dull and oppress it
If thou findest these ill Symptoms, consider whether
too much meat, or too much Drink occasions it, or
both, and abate by little and little, till thou findest
the inconveniency removed.

Keep out of the Sight of Feasts and Banquets as
much as may be; for it is more difficult to refrain
good-cheer, when it's present, than from the Desire
of it when it is away; the like you may observe in the
objects of all the other senses
If a man casually exceeds, let him fast the next Meal,
and all may be well again, provided it be not too often
done; asif he exceedat dinner, let him refrain at supper.

A temperate diet frees from diseases; such are
seldom ill, but if they are surprised with sickness,
they bear it better and recover sooner; for most dis-
tempers have their original from repletion
Use now and then a little Exercise a quarter of an
hour before meals, as to swing a Weight; or swing
your arms about with a small weight in each hand; to
leap, or the like, for that stirs the muscles of the breast.

A temperate diet arms the body against all external
accidents; so that they are not so easily hurt by

Heat, Cold or Labor; if they at any time should be prejudiced, they are more easily cured either of wounds, dislocations or bruises

A Sober Diet makes a man die without pain; it maintains the Senses in Vigor; it mitigates the violence of the Passions and Affections

———

BEFORE I enter upon my public appearance in business, it may be well to let you know the then state of my mind with regard to my principles and morals, that you may see how far those influenced the future events of my life. My parents had early given me religious impressions, and brought me through my childhood piously in the Dissenting way. But I was scarce fifteen when, after doubting by turns of several points, as I found them disputed in the different books I read, I began to doubt of revelation itself. Some books against Deism fell into my hands; they were said to be the substance of sermons preached at Boyle's Lectures. It happened that they wrought an effect on me quite contrary to what was intended by them; for the arguments of the Deists, which were quoted to be refuted, appeared to me much stronger than the refutations; in short, I soon became a thorough Deist

I grew convinced that truth, sincerity and integrity in dealings between man and man were of the utmost importance to the felicity of life; and I formed written resolutions, which still remain in my journal book, to practise them ever while I lived

Revelation had indeed no weight with me, as such; but I entertained an opinion that, though certain actions might not be bad because they were forbidden by it, or good because it commanded them, yet probably these actions might be forbidden because they were bad for us, or commanded because they were beneficial to us, in their own natures, all the circumstances of things considered. And this persuasion, with the kind hand of Providence, or some guardian angel, or accidental favorable circumstances and situations, or all together, preserved me, through this dangerous time of youth, and the hazardous situations I was sometimes in among strangers, remote from the eye and advice of my father, without any wilful gross immorality or injustice, that might have been expected from my want of religion. I say wilful, because the instances I have mentioned had something of necessity in them, from my youth, inexperience and the knavery of others. I had therefore a tolerable character to begin the world with; I valued it properly, and determined to preserve it

HUMAN felicity is produced not so much by great pieces of good fortune that seldom happen, as by little advantages that occur every day. Thus, if you teach a poor young man to shave himself, and keep his razor in order, you may contribute more to the happiness of his life than in giving him a thousand guineas. The money may be soon spent, the regret only remaining of having foolishly consumed it; but in the other case, he escapes the foolish vexations of waiting for barbers, and of their sometimes dirty fingers, offensive breaths and dull razors; he shaves when most convenient to him, and enjoys daily the pleasure of its being done with a good instrument. With these sentiments I have hazarded the few preceding pages, hoping they may afford hints which some time or other may be useful to a city I love, having lived many years in it very happily, and perhaps to some of our towns in America

I HAD been religiously educated as a Presbyterian; and though some of the dogmas of that persuasion, such as the eternal decrees of God, election, reprobation, etc., appeared to me unintelligible, others doubtful, and I early absented myself from the public assemblies of the sect, Sunday being my studying day, I never was without some religious principles.

I never doubted, for instance, the existence of the Deity; that He made the world, and governed it by His Providence; that the most acceptable service of God was the doing good to man; that our souls are immortal; and that all crime will be punished, and virtue rewarded, either here or hereafter. These I esteemed the essentials of every religion; and, being to be found in all the religions we had in our country, I respected them all, though with different degrees of respect, as I found them more or less mixed with other articles which, without any tendency to inspire, promote or confirm morality, served principally to divide us, and make us unfriendly to one another.

This respect to all, with an opinion that the worst had some good effects, induced me to avoid all discourse that might tend to lessen the good opinion another might have of his own religion; and as our province increased in people, and new places of worship were continually wanted, and generally erected by voluntary contributions, my mite for such purpose, whatever might be the sect, was never refused. Though I seldom attended any public worship, I had still an opinion of its propriety, and of its utility when rightly conducted, and I regularly paid my annual subscription for the support of the only Presbyterian minister or meeting we had in Philadelphia. He used to visit me sometimes as a friend, and admonish me to attend his administrations, and I was now and then prevailed on to do so, once for five Sundays successively. Had he been in my opinion a good preacher, perhaps I might have continued, notwithstanding the occasion I had for the Sunday's leisure in my course of study; but his discourses were either polemic arguments, or explications of the peculiar doctrines of our sect, and were all to me very dry, uninteresting and unedifying, since not a single moral principle was inculcated or enforced, their aim seeming to be rather to make us Presbyterians than good citizens

At length, he took for his text that verse of the fourth chapter of Philippians, " Finally, brethren, whatsoever things are true, honest, just, pure, lovely, or of good report, if there be any virtue, or any praise, think on these things." And I imagined, in such a sermon on such a text, we could not miss of having some morality. But he confined himself to five points only, as meant by the apostle, viz. : (1) Keeping holy the Sabbath day. (2) Being diligent in reading the Holy Scriptures. (3) Attending duly the Public Worship. (4) Partaking of the Sacrament. (5) Paying a due respect to God's ministers. These might be all good things ; but, as they were not the kind of things that I expected from that text, I despaired of ever meeting with them from any other, was disgusted, and attended his preaching no more.

I had some years before composed a little Liturgy, or form of prayer, for my own private use, viz., in Seventeen Hundred Twenty-eight, entitled, " Articles of Belief and Acts of Religion." I returned to the use of this, and went no more to the public assemblies. My conduct might be blamable, but I leave it, without attempting further to excuse it, my present purpose being to relate facts, not to make apologies for them.

IT was about this time I conceived the bold and arduous project of arriving at moral perfection. I wished to live without committing any fault at any time ; I would conquer all that either natural inclination, custom or company might lead me into. As I knew, or thought I knew, what was right and wrong, I did not see why I might not always do the one and avoid the other. But I found I had undertaken a task more difficult than I had imagined. While my care was employed in guarding against one fault, I was often surprised by another; habit took the advantage of inattention; inclination was sometimes too strong for reason

I concluded, at length, that the mere speculative conviction that it was our interest to be completely virtuous, was not sufficient to prevent our slipping; and that the contrary habits must be broken, and good ones acquired and established, before we can have any dependence on a steady, uniform rectitude of conduct. For this purpose I therefore contrived the following method.

These names of virtues with their precepts were:

1. *Temperance.*—Eat not to dulness; drink not to elevation

2. *Silence.*—Speak not but what may benefit others or yourself; avoid trifling conversation

3. *Order.*—Let all your things have their places; let each part of your business have its time

4. *Resolution.*—Resolve to perform what you ought; perform without fail what you resolve

5. *Frugality.*—Make no expense but to do good to others or yourself; i. e., waste nothing

6. *Industry.*—Lose no time; be always employed in something useful; cut off all unnecessary actions

7. *Sincerity.*—Use no hurtful deceit; think innocently and justly, and, if you speak, speak accordingly

8. *Justice.*—Wrong none by doing injuries, or omitting the benefits that are your duty

9. *Moderation.*—Avoid extremes; forbear resenting injuries so much as you think they deserve

10. *Cleanliness.*—Tolerate no uncleanliness in body, clothes or habitation

11. *Tranquillity.*—Be not disturbed at trifles, or at accidents common or unavoidable

12. *Humility.*—Imitate Jesus and Socrates

Y intention being to acquire the habitude of all these virtues, I judged it would be well not to distract my attention by attempting the whole at once, but to fix it on one of them at a time, and, when I should be master of that, then to proceed to another, and so on, till I should have gone through all, and, as the previous acquisition of some might facilitate the acquisition of others, I arranged them with that view, as they stand above.

Temperance first, as it tends to procure that coolness and clearness of head which is so necessary where constant vigilance is to be kept up, and guard maintained against the unremitting attraction of ancient habits, and the force of perpetual temptations. This being acquired and established, Silence would be more easy ; and my desire being to gain knowledge at the same time that I improved in virtue, and considering that in conversation it was obtained rather by the use of the ears than of the tongue, and therefore wishing to break a habit I was getting into of prattling, punning and joking, which only made me acceptable to trifling company, I gave Silence the second place. This and the next, Order, I expected would allow me more time for attending to my project and my studies. Resolution, once become habitual, would keep me firm in my endeavors to obtain all the subsequent virtues ; Frugality and Industry freeing me from my remaining debt, and producing affluence and independence, would make more easy the practise of Sincerity and Justice, etc., etc.

OBSERVATIONS on my reading history, in Library, May Nineteenth, Seventeen Hundred Thirty-one

That the great affairs of the world, the wars, revolutions, etc., are carried on and effected by parties.

That the view of these parties is their present general interest, or what they take to be such That the different views of these different parties occasion all confusion.

That while a party is carrying on a general design,

each man has his particular private interest in view.

❡ That as soon as a party has gained its general point, each member becomes intent upon his particular interests; which, thwarting others, breaks that party into divisions, and occasions more confusion.

❡ That few in public affairs act from a mere view of the good of their country, whatever they may pretend; and, though their actings bring real good to their country, yet men primarily considered that their own and their country's interest was united, and did not act from a principle of benevolence

That fewer still, in public affairs, act with a view to the good of mankind

There seems to me at present to be great occasion for raising a United Party for Virtue, by forming the virtuous and good men of all nations into a regular body, to be governed by suitable good and wise rules, which good and wise men may probably be more unanimous in their obedience to, than common people are to common laws.

❡ I at present think that whoever attempts this aright, and is well qualified, can not fail of pleasing God, and of meeting with success.

❡ The most acceptable service of God is doing good to man

❦

MBARRASSMENTS that the Quakers suffered from having established it and published it as one of their principles that no kind of war was lawful, and which, being once published, they could not afterwards, however much they might change their minds, easily get rid of, reminds me of what I think a more prudent conduct in another sect among us, that of the Dunkers.

❡ I was acquainted with one of its founders, Michael Welfare, soon after it appeared. He complained to me that they were grievously calumniated by the zealots of other persuasions, and charged with abominable principles and practises, to which they were utter strangers

I told him this had always been the case with new sects, and that, to put a stop to such abuse, I imagined it might be well to publish the articles of belief, and the rules of their discipline. He said that it had been proposed among them, but not agreed to, for this reason: " When we were first drawn together as a Society," says he, " it had pleased God to enlighten our minds so far as to see that some doctrines which we once esteemed truths, were errors; and that others, which we had esteemed errors, were real truths

From time to time He has been pleased to afford us further light, and our principles have been improving, and our errors diminishing. Now we are not sure that we have arrived at the end of this progression, and at the perfection of spiritual or theological knowledge; and we fear that, if we should once print our confession of faith, we should feel ourselves as if bound and confined by it, and perhaps be unwilling to receive further improvement, and our successors still more so, as conceiving what we their elders and founders had done, to be something sacred, never to be departed from."

This modesty in a sect is perhaps a singular instance in the history of mankind, every other sect supposing itself in the possession of all truth, and that those who differ are so far in the wrong; like a man traveling in foggy weather, those at some distance before him on the road he sees wrapped up in the fog, as well as those behind him, and also the people in the fields on each side, but near him all appears clear, though, in truth, he is as much in the fog as any of them

Mankind are very odd creatures: One half censure what they practise, the other half practise what they censure; the rest always say and do as they ought.

HINTS to Those That Would Be Rich.— The use of money is all the advantage there is in having money

For six pounds a year you may have the use of one hundred pounds, if you are a man of known prudence and honesty.

He that spends a groat a day idly, spends idly above six pounds a year, which is the price of using one hundred pounds

He that wastes idly a groat's worth of his time per day, one day with another, wastes the privilege of using one hundred pounds each day.

He that idly loses five shillings' worth of time loses five shillings, and might as prudently throw five shillings into the river

He that loses five shillings not only loses that sum, but all the other advantage that might be made by turning it in dealing, which, by the time a young man becomes old, amounts to a comfortable bag of money.

Again, he that sells upon credit asks a price for what he sells equivalent to the principal and interest of his money for the time he is like to be kept out of it; therefore, he that buys upon credit pays interest for what he buys, and he that pays ready money might let that money out to use; so that,

He that possesses anything he has bought, pays interest for the use of it

Consider, then, when you are tempted to buy any unnecessary household stuff, or any superfluous thing, whether you will be willing to pay interest, and interest upon interest for it as long as you live, and more if it grows worse by using

Yet, in buying goods, 't is best to pay ready money, because,

He that sells upon credit expects to lose five per cent by bad debts; therefore he charges upon all he sells upon credit, an advance that shall make up that deficiency

Those who pay for what they buy upon credit pay
their share of this advance.

❧ He that pays ready money escapes, or may escape,
that charge. Save and have

A penny saved is twopence clear. A pin a day is a
groat a year

Every little makes a mickle

⟡

Anger is never without a reason, but seldom with
a good one

⟡

No man ever was glorious who was not laborious.

⟡

Better slip with foot than tongue

⟡

Innocence is its own defense

⟡

There is neither honor nor gain got in dealing with
a villain

⟡

Keep your mouth wet, feet dry

⟡

He 's the best physician that knows the worthlessness
of the most medicines

⟡

Drive thy business, or it will drive thee

⟡

The same man can not be both friend and flatterer.

⟡

He who multiplies Riches multiplies Cares

⟡

An old man in a House is a good Sign

⟡

Those that are feared, are hated

⟡

The things which hurt, instruct

⟡

The eye of a master will do more work than his hand.

Courage would fight, but Discretion won't let him.

A soft tongue may strike hard

We are not so sensible of the greatest Health as of the least Sickness

A poor example is the best sermon

Despair ruins some, Presumption many

He that won't be counseled, can't be helped

Craft must be at charge for clothes, but Truth can go naked

Write injuries in dust, benefits in marble

Many a man thinks he is buying Pleasure, when he is really selling himself a slave to it

'T is hard (but glorious) to be poor and honest: An empty sack can hardly stand upright; but if it does, 't is a stout one!

He that can bear a reproof, and mend by it, if he is not wise, is in a fair way of being so

He that spills the rum loses that only; he that drinks it, often loses both that and himself

He that would catch fish must venture his bait

You can bear your own faults, and why not a fault in your wife?

Work as if you were to live one hundred years, pray as if you were to die tomorrow

Pride breakfasted with plenty, dined with poverty, supped with infamy

One today is worth two tomorrows

The way to be safe is never to be secure

Retirement does not always secure virtue; Lot was upright in the city; wicked in the mountain

He that has a trade has an office of profit and honor.

HE wit of conversation consists more in finding it in others, than in showing a great deal yourself. He who goes out of your company, pleased with his own facetiousness and ingenuity, will the sooner come into it again. Most men had rather please than admire you, and seek less to be instructed and diverted than approved and applauded, and it is certainly the most delicate sort of pleasure, to please another But that sort of wit, which employs itself insolently in criticizing and censuring the words and sentiments of others in conversation, is absolute folly; for it answers none of the ends of conversation. He who uses it neither improves others, is improved himself, nor pleases any one

Be civil to all; sociable to many; familiar with few; friend to one; enemy to none

Onions can make even heirs and widows weep

The family of fools is ancient

Necessity never made a good bargain

The poor man must walk to get meat for his stomach; the rich man to get a stomach to his meat

If pride leads the van, beggary brings up the rear.

Three may keep a secret if two of them are dead.

Sloth and silence are a fool's virtues

Approve not of him who commends all you say

By diligence and patience, the mouse bit in two the cable

He that goes far to marry, will either deceive or be deceived

Eyes and priests bear no jests

The thrifty maxim of the wary Dutch is to save all the money they can touch

He that waits upon fortune is never sure of a dinner.

A learned blockhead is a greater blockhead than an ignorant one

Avarice and happiness never saw each other; how then should they become acquainted?

Necessity has no law; I know some attorneys of the same

To be humble to superiors is a duty, to equals courtesy, to inferiors nobleness

Here comes the orator, with his flood of words, and his drop of reason

Are you angry that others disappoint you? Remember that you can not depend upon yourself

One mend-fault is worth two find-faults; but one find-fault is better than two make-faults

Forewarned, forearmed

He is no clown that drives the plow, but he that doth clownish things

Great famine when wolves eat wolves

He that lieth down with dogs shall rise up with fleas.

Search others for their virtues, thyself for thy vices.

God heals, and the doctor takes the fee

If you desire many things, many things will seem but a few

Mary's mouth costs her nothing, for she never opens it but at others' expense

Receive before you write, but write before you pay.

I saw few die of hunger, of eating—one hundred thousand

He that lives well is learned enough

Poverty, poetry and new titles of honor make men ridiculous

He that scatters thorns, let him not go barefoot

The rotten apple spoils his companion

Don't throw stones at your neighbors, if your own windows are glass

He that sells upon trust loses many friends, and always wants money

Lovers, travelers and poets will give money to be heard

He that speaks much is much mistaken

Reading makes a full man—meditation a profound man—discourse a clear man

Creditors have better memories than debtors

If any man flatters me, I'll flatter him again, though he were my best friend

None but the well-bred man knows how to confess a fault, or acknowledge himself in an error

There is much difference between imitating a good man and counterfeiting him

Wink at small faults—remember thou hast great ones.

Wish not so much to live long as to live well

As we must account for every idle word, so we must for every idle silence

I have never seen the Philosopher's Stone that turns lead into gold, but I have known the pursuit of it turn a man's gold into lead

Never entreat a servant to dwell with thee

Write with the learned, pronounce with the vulgar.

Time is an herb that cures all diseases

Keep your eyes wide open before marriage, half shut afterwards

Let thy vices die before thee

The ancients tell us what is best; but we must learn of the moderns what is fittest

Since I can not govern my own tongue, though within my own teeth, how can I hope to govern the tongues of others?

Since thou art not sure of a minute, throw not away an hour

If you do what you should not, you must hear what you would not

Fly pleasures, and they 'll follow you

Hast thou virtue?—acquire also the graces and beauties of virtue

If thou hast wit and learning, add to it wisdom and modesty

You may be more happy than princes, if you will be more virtuous

If you would not be forgotten, as soon as you are dead and rotten, either write things worth reading, or do things worth the writing

Sell not virtue to purchase wealth, nor liberty to purchase power

The creditors are a superstitious sect, great observers of set days and times

The noblest question in the world is, What good may I do in it?

Great talkers should be cropped, for they have no need of ears

Who has deceived thee so oft as thyself?

Is there anything men take more pains about than to make themselves unhappy?

Nothing brings more pain than too much pleasure; nothing more bondage than too much liberty (or libertinism)

He that builds before he counts the cost, acts foolishly; and he that counts before he builds, finds that he did not count wisely

A pair of good ears will drain dry a hundred tongues.

Serving God is doing good to man, but praying is thought an easier service, and therefore more generally chosen

Nothing humbler than ambition when it is about to climb

When Prosperity was well mounted, she let go the Bridle, and soon came tumbling out of the saddle

It is not Leisure that is not used

Ignorance leads men into a party, and Shame keeps them from getting out again

When out of Favor, none know thee; when in, thou dost not know thyself

Setting too good an example is a kind of slander
seldom forgiven; 't is *Scandalum Magnatum*

Haste makes waste

Severity is often clemency; Clemency severity

Success has ruined many a man

A great talker may be no fool, but he is one that
relies on him

All things are easy to industry; all things difficult
to sloth

The old man has given all to his son. O fool! to undress
thyself before thou art going to bed

What one relishes, nourishes

Would you live with ease, do what you ought, and
not what you please

He has lost his boots, but saved his spurs

In success be moderate

Many dishes, many diseases. Many medicines, few
cures

God works wonders now and then; Behold! a lawyer,
an honest man

To lengthen thy life, lessen thy meals

He has changed his one-eyed horse for a blind one.

Eat to live, and not live to eat

Beware of the young doctor and the old barber

Idleness is the Dead Sea that swallows all virtues:
Be active in business, that temptation may miss her
aim; the bird that sits is easily shot

Kings and bears often worry their keepers

Bucephalus, the horse of Alexander, hath as lasting
fame as his master

He does not possess wealth: it possesses him

He that can not obey, can not command

Fools multiply folly

Anger warms the invention, but overheats the oven.

Beauty and folly are old companions

Tell me my faults and mend your own

Many a man's own tongue gives evidence against
his understanding

The royal crown cures not the Headache

Samson with his strong body had a weak head, or he
would not have laid it in a harlot's lap

Nothing dries sooner than a tear

When a friend deals with a friend, let the bargain
be clear and well-penned, that they may continue
friends to the end

Trouble springs from idleness; toil from ease

An honest man will receive neither money nor praise
that is not his due

Saying and doing have quarreled and parted

Laws too gentle are seldom obeyed; too severe, seldom executed

A wise man will desire no more than what he can
get justly, use soberly, distribute cheerfully and
leave contentedly

Tomorrow every fault is to be amended; but that
Tomorrow never comes

A flatterer never seems absurd: the flattered always
take his word

Never praise nor dispraise, till seven Christmases
be over

Learn of the skilful: he that teaches himself hath a
fool for a master

Be always ashamed to catch thyself idle

Love and be loved

They who have nothing to be troubled at, will be
troubled at nothing

Lying rides upon debt's back

> If evils come not, then our fears are vain;
> And if they do, fear but augments the pain.

Nick's passions grow fat and hearty: his understanding looks consumptive

If you would keep your secret from an enemy, tell it not to a friend

⌒

Quarrels never could last long,
If on one side only lay the wrong.

⌒

Strange! that a Man who has wit enough to write a Satire should have folly enough to publish it

⌒

Rob not for burnt offerings

⌒

Doing an injury puts you below your enemy; revenging one makes you but even with him; forgiving it sets you above him

⌒

All would live long, but none would be old

⌒

Great good-nature, without Prudence, is a great Misfortune

⌒

The golden age never was the present age

⌒

What signifies knowing the names, if you know not the nature of things?

⌒

We may give advice, but we can not give conduct.

⌒

Honors change manners

⌒

Youth is pert and positive, age modest and doubting. So ears of corn, when young and light, stand bolt upright, but hang their heads when weighty, full and ripe

⌒

Don't judge of Men's Wealth or Piety, by their Sunday appearance

⌒

Nine men in ten are suicides

Not to oversee workmen is to leave your purse open to them

The wise and brave dares own that he was wrong.

Sorrow is good for nothing but sin

Friendship increases by visiting friends, but by visiting seldom

A brother may not be a friend, but a friend will always be a brother

Cunning proceeds from want of capacity

An hundred thieves can not strip one naked man, especially if his skin 's off

Be at war with your vices, at peace with your neighbors, and let every New Year find you a better man.

Today is yesterday's pupil

A change of fortune hurts a wise man no more than a change of moon

Think of three things: whence you came, where you are going, and to whom you must account

Who is wise? He that learns from every one. Who is powerful? He that governs his passions. Who is rich? He that is content. Who is that? Nobody

Generous minds are all of a kin

The end of Passion is the beginning of Repentance.

Meanness is the parent of insolence

To be intimate with a foolish friend is like going to
bed with a razor

The doors of wisdom are never shut

Where there is hunger, law is not regarded ; and where
law is not regarded, there will be hunger

Would you be loved, love and be lovable

In the affairs of this world men are saved, not by
Faith, but by the want of it

Friendship can not live with ceremony, nor without
civility

He that would travel much, should eat little

The learned fool writes his nonsense in better language than the unlearned, but still 't is nonsense.

God gives all things to industry

Willows are weak, but they bind the fagot

Eat few suppers, and you 'll need few Medicines

Two dry sticks will burn a green one

How few there are who have courage enough to own
their Faults, or resolution enough to mend them!

Little rogues easily become great ones

Many a long dispute among Divines may be thus
abridged : It is so ; it is not so : It is so ; it is not so.

Praise little, dispraise less

Men differ daily about things which are subject to sense. Is it likely then they should agree about things invisible?

Who is strong? He that can conquer his bad Habits.

He that speaks ill of the mare will buy her

If you 'd be wealthy, think of saving, more than of getting : the Indies have not made Spain rich, because her Outgoes equal her Incomes

You may drive a gift without a gimlet

If you 'd lose a troublesome visitor, lend him money.

The sleeping fox catches no poultry. UP! UP!

If you 'd have it done, go; if not, send

Tart words make no friends : spoonful of honey will catch more flies than gallon of vinegar

Make haste slowly

Dine with little, sup with less; do better still : sleep supperless

What you would seem to be, be really

Industry, perseverance and frugality make fortune yield

Keep thou from the Opportunity, and God will keep thee from the Sin

If you 'd be beloved, make yourself amiable. A true friend is the best possession

It's common for men to give pretended reasons, instead of one real one

He's a fool that can not conceal his Wisdom

You may talk too much on the best of subjects

All blood is alike ancient

A man without ceremony has need of great merit in its place

> Speak with contempt of none, from slave to
> king,
> The meanest bee hath, and will use, a sting.

To God we owe fear and love; to our neighbors justice and character; to ourselves prudence and sobriety.

No gains without pains

Light-heeled mothers make leaden-heeled daughters.

When the well's dry we know the worth of water.

Silks and satins put out the kitchen fire

The generous mind least regards money, and yet most feels the want of it

Who is rich? He that rejoices in his portion

Wealth and Content are not always Bedfellows. Wise men learn by others' harms; Fools by their own

Great spenders are bad lenders

Virtue and Happiness are Mother and Daughter

Words may show a man's Wit, but Actions his meaning

Content makes poor men rich; Discontent makes rich men poor

Vice knows she's ugly, so puts on her mask

A man has no more Goods than he gets Good by

Dost thou love life? Then do not squander time; for that's the stuff Life is made of

Welcome, mischief, if thou comest alone

Good sense is a thing all need, few have, and none think they want

What's proper is becoming: see the Blacksmith with his white silk apron!

Want of care does us more damage than want of knowledge

A life of leisure and a life of laziness are two things.

A light purse is a heavy curse

Take courage, Mortal! Death can't banish thee out of the universe

The sting of a reproach is the Truth of it

The most exquisite folly is made of wisdom spun too fine

Mad kings and mad bulls are not to be held by treaties and packthread

Changing countries or beds cures neither a bad manager nor a fever

Do me the favor to deny me at once

A true great man will neither trample on a worm nor sneak to an Emperor

Half-hospitality opens his Door and shuts up his countenance

Strive to be the greatest man in your country, and you may be disappointed; strive to be the best and you may succeed: he may well win the race that runs by himself

Time enough always proves little enough

Gifts burst rocks

He that by the Plow would thrive, himself must either hold or drive

Life with fools consists in Drinking; with the wise man, Living 's Thinking

If Jack 's in love, he 's no judge of Jill's Beauty

Pardoning the Bad is injuring the Good

THOSE who govern, having much business on their hands, do not generally like to take the trouble of considering and carrying into execution new projects. The best public measures are therefore seldom adopted from previous wisdom, but forced by the occasion

A Mob 's a Monster; Heads enough, but no Brains.

HEN men are employed, they are best contented; for on the days they work, they are good-natured and cheerful, and, with the consciousness of having done a good day's work, they spend the evening jollily; but on idle days they are mutinous and quarrelsome, finding fault with their pork, the bread, etc., and in continual ill-humor, which puts me in mind of a sea-captain, whose rule it was to keep his men constantly at work; and, when his mate once told him that they had done everything, and there was nothing further to employ them about, " Oh," said he, " make them scour the anchor."

N order to secure my credit and character as a tradesman, I took care not only to be in reality industrious and frugal, but to avoid all appearances to the contrary. I dressed plainly; I was seen at no places of idle diversion. I never went out a-fishing or shooting; a book indeed sometimes debauched me from my work, but that was seldom, snug, and gave no scandal; and, to show that I was not above my business, I sometimes brought home the paper I purchased at the stores through the streets on a wheelbarrow. Thus being esteemed an industrious, thriving young man, and paying duly for what I bought, the merchants who imported stationery solicited my custom; others proposed supplying me with books, and I went on swimmingly

---

It is wise not to seek a secret, and honest not to reveal it

Here comes Courage! that seized the lion absent, and ran away from the present mouse

---

Why does the blind man's wife paint herself?

He that can have patience can have what he will.

Now I have a sheep and a cow, everybody bids me good-morrow

None preaches better than the ant, and she says nothing

The absent are never without fault, nor the present without excuse

Wealth is not his that has it, but his that enjoys it.

'T is easy to see, hard to foresee

In a discreet man's mouth a public thing is private.

Let thy maidservant be faithful, strong and homely.

Bargaining has neither friends nor relations

There 's more old drunkards than old doctors

If you know how to spend less than you get, you have the philosopher's stone

The good paymaster is lord of another man's purse.

He that has neither fools nor beggars among his kindred is the son of thunder-gust

Diligence is the mother of good luck

Do not do that which you would not have known.

Ever since follies have pleased, fools have been able to divert

A man is never so ridiculous by those qualities that are his own as by those that he affects to have.

It is better to take many injuries than to give one.

Deny self for self's sake

You may give a man an office, but you can not give him discretion

When reason preaches, if you don't hear her she 'll box your ears

Old boys have their playthings as well as young ones; the difference is only in the price

He 's a fool that makes his doctor his heir

Don't value a man for the quality he is made of, but for the qualities he possesses

Promises may get thee friends, but non-performance will turn them into enemies

Love your enemies, for they tell you their faults

Lend money to an enemy, and thou 'lt gain him; to a friend, and thou 'lt lose him

Anger and folly walk cheek by jowl; repentance treads on both their heels

When knaves fall out, honest men get their goods: when priests dispute we come at the truth

He that riseth late must trot all day, and shall scarce overtake his business at night

A quarrelsome man has no good neighbors

Employ thy time well, if thou meanest to gain leisure.

Experience keeps a dear school, yet fools will learn in no other

Beware of little expenses: a small leak will sink a great ship

Many complain of their memory, few of their judgment

None know the unfortunate, and the fortunate do not know themselves

What signifies your patience if you can't find it when you want it?

He is not well bred that can not bear Ill-Breeding in others

Many a man would have been worse, if his estate had been better

The busy man has few idle visitors; to the boiling pot the flies come not

Calamity and prosperity are the touchstones of integrity

Some are justly laughed at for keeping their money foolishly; others for spending it idly: He is the greatest fool that lays it out in a purchase of repentance.

Don't overload gratitude; if you do, she 'll kick

At twenty years of age the will reigns; at thirty the wit; at forty the judgment

Christianity commands us to pass by injuries; policy to let them pass by us

Up, sluggard, and waste not life; in the grave will be sleeping enough

The world is full of fools and faint hearts; and yet every one has courage enough to bear the misfortunes, and wisdom enough to manage the affairs of his neighbor

Fools make feasts and wise men eat them

It 's the easiest thing in the world for a man to deceive himself

The tongue is ever turning to the aching tooth

There is no man so bad but he secretly respects the good

Most fools think they are only ignorant

Most people return small favors, acknowledge middling ones, and repay great ones with ingratitude.

Who judges best of a man—his enemies or himself?

There 's a time to wink as well as to see

The honest man takes pains, and then enjoys pleasures; the knave takes pleasures, and then suffers pains.

He is ill clothed that is bare of virtue

If you would be revenged of your enemy, govern yourself

The favor of the great is no inheritance

He that never eats too much will never be lazy

An innocent plowman is more worthy than a vicious prince

Teach your child to hold his tongue, he 'll learn fast enough to speak

Where there 's marriage without love, there will be love without marriage

The tongue offends and the ears get the cuffing

It is ill-mannered to silence a fool, and cruelty to let him go on

Fear to do ill, and you need fear naught else

> To whom thy secret thou dost tell,
> To him thy freedom thou dost sell

If you 'd have a servant that you like, serve yourself.

He that pursues two hares at once, does not catch one and lets t' other go

If you have time, don't wait for time

Don't go to the doctor with every distemper, nor to the lawyer with every quarrel, nor to the pot for every thirst

At the workingman's house hunger looks in, but dares not enter

The worst wheel of the cart makes the most noise.

Don't misinform your doctor nor your lawyer

The masterpiece of man is to live to the purpose.

A countryman between two lawyers is like a fish
between two cats

Tomorrow you 'll reform, you always cry;
In what far country does this morrow lie,
That 't is so mighty long ere it arrive?
Beyond the Indies does this morrow live?
'T is so far-fetched this morrow that I fear
'T will be both very old, and very dear.
Tomorrow I 'll reform, the fool does say;
Today itself 's too late—the wise did yesterday.

He that can compose himself is wiser than he that
composed books

Poor Dick eats like a well man, and drinks like a sick.

Love, cough and a smoke can't well be hid

No better relation than a prudent and faithful friend.

Well done is better than well said

Each year one vicious habit rooted out,
In time might make the worst man good
throughout

Trust thyself, and another shall not betray thee.

Historians relate, not so much what is done, as what
they would have believed

Grace thou thy house, and let not that grace thee.

Thou can'st not joke an enemy into a friend, but
thou may'st a friend into an enemy

He that falls in love with himself will have no rivals.

Let thy child's first lesson be obedience and the second will be what thou wilt

Blessed is he that expects nothing, for he shall never be disappointed

Rather go to bed supperless than run in debt for a breakfast

No resolution of repenting hereafter can be sincere.

Let thy discontents be secrets

Honor thy father and mother; that is, live so as to be an honor to them though they are dead

If thou injurest conscience, it will have its revenge on thee

Hear no ill of a friend, nor speak any of an enemy.

Pay what you owe, and you'll know what is your own

Be not niggardly of what costs thee nothing, as courtesy, counsel and countenance

Beware of him that is slow to anger: He is angry for something, and will not be pleased for nothing

Thirst after desert—not reward

Who says Jack is not generous? He is always fond of giving, and cares not for receiving—what?—why, advice

Thou hadst better eat salt with the philosophers of Greece, than sugar with the courtiers of Italy

Let our fathers and grandfathers be valued for their goodness, ourselves for our own

Sin is not hurtful because it is forbidden, but it is forbidden because it is hurtful

Nor is a duty beneficial because it is commanded, but it is commanded because it is beneficial

Industry need not wish

O Lazybones! Dost thou think God would have given thee arms and legs, if He had not designed thou should'st use them?

An empty bag can not stand upright

Happy that nation, fortunate that age, whose history is not diverting

None are deceived but those that confide

There are lazy minds as well as lazy bodies

Tricks and treachery are the practise of fools that have not wit enough to be honest

One Nestor is worth two Ajaxes

When knaves betray each other, one can be blamed or the other pitied

He that carries a small Crime easily, will carry it on when it comes to be an Ox

Great Modesty often hides Great Merit

Pride gets into the Coach, and Shame mounts behind.

Fools need advice most, but Wise Men only are the better for it

Silence is not always a Sign of Wisdom, but Babbling is ever a Folly

You may delay, but Time will not

Virtue may always make a Face handsome, but Vice will certain make it ugly

Prodigality of Time produces Poverty of Mind as well as of Estate

When you 're an Anvil, hold you still;
When you 're a Hammer, strike your fill.

Content is the Philosopher's Stone, that turns all it touches into gold

He that 's content hath enough

The first Mistake in Public Business is the going into it

Half the Truth is often a great Lie

The way to see by Faith is to shut the Eye of Reason.

He that complains has too much

The morning Daylight appears plainer when you put out your candle

The Eagle snatched a coal from the Altar, but it fired her Nest

Good-Will, like the Wind, floweth where it listeth.

In a corrupt Age, the putting the world in order
would breed Confusion; then e'en mind your own
Business

To serve the Public faithfully, and at the same time
to please it entirely, is impracticable

Death takes no bribes

Men often mistake themselves, seldom forget themselves

The Idle Man is the Devil's Hireling, whose Livery
is Rags, whose Diet and Wages are Famine and
Diseases

OURTEOUS READER: I have heard that
nothing gives an Author so great Pleasure
as to find his works respectfully quoted by
other learned Authors. This pleasure I have
seldom enjoyed, for though I have been, if I may
say it without Vanity, an eminent Author of Almanacs annually now a full quarter of a Century, my
Brother Authors in the same Way, for what Reason
I know not, have ever been very sparing in their
Applauses; and no other Author has taken the least
notice of me, so that, did not my Writings produce
me some solid Pudding, the great Deficiency of Praise
would have quite discouraged me.

I concluded at length that the People were the
best judges of my Merit; for they buy my Works;
and besides, in my Rambles, where I am not personally known, I have frequently heard one or other of
my Adages repeated with, as Poor Richard says, at
the End on't; this gave me some Satisfaction, as it
showed not only that my Instructions were regarded,
but Discovered likewise some Respect for my Authority; and I own that to encourage the practise of

remembering and repeating those wise Sentences, I have sometimes quoted myself with great gravity. ⟨ Judge, then, how much I must have been gratified by an Incident I am going to relate to you. I stopped my horse lately where a great Number of people were collected at a Vendue of Merchant Goods. The Hour of Sale not being come, they were conversing on the Badness of the Times, and one of the Company called to a plain, clean, old Man, with white Locks: " Pray, Father Abraham, what think you of the Times? Won't these heavy Taxes quite ruin the Country? How shall we be ever able to pay them? What would you advise us to? " Father Abraham stood up, and replied, " If you 'd have my Advice, I 'll give it you in short, for a word to the Wise is enough, and many Words won't fill a bushel, as Poor Richard says."

⟨ They joined in desiring him to speak his Mind, and gathering round him, he proceeded as follows : 'RIENDS," says he, " and Neighbors, the Taxes are indeed very heavy, and if those laid on by the Government were the only ones we had to pay, we might more easily discharge them; but we have many others, and much more grievous to some of us. We are taxed twice as much by our Idleness, three times as much by our Pride, and four times as much by our Folly, and from these taxes the Commissioners can not ease or deliver us by allowing an Abatement. However, let us hearken to good Advice, and something may be done for us; God helps them that help themselves, as Poor Richard says in his Almanac of Seventeen Hundred Thirty-three

" It would be thought a hard Government that should tax its People one-tenth Part of their Time, to be employed in its Service. But Idleness taxes many of us much more, if we reckon all that is spent in absolute Sloth, or doing of nothing, with that which is spent in idle Employments or Amusements, that amount to nothing. Sloth, by bringing on Diseases, absolutely shortens Life. Sloth, like Rust, consumes faster than Labor wears, while the used key is always bright, as Poor Richard says. But, dost thou love Life, then do not squander Time, for that's the Stuff Life is made of, as Poor Richard says. How much more than is necessary do we spend in Sleep! forgetting that the Sleeping Fox catches no Poultry, and that there will be sleeping enough in the Grave, as Poor Richard says. If Time be of all Things the most Precious, wasting of Time must be, as Poor Richard says, the greatest Prodigality, since, as he elsewhere tells us, Lost time is never found again, and what we call Time enough, always proves little enough. Let us then be up and doing, and doing to the Purpose; so by Diligence shall we do more with less Perplexity. Sloth makes all things difficult, but Industry all Things easy, as Poor Richard says: and He that riseth late must trot all Day, and shall scarce overtake his business at Night. While Laziness travels so slowly that Poverty soon overtakes him, as we read in Poor Richard, who adds, Drive thy Business, let not that drive thee; and Early to Bed and early to rise, makes a Man healthy, wealthy and wise

O what signifies wishing and hoping for better times? We may make these Times better if we bestir ourselves. Industry need not wish, as Poor Richard says, and He that lives upon Hope will die fasting. There are no gains, without Pains; then Help Hands for I have no Lands, or if I have, they are smartly taxed. And as Poor Richard likewise observes, He that hath a trade hath an Estate; he that hath a Calling hath an Office of Profit and Honor; but then the Trade must be worked at, and the Calling well followed, or neither the Estate nor the Office will enable us to pay our Taxes. If we are industrious we shall never starve; for, as Poor Richard says, At the Workingman's house Hunger looks in, but dares not enter. Nor will the Bailiff nor the

Constable enter, for Industry pays Debts while Despair increaseth them, says Poor Richard. What though you have found no Treasure, nor has any Rich Relation left you a Legacy, Diligence is the Mother of Good-Luck, as Poor Richard says, and God gives all things to Industry. Then plow deep, while Sluggards sleep, and you shall have Corn to sell and to keep, says Poor Dick. Work while it is called Today, for you know not how much you may be hindered tomorrow, which makes Poor Richard say, One Today is worth two Tomorrows; and farther, Have you somewhat to do Tomorrow, do it Today. If you were a Servant would you not be ashamed that a good Master should catch you idle? Are you then your own Master, be ashamed to catch yourself idle, as Poor Dick says. When there is so much to be done for yourself, your Family, your Country, and your gracious King, be up by Peep of Day; Let not the sun look down and say, Inglorious here he lies. Handle your Tools without Mittens; remember that the Cat in Gloves catches no mice, as Poor Richard says. 'T is true there is much to be done, and perhaps you are weak-handed, but stick to it steadily, and you will see great Effects, for constant Dropping wears away Stones, and by Diligence and Patience the Mouse ate in two the Cable; and little strokes fell great Oaks, as Poor Richard says in his Almanac, the Year I can not just now remember

METHINKS I hear some of you say, Must a man afford himself no leisure? I will tell thee, my friend, what Poor Richard says, Employ thy Time well if thou meanest to gain Leisure; and, since thou art not sure of a Minute, throw not away an Hour. Leisure is Time for doing something useful; this Leisure the diligent man will obtain, but the lazy man never; so that, as Poor Richard says, a Life of Leisure and a Life of Labor are two Things. Do you imagine that Sloth will afford you more comfort than

Labor? No; for as Poor Richard says, Trouble springs
from Idleness, and grievous Toil from needless Ease.
Many without Labor would live by their Wits only,
but they break for want of stock. Whereas Industry
gives Comfort, and Plenty, and Respect. Fly Pleasure,
and they 'll follow you. The diligent Spinner has a
large Shift; and now I have a Sheep and a Cow, everybody bids me Good-morrow, all of which is well said
by Poor Richard. " But with our Industry we must
likewise be steady, settled and careful, and oversee
our own Affairs with our own eyes, and not trust too
much to others; for as Poor Richard says,

> I never saw an oft-removed Tree,
> Nor yet an oft-removed Family,
> That throve so well as those that settled be.

And again, Three Removes is as bad as a Fire; and
again, Keep thy Shop, and thy Shop will keep thee;
and again, If you would have your business done, go;
if not, send. And again,

> He that by the Plow must thrive,
> Himself must either hold or drive.

And again, The Eye of a Master will do more work
than both his Hands; and again, Want of Care does
us more damage than want of Knowledge; and again,
Not to oversee Workmen is to leave them your Purse
open. Trusting too much to others' care is the Ruin of
Many; for as the Almanac says, In the affairs of this
world men are saved, not by Faith, but by the Want
of it; but a Man's own Care is profitable; for, saith
Poor Dick, Learning is to the Studious, and Riches
to the Careful, as well as Power to the Bold, and
Heaven to the Virtuous. And farther, If you would
have a faithful Servant, and one that you like, serve
yourself. And again, he adviseth to Circumspection
and Care, even in the smallest Matters, because
sometimes a little Neglect may breed great Mischief,
adding, For want of a Nail the Shoe was lost; for
want of a Shoe the Horse was lost, and for want of

a Horse the Rider was lost, being overtaken and slain
by the Enemy, all for want of care about a Horse-
shoe-Nail

O much for Industry, my Friends, and attention
to one's own Business; but to these we must add
Frugality, if we would make our Industry more
certainly successful. A man may, if he knows not
how to save as he gets, Keep his nose all his Life to
the Grindstone, and die not worth a Groat at last. A fat
Kitchen makes a lean Will, as Poor Richard says, and,

> Many estates are spent in the Getting,
> Since women for Tea forsook Spinning and
>   Knitting,
> And men for Punch forsook Hewing and
>   Splitting

If you would be wealthy, says he, in another Almanac,
think of Saving as well as of Getting: the Indies have
not made Spain rich, because her Outgoes are greater
than her Incomes. Away, then, with your expensive
Follies; you will not have so much cause to complain of hard Times, Heavy Taxes, and chargeable
Families; for, as Poor Dick says,

> Women and Wine, Game and Deceit,
> Make the Wealth small, and the Wants great

And farther, What maintains one Vice would bring
up two Children. You may think, perhaps, that a
little Tea or a little Punch now and then, Diet a little
more Costly, Clothes a little finer, and a little Entertainment now and then, can be no great Matter;
but remember what Poor Richard says, Many a
Little makes a Mickle; and farther, Beware of Little
Expenses; a small Leak will sink a great Ship; and
again, Who Dainties love, shall Beggars prove; and
moreover, Fools make feasts and wise Men eat them.

ERE you are all got together at this Vendue of
Fineries and Knicknacks. You call them Goods,
but if you do not take care, they will prove Evil
to some of you. You expect they will be sold cheap,

and perhaps they may for less than they cost; but
if you have no Occasion for them, they must be Dear
to you. Remember what Poor Richard says, Buy
what thou hast no need of, and ere long thou shalt
sell thy Necessaries. And again, At a great Penny-
worth pause a while: he means, that perhaps the
cheapness is apparent only, and not real, or the
Bargain, by straitening thee in thy Business, may
do thee more Harm than Good. For in another Place
he says, Many have been ruined by buying good
Pennyworths. Again Poor Richard says, 'T is foolish
to lay out Money in a purchase of Repentance; and
yet this Folly is practised every day at Vendues,
for want of minding the Almanac. Wise men, as Poor
Dick says, learn by others' Harms, Fools scarcely by
their own; but *Felix quem faciunt aliena Pericula
cautum*. Many a one, for the sake of Finery on the
Back, have gone with a hungry Belly, and half-starved
their Families; Silks and Satins, Scarlet and Velvets,
as Poor Richard says, Put out the Kitchen Fire
These are not the Necessaries of Life; they can
scarcely be called the Conveniences, and yet only
because they look Pretty, how many want to have
them. The artificial Wants of Mankind thus become
more numerous than the natural; and as Poor Dick
says, For one poor person, there are a hundred indi-
gent. By these, and other Extravagances, the Genteel
are reduced to Poverty, and forced to borrow of those
whom they formerly despised, but who through Industry and Frugality have maintained their Standing;
in which case it appears plainly that a Plowman on
his Legs is higher than a Gentleman on his Knees, as
Poor Richard says. Perhaps they have had a small
estate left them, which they knew not the getting of
—they think 't is Day and will never be Night; that
a little to be spent out of so much, is not worth minding (a Child and a Fool, as Poor Richard says, imagine
that Twenty Shillings and Twenty Years can never

be spent); but, always taking out of the Meat-tub,
and never putting in, soon comes to the Bottom;
then, as Poor Dick says, When the Well's dry, they
know the Worth of Water. But this they might have
known before if they had taken his Advice: If you
would know the Value of Money, go and try to borrow
some; for he that goes a-borrowing goes a-sorrowing;
and indeed, so does he that lends to such People,
when he goes to get it in again. Poor Dick farther
advises and says,

> Fond Pride of Dress is sure a very Curse;
> Ere Fancy you consult, consult your Purse.

And again, Pride is as loud a Beggar as Want, and
a great deal more saucy. When you have bought one
fine Thing you must buy ten more, that your appearance may be all of a Piece; but Poor Dick says, 'T is
easier to suppress the first Desire than to satisfy all
that follow it. And 't is truly folly for the Poor to
ape the Rich, as for the Frog to swell, in order to
equal the Ox

> Great Estates may venture more,
> But little Boats should keep near Shore.

'T is, however, a Folly soon punished; for Pride that
dines on Vanity sups on Contempt, as Poor Richard
says. And in another place, Pride breakfasted with
Plenty, dined with Poverty, and supped with Infamy.
And after all, of what Use is this Pride of Appearance?
for which so much is risked, so much is suffered! It
can not promote Health or ease Pain; it makes no
increase of merit in the Person, creates Envy, it
hastens Misfortune

> What is a Butterfly? At best
> He's but a caterpillar dressed.
> The gaudy Fop's his Picture just,

as Poor Richard says

BUT what Madness must it be to run in Debt for
these Superfluities! We are offered by the terms
of this Vendue, Six Months' Credit; and that perhaps

has induced some of us to attend it, because we can not spare the ready Money and hope now to be fine without it. But, ah, think what you do when you run in debt; You give to another Power over your Liberty. If you can not pay at the Time, you will be ashamed to see your Creditor; you will be in Fear when you speak to him; you will make poor, pitiful, sneaking Excuses, and by Degrees come to lose your Veracity, and sink into base downright lying; for as Poor Richard says, The second Vice is Lying, the first is running in Debt. And again, to the same purpose, Lying rides upon Debt's back. Whereas a freeborn Englishman ought not to be ashamed or afraid to see or speak to any Man living, But Poverty often deprives a Man of all Spirit and Virtue; 'T is hard for an empty Bag to stand upright, as Poor Richard truly says. What would you think of that Prince, or that Government, who should issue an Edict forbidding you to dress like a Gentleman, or a Gentlewoman, on Pain of Imprisonment or Servitude! Would you not say, that you are Free, have a right to dress as you please, and that such an Edict would be a Breach of your Privileges, and such a Government tyrannical! And yet you are about to put yourself under that Tyranny when you run in debt for such Dress! Your Creditor has authority at his Pleasure to deprive you of your Liberty, by confining you in Jail for Life, or to sell you for a Servant, if you should not be able to pay him! When you have got your Bargain, you may, perhaps, think little of Payment! but Creditors, Poor Richard tells us, have better memories than Debtors; and in another Place says, Creditors are a superstitious Sect, great Observers of set Days and Times. The Day comes round before you are aware, and the Demand is made before you are prepared to satisfy it. Or, if you bear your Debt in Mind, the Term which at First seemed so long will, as it lessens, appear extremely short. Time will seem to have added wings to his Heels as well as Shoulders. Those hath a short Lent, saith Poor Richard, who owe Money to be paid at Easter Then since, as he says, the Borrower is a slave to the Lender, and the Debtor is the creditor, disdain the Chain, preserve your Freedom, and maintain your Independency. Be Industrious and free; be frugal and free. At present, perhaps, you may think yourself in thriving Circumstances, and that you can bear a little Extravagance without Injury; but,

For Age and Want save while you may;
No Morning Sun lasts a whole Day,

as Poor Richard says. Gain may be temporary and uncertain, but ever while you live Experience is constant and certain; and, 't is easier to build two Chimneys than to keep one in fuel, as Poor Richard says. So rather go to bed supperless than rise in Debt.

Get what you can, and what you get hold.
'T is the stone that will turn all your Lead into
Gold,

as Poor Richard says. And when you have got the Philosopher's Stone, sure you will no longer complain of the bad Times, or the Difficulty of paying Taxes.

THIS Doctrine, my Friends, is Reason and Wisdom; but after all, do not depend too much on your own Industry, and Frugality, and Prudence, though excellent Things; for they may all be blasted without the Blessing of Heaven; and therefore, ask that Blessing humbly, and be not uncharitable to those that at present seem to want it, but comfort and help them. Remember Job suffered and was afterwards prosperous

"And now to conclude, Experience keeps a dear School, but Fools will learn in no other, and scarce in that; for it is true, we may give Advice, but we can not give Conduct, as Poor Richard says. However, remember this, They that won't be counseled can't be helped, as Poor Richard says: and farther, That

if you will not hear Reason, she 'll surely rap your
Knuckles."

THUS the old Gentleman ended his Harangue.
The People heard it and approved the Doctrine,
and immediately practised the contrary, just as if
it had been a common Sermon ; for the Vendue opened,
and they began to buy extravagantly, notwithstanding all his Cautions, and their own Fear of Taxes.
I found the good Man had thoroughly studied my
Almanacs and digested all I had dropped on those
Topics during the course of Five-and-Twenty Years.
The frequent mention he made of me must have tried
any one else, but my Vanity was wonderfully delighted with it, though I was conscious that not a
Tenth part of this Wisdom was my own which he
ascribed to me, but rather the Gleanings I had made
of the sense of all Ages and Nations. However, I
resolved to be the better for the Echo of it ; and though
I had at first determined to buy stuff for a new Coat,
I went away resolved to wear my old one a little
longer. Reader, if thou wilt do the same, thy profit
will be as great as mine

IN time, perhaps, mankind may be wise enough
to let trade take its own course, find its own
channels, and regulate its own proportions, etc. At
present, most of the edicts of princes, placærts, laws
and ordinances of kingdoms and States for the purpose prove political blunders, the advantages they
produce not being general for the Commonwealth,
but particular to private persons or bodies in the
State who procure them, and at the expense of the
rest of the people

I JOIN with you most cordially in rejoicing at
the return of peace. I hope that it will be lasting,
and that mankind will at length, as they call themselves reasonable creatures, have reason and sense

enough to settle their differences without cutting throats; for, in my opinion, there never was a good war or a bad peace. What vast additions to the conconveniences and comforts of living might mankind have acquired, if the money spent in wars had been employed in works of public utility ! What an extension of agriculture, even to the tops of our mountains ; what rivers rendered navigable, or joined by canals ; what bridges, aqueducts, new roads and other public works, edifices and improvements, rendering England a complete paradise, might have been obtained by spending those millions in doing good, which in the last war have been spent in doing mischief ; in bringing misery to thousands of families, and destroying the lives of so many thousands of working people, who might have performed the useful labor

When the well 's dry we know the worth of water

It were to be wished that commerce were as free between all nations of the world as it is between the several counties of England : so would all by mutual communication obtain more enjoyment. These counties do not ruin one another by trade ; neither would the nations

Let us be attentive to these (our natural advantages) and then the power of rivals, with all their restraining and prohibiting acts, can not much hurt us. We are sons of the earth and seas, and the touch of our parents will communicate to us fresh strength and vigor to renew the contest

THE GOSPEL ACCORDING TO
THOMAS JEFFERSON

The God who gave us life gave us liberty
at the same time: the hand of force
may destroy, but can not disjoin them.

Jefferson

WHEN, in the course of human events, it becomes necessary for one people to dissolve the political bands which have connected them with another, and to assume among the powers of the earth the separate and equal station to which the Laws of Nature and of Nature's God entitle them, a decent respect to the opinions of mankind requires that they should declare the causes which impel them to the separation.

We hold these truths to be self-evident: that all men are created equal; that they are endowed by their Creator with inherent and inalienable rights; that among these are Life, Liberty, and the pursuit of Happiness; that to secure these rights, governments are instituted among men, deriving their just powers from the consent of the governed; that whenever any form of government becomes destructive of these ends, it is the right of the people to alter or to abolish it, and to institute new government, laying its foundation on such principles, and organizing its powers in such form, as to them shall seem most likely to effect their safety and happiness Prudence, indeed, will dictate that governments long established should not be changed for light and transient causes; and accordingly all experience hath shown that mankind are more disposed to suffer, while evils are sufferable, than to right themselves by abolishing the forms to which they are accustomed. But when a long train of abuses and usurpations (begun at a distinguished period and pursuing invariably the same object) evinces a design to reduce them under absolute despotism, it is their right, it is their duty, to throw off such government, and to provide new guards for their future security. Such has been the patient sufferance of these Colonies; and such is now the necessity which constrains them to expunge their former systems of government. The history of the present King of Great Britain is a history of unremitting injuries and usurpations, among which appears no solitary fact to contradict the uniform tenor of the rest, but all have in direct object, the establishment of an absolute tyranny over these States. To prove this, let facts be submitted to a candid world, for the truth of which we pledge a faith yet unsullied by falsehood.

HE has refused his assent to laws the most wholesome and necessary for the public good
He has forbidden his Governors to pass laws of immediate and pressing importance, unless suspended in their operation till his assent should be obtained; and, when so suspended, he has utterly neglected to attend to them.

He has refused to pass other laws for the accommodation of large districts of people, unless those people would relinquish the right of representation in the Legislature, a right inestimable to them, and formidable to tyrants only
He has called together legislative bodies at places unusual, uncomfortable, and distant from the depository of their public records, for the sole purpose of fatiguing them into compliance with his measures
He has dissolved representative houses repeatedly and continually for opposing with manly firmness his invasions on the rights of the people.

He has refused for a long time after such dissolutions to cause others to be elected, whereby the legislative powers, incapable of annihilation, have returned to the people at large for their exercise, the State remaining, in the meantime, exposed to all the dangers of invasions from without and convulsions within
He has endeavored to prevent the population of these States; for that purpose obstructing the laws for naturalization of foreigners, refusing to pass others

to encourage their migrations hither, and raising the conditions of new appropriations of lands

He has suffered the administration of justice totally to cease in some of these States, refusing his assent to laws for establishing judiciary powers.

He has made our judges dependent upon his will alone for the tenure of their offices, and the amount and payment of their salaries

He has erected a multitude of new offices, by a self-assumed power, and sent hither swarms of new officers to harass our people and eat out their substance

He has kept among us in times of peace standing armies and ships of war without the consent of our Legislatures

He has affected to render the military independent of, and superior to, the civil power.

He has combined with others to subject us to a jurisdiction foreign to our constitutions and unacknowledged by our laws, giving his assent to their acts of pretended legislation for quartering large bodies of armed troops among us ; for protecting them by a mock trial from punishment for any murders which they should commit on the inhabitants of these States ; for cutting off our trade with all parts of the world ; for imposing taxes on us without our consent ; for depriving us of the benefits of trial by jury ; for transporting us beyond seas to be tried for pretended offenses ; for abolishing the free system of English laws in a neighboring province, establishing therein an arbitrary government, and enlarging its boundaries, so as to render it at once an example and fit instrument for introducing the same absolute rule into these States ; for taking away our charters, abolishing our most valuable laws, and altering fundamentally the forms of our governments ; for suspending our own Legislatures, and declaring themselves invested with power to legislate for us in all cases whatsoever

He has abdicated government here, withdrawing his governors, and declaring us out of his allegiance and protection

He has plundered our seas, ravaged our coasts, burnt our towns, and destroyed the lives of our people

He is at this time transporting large armies of foreign mercenaries to complete the works of death, desolation and tyranny already begun with circumstances of cruelty and perfidy unworthy the head of a civilized nation. He has constrained our fellow-citizens, taken captive on the high seas, to bear arms against their country, to become the executioners of their friends and brethren, or to fall themselves by their hands

He has endeavored to bring on the inhabitants of our frontiers, the merciless Indian savages, whose known rule of warfare is an undistinguished destruction of all ages, sexes, and conditions of existence

He has incited treasonable insurrections of our fellow-citizens, with the allurements of forfeiture and confiscation of our property.

He has waged cruel war against human nature itself, violating its most sacred rights of life and liberty in the persons of a distant people who never offended him, captivating and carrying them into slavery in another hemisphere, or to incur miserable death in their transportation thither. This piratical warfare, the opprobrium of *Infidel* powers, is the warfare of the *Christian* king of Great Britain. Determined to keep open a market where *Men* should be bought and sold, he has prostituted his negative for suppressing every legislative attempt to prohibit or to restrain this execrable commerce. And that this assemblage of horrors might want no fact of distinguished die, he is now exciting those very people to rise in arms among us, and to purchase that liberty of which he has deprived them, by murdering the people on whom he also obtruded them: thus paying off former crimes committed against the *liberties* of one people, with crimes which he urges them to commit against the *lives* of another.

IN every stage of these oppressions we have petitioned for redress in the most humble terms: our repeated petitions have been answered only by repeated injuries. A prince whose character is thus marked by every act which may define a tyrant is unfit to be the ruler of a people who mean to be free. Future ages will scarcely believe that the hardiness of one man adventured, within the short compass of twelve years only, to lay a foundation so broad and so undisguised for tyranny, over a people fostered and fixed in principles of freedom

Nor have we been wanting in attentions to our British brethren. We have warned them from time to time of attempts by their Legislature to extend a jurisdiction over these our States. We have reminded them of the circumstances of our emigration and settlement here, no one of which could warrant so strange a pretension: that these were effected at the expense of our own blood and treasure, unassisted by the wealth or the strength of Great Britain: that in constituting indeed our several forms of government, we had adopted one common king, thereby laying a foundation for perpetual league and amity with them: but that submission to their parliament was no part of our constitution, nor ever in idea, if history may be credited: and we appealed to their native justice and magnanimity as well as to the ties of our common kindred to disavow these usurpations which were likely to interrupt our connection and correspondence. They, too, have been deaf to the voice of Justice and of consanguinity, and when occasions have been given them, by the regular course of their laws, of removing from their councils the disturbers of our harmony, they have, by their free election, re-established them in power. At this very time, too, they are permitting their chief magistrate to send over not only soldiers of our common blood, but Scotch and foreign mercenaries to invade and destroy us. These facts have given the last stab to agonizing affection, and manly spirit bids us to renounce forever these unfeeling brethren. We must endeavor to forget our former love for them, and hold them as we hold the rest of mankind, enemies in war, in peace friends. We might have been a free and a great people together; but a communication of grandeur and of freedom, it seems, is below their dignity. Be it so, since they will have it. The road to happiness and to glory is open to us, too. We will tread it apart from them, and acquiesce in the necessity which pronounces our eternal separation!

E, therefore, the representatives of the United States of America in General Congress assembled, do in the name, and by the authority of the good people of these States, reject and renounce all allegiance and subjection to the kings of Great Britain and all others who may hereafter claim by, through or under them; we utterly dissolve all political connection which may heretofore have subsisted between us and the people or parliament of Great Britain: and finally we do assert and declare these Colonies to be free and independent States, and that as free and independent States they have full power to levy war, conclude peace, contract alliances, establish commerce, and to do all other acts and things which independent States may of right do.

And for the support of this declaration, we mutually pledge to each other our lives, our fortunes, and our sacred honor.—*Jefferson's First Draft of the Declaration of Independence.*

HERE are extraordinary situations which require extraordinary interposition. An exasperated people who feel that they possess power are not easily restrained within limits strictly regular

LET those flatter who fear: it is not an American art. To give praise where it is not due might be well from the venal, but would ill beseem those who are asserting the rights of human nature. They know, and will, therefore, say, that kings are the servants, not the proprietors of the people

⟵

THE great principles of right and wrong are legible to every reader; to pursue them requires not the aid of many counselors. The whole art of government consists in the art of being honest. Only aim to do your duty, and mankind will give you credit where you fail

⟵

It is a certain position in law that allegiance and protection are reciprocal, the one ceasing when the other is withdrawn.

⟵

I PROPOSED to abolish the law of primogeniture, and to make real estate descendible in parcenary to the next of kin, as personal property is, by the statute of distribution. Mr. Pendleton wished to preserve the right of primogeniture, but seeing at once that that could not prevail, he proposed we should adopt the Hebrew principle, and give a double portion to the elder son. I observed that if the eldest son could eat twice as much, or do double work, it might be a natural evidence of his right to a double portion; but being on a par, in his powers and wants, with his brothers and sisters, he should be on a par also in the partition of the patrimony; and such was the decision of the other members

⟵

THE bill for establishing religious freedom in the United States, the principles of which had, to a certain degree, been enacted before, I had drawn in all the latitude of reason and right. It still met with opposition; but, with some mutilations in the

preamble, it was finally passed; and a singular proposition proved that its protection of opinion was meant
to be universal. Where the preamble declares that
coercion is a departure from the plan of the holy
author of our religion, an amendment was proposed,
by inserting the words "Jesus Christ," so that it should
read, "a departure from the plan of Jesus Christ, the
holy author of our religion"; the insertion was rejected
by a great majority, in proof that they meant to comprehend, within the mantle of its protection, the Jew
and the Gentile, the Christian and Mohammedan,
the Hindoo, and Infidel of every denomination

I REPAIR, then, fellow-citizens, to the post
you have assigned me. With experience
enough in subordinate offices to have seen
the difficulties of this, the greatest of all,
I have learned to expect that it will rarely fall to the
lot of imperfect man to retire from this station with
the reputation and favor which bring him into it.
Without pretensions to that high confidence reposed
in our first and great Revolutionary character, whose
pre-eminent services had entitled him to the first
place in his country's love, and destined for him the
fairest page in the volume of faithful history, I ask
so much confidence only as may give firmness and
effect to the legal administration of your affairs.
I shall often go wrong through defect of judgment.
When right, I shall often be thought wrong by those
whose positions will not command a view of the whole
ground. I ask your indulgence for my own errors,
which will never be intentional; and your support
against the errors of others, who may condemn what
they would not if seen in all its parts. The approbation
implied by your suffrage is a consolation to me for
the past; and my future solicitude will be to retain
the good opinion of those who have bestowed it in
advance, to conciliate that of others by doing them

all the good in my power, and to be instrumental
to the happiness and freedom of all

Relying, then, on the patronage of your good-will,
I advance with obedience to the work, ready to retire
from it whenever you become sensible how much
better choice it is in your power to make. And may
that Infinite Power which rules the destinies of the
universe lead our councils to what is best, and give
them a favorable issue for your peace and prosperity.
—*Extract From Inaugural Address.*

IT is not enough that honest men are appointed
judges. All know the influence of interest on
the mind of man, and how unconsciously his
judgment is warped by that influence. To
this bias add that of the esprit de corps, of their
peculiar maxim and creed, that " it is the office of
a good judge to enlarge his jurisdiction," and the
absence of responsibility; and how much can we
expect in impartial decision between the General
Government, of which they are themselves so eminent
a part, and an individual State, from which they have
nothing to hope or fear? We have seen, too, that,
contrary to all correct example, they are in the habit
of going out of the question before them, to throw
an anchor ahead, and grapple further hold for future
advances of power. They are then, in fact, the corps
of sappers and miners, steadily working to undermine
the independent rights of the States, and to con-
solidate all power in the hands of that government
in which they have so important a freehold estate.
But it is not by the consolidation or concentration
of powers, but by their distribution, that good government is effected. Were not this great country already
divided into States, that division must be made,
that each might do for itself what concerns itself
directly, and what it can so much better do than a
distant authority. Every State again is divided into

counties, each to take care of what lies within its local bounds; each county again into townships or wards, to manage minuter details; and every ward into farms, to be governed each by its individual proprietor. Were we directed from Washington when to sow, and when to reap, we should soon want bread. It is by this partition of cares, descending in gradation from general to particular, that the mass of human affairs may be best managed, for the good and prosperity of all. I repeat that I do not charge the judges with wilful and ill-intentioned error; but honest error must be arrested, where its toleration leads to public ruin. As, for the safety of society, we commit honest maniacs to Bedlam, so judges should be withdrawn from their bench, whose erroneous biases are leading us to dissolution. It may, indeed, injure them in fame or in fortune; but it saves the Republic, which is the first and supreme law

I AM not prepared to say that the first magistrate of a nation can not commit treason against his country, or is unamenable to its punishment; nor yet that, where there is no written law, no regulated tribunal, there is not a law in our hearts, and a power in our hands, given for righteous employment in maintaining right, and redressing wrong

ONE free and independent legislature hereby takes upon itself to suspend the powers of another, free and independent as itself, thus exhibiting a phenomenon unknown in Nature, the creator and creature of its own power. Not only the principles of commonsense, but the common feelings of human nature must be surrendered up, before his Majesty's subjects here can be persuaded to believe that they hold their political existence at the will of a British Parliament. Shall these governments be dissolved, their property annihilated, and their people reduced to a state of Nature, at the imperious breath of a body of men whom they never saw, in whom they never confided, and over whom they have no powers of punishment or removal, let their crimes against the American public be ever so great? Can any one reason be assigned why one hundred and sixty thousand electors in the island of Great Britain should give law to four millions in the States of America, every individual of whom is equal to every individual of them in virtue, in understanding and in bodily strength? Were this to be admitted, instead of being a free people, as we have hitherto supposed, and mean to continue ourselves, we should suddenly be found the slaves, not of one but of one hundred and sixty thousand tyrants; distinguished, too, from all others, by this singular circumstance, that they are removed from the reach of fear, the only motive which holds the hand of a tyrant.

⸺

I SERVED with General Washington in the Legislature of Virginia, before the Revolution, and, during it, with Doctor Franklin in Congress. I never heard either of them speak ten minutes at a time, nor to any but the main point, which was to decide the question
They laid their shoulders to the great points, knowing that the little ones would follow of themselves. If the present Congress errs in too much talking, how can it be otherwise, in a body to which the people send one hundred and fifty lawyers, whose trade it is to question everything, yield nothing, and talk by the hour? That one hundred and fifty lawyers should do business together ought not to be expected.

⸺

THE appeal to the rights of man, which had been made in the United States, was taken up by France, first of the European nations. From her, the spirit has spread over those of the South. The tyrants of the North have allied indeed against it; but it is irresistible. Their opposition will only multiply its millions of human victims; their own satellites will catch it, and the condition of man through the civilized world will be finally and greatly ameliorated. This is a wonderful instance of great events from small causes. So inscrutable is the arrangement of causes and consequences in this world, that a two-penny duty on tea, unjustly imposed in a sequestered part of it, changes the condition of all its inhabitants.

⌖

The bulk of mankind are schoolboys through life.

⌖

HERE are three epochs in history, signalized by the total extinction of national morality. The first was of the successors of Alexander, not omitting himself. The next, the successors of the first Cæsar. The third, our own age. This was begun by the partition of Poland, followed by that of the treaty of Pillnitz; next the conflagration of Copenhagen; then the enormities of Bonaparte, partitioning the earth at his will, and devastating it with fire and sword; now the conspiracy of kings, the successors of Bonaparte, blasphemously calling themselves the Holy Alliance, and treading in the footsteps of their incarcerated leader; not yet, indeed, usurping the governments of other nations, avowedly and in detail, but controlling by their armies the forms in which they will permit them to be governed; and reserving, *in petto*, the order and extent of the usurpations further meditated

⌖

I HAVE sometimes asked myself whether my country is the better for my having lived at all? I do not know that it is. I have been the instrument of doing the following things; but they would have been done by others—some of them, perhaps, a little better: The Rivanna had never been used for navigation; scarcely an empty canoe had ever passed down it. Soon after I came of age, I examined its obstructions, set on foot a subscription for removing them, got an Act of Assembly passed, and the thing effected, so as to be used completely and fully for carrying down all our produce

The Declaration of Independence.

I proposed the demolition of the Church establishment, and the freedom of religion. It could only be done by degrees; to wit, the act of 1776, c 2, exempted dissenters from contributions to the Church, and left the Church clergy to be supported by voluntary contributions of their own sect; was continued from year to year, and made perpetual 1779, c 36.

The act putting an end to entails

The act prohibiting the importation of slaves.

The act concerning citizens, and establishing the natural right of man to expatriate himself, at will

The act changing the course of descents, and giving the inheritance to all the children, etc., equally, I drew as part of the revisal.

In 1789 and 1790, I had a great number of olive-plants, of the best kind, sent from Marseilles to Charleston, for South Carolina and Georgia. They were planted and are flourishing; and, though not yet multiplied, they will be the germ of that cultivation in those States

In 1790, I got a cask of heavy upland rice, from the River Denbigh, in Africa, about lat. 9° 30′ North, which I sent to Charleston, in hopes it might supersede the culture of the wet rice, which renders South Carolina and Georgia so pestilential through the Summer. It was divided and a part sent to Georgia. I know not whether it has been attended to in South Carolina; but it has spread in the upper parts of Georgia, so as to have become almost general, and is highly prized. Perhaps it may answer in Tennessee and Kentucky. The greatest service which can be rendered any country is, to add a useful plant to its culture, especially a bread grain ; next in value to bread is oil. Whether the act for the more general diffusion of knowledge will ever be carried into complete effect, I know not. It was received by the Legislature with great enthusiasm at first ; and a small effort was made in 1796, by the act to establish public schools, to carry a part of it into effect, viz., that for the establishment of free English schools ; but the option given to the courts has defeated the intention of the act

Those who labor in the earth are the chosen people of God

I steer my bark with Hope in the head, leaving Fear astern

ONESTY, disinterestedness and good-nature are indispensable to procure the esteem and confidence of those with whom we live, and on whose esteem our happiness depends. Never suffer a thought to be harbored in your mind which you would not avow openly. When tempted to do anything in secret, ask yourself if you would do it in public ; if you would not, be sure it is wrong. In little disputes with your companions, give way rather than insist on trifles, for the love and the approbation of others will be worth more to you than the trifle in dispute. Above all things, and at all times, practise yourself in good humor ; this, of all human qualities, is the most amiable and endearing to society. Whenever you feel a warmth of temper arising, check it at once and suppress it, recollecting it would make you unhappy within yourself and disliked by others. Nothing gives one person so great an advantage over another under all circumstances. Think of these things, practise them, and you will be rewarded by the love and confidence of the world

YOU say that in taking General Washington on your shoulders, to bear him harmless through the Federal coalition, you encounter a perilous topic. I do not think so. You have given the genuine history of the course of his mind through the trying scenes in which it was engaged, and of the seductions by which it was deceived, but not depraved. I think I knew General Washington intimately and thoroughly; and were I called on to delineate his character, it should be in terms like these:

His mind was great and powerful without being of the very first order; his penetration strong, though not so acute as that of a Newton, Bacon or Locke; and, as far as he saw, no judgment was ever sounder. It was slow in operation, being little aided by imagination or invention, but sure in conclusion. Hence the common remark of his officers, of the advantage he derived from councils of war, where, hearing all suggestions, he selected whatever was best; and certainly, no general ever planned his battles more judiciously. But if deranged during the course of the action, if any member of his plan was dislocated by sudden circumstances, he was slow in a readjustment. The consequence was that he often failed in the field, and rarely against an enemy in station, as at Boston and York. He was incapable of fear, meeting personal danger with the calmest unconcern

Perhaps the strongest feature in his character was prudence, never acting until every circumstance, every consideration, was maturely weighed; refraining if he saw a doubt, but, when once decided, going through with his purpose, whatever obstacles opposed. His integrity was most pure, his justice the most inflexible I have ever known, no motives of interest or consanguinity, of friendship or hatred, being able to bias his decision. He was, indeed, in every sense of the words, a wise, a good and a great man. His temper was naturally irritable and high-toned; but reflection and resolution had obtained a firm and habitual ascendancy over it. If ever, however, it broke its bonds, he was most tremendous in his wrath. In his expenses he was honorable, but exact; liberal in contribution to whatever promised utility; but frowning and unyielding on all visionary projects, and all unworthy calls on his charity. His heart was not warm in its affections; but he exactly calculated every man's value, and gave him a solid esteem proportioned to it.

His person, you know, was fine; his stature exactly what one would wish; his deportment easy, erect and noble; the best horseman of his age, and the most graceful figure that could be seen on horseback Although in the circle of his friends, where he might be unreserved with safety, he took a free share in conversation, his colloquial talents were not above mediocrity, possessing neither copiousness of ideas nor fluency of words. In public, when called on for a sudden opinion, he was unready, short and embarrassed. Yet he wrote readily, rather diffusely, in an easy and correct style. This he had acquired by conversation with the world, for his education was merely reading, writing and common arithmetic, to which he added surveying at a later day. His time was employed in action chiefly, reading little, and that only in agriculture and English history. His correspondence became necessarily extensive, and, with journalizing his agricultural proceedings, occupied most of his leisure hours within doors On the whole, his character was, in its mass, perfect; in nothing bad, in few points indifferent; and it may truly be said that never did Nature and fortune combine more perfectly to make a man great, and to place him in the same constellation with whatever worthies have merited from man an everlasting remembrance. For his was the singular destiny and merit of leading the armies of his country successfully

through an arduous war, for the establishment of its
independence; of conducting its councils through the
birth of a Government new in its forms and principles,
until it had settled down into a quiet and orderly
train; and of scrupulously obeying the laws through
the whole of his career, civil and military, of which
the history of the world furnishes no other example.
How then can it be perilous for you to take such a
man on your shoulders?

He has often declared to me that he considered our
new constitution as an experiment on the practi-
cability of republican government, and with what
dose of liberty man could be trusted for his own good;
that he was determined the experiment should have
a fair trial, and would lose the last drop of his blood
in support of it. I do believe that General Washington
had a firm confidence in the durability of our Government. I felt on his death, with my countrymen, that
"Verily a great man hath fallen this day in Israel."
—*Jefferson's Character of Washington.*

I KNOW that laws and institutions must go
hand in hand with the progress of the human
mind. As that becomes more developed,
more enlightened, as new discoveries are
made, new truths disclosed, and manners and opinions
change with the change of circumstances, *institutions
must advance also*, and keep pace with the times.
We might as well require a man to wear still the coat
which fitted him when a boy, as civilized society to
remain ever under the regimen of their barbarous
ancestors. It is this preposterous idea which has
lately deluged Europe in blood.

Their monarchs, instead of wisely yielding to the
gradual changes of circumstances, of favoring progressive accommodation to progressive improvement,
have clung to old abuses, entrenched themselves
behind steady habits, and obliged their subjects to

seek through blood and violence rash and ruinous innovations, which, had they been referred to the peaceful deliberations and collected wisdom of the nation, would have been put into acceptable and salutary forms

Let us follow no such examples, nor weakly believe that one generation is not as capable as another of taking care of itself, and of ordering its own affairs.

I have ever found, in my progress through life, that acting for the public if we always do what is right, the approbation denied in the beginning will surely follow in the end

HE station which we occupy among the nations of the earth is honorable, but awful. Trusted with the destinies of this solitary republic of the world, the only monument of human rights and the sole depository of the sacred fire of freedom and self-government, from hence it is to be lighted up in other regions of the earth, if other regions of the earth ever become susceptible to its benign influence. All mankind ought then, with us, to rejoice in its prosperous, and sympathise in its adverse, fortunes, as involving everything that is dear to man. And to what sacrifices of interest or commerce ought not these considerations to animate us? To what compromises of opinion and inclination, to maintain harmony and union among ourselves, and to preserve from all danger this hallowed ark of human hope and of human happiness? That differences of opinion should arise among men, on politics, on religion, and on every other topic of human inquiry, and that these should be freely expressed in a country where all our faculties are free, is to be expected

The land belongs in usufruct to the living, and the dead have no power over it

I KNOW, indeed, that some honest men fear that a Republican Government can not be strong; that this Government is not strong enough. But would the honest patriot, in the full tide of successful experiment, abandon a government which has so far kept us free and firm, on the theoretic and visionary fear that this Government, the world's best hope, may by possibility want energy to preserve itself? I trust not. I believe this, on the contrary, the strongest Government on earth. I believe it the only one where every man, at the call of the laws, would fly to the standard of the law, and would meet invasions of the public order as his own personal concern

THOSE who labor in the earth are the chosen people of God, if he ever had chosen people, whose breasts he has made the peculiar deposit for substantial and genuine virtue. It is the focus in which he keeps alive that sacred fire, which otherwise might escape from the earth. Corruption of morals in the mass of cultivators is a phenomenon of which no age or nation has furnished an example. Generally speaking, the proportion which the aggregate of the other classes of citizens bears in any State to that of its husbandmen, is the proportion of its unsound and healthy parts, and it is a good enough barometer whereby to measure its degree of corruption.

LET us, then, with courage and confidence, pursue our own Federal and Republican principles, our attachment to our Union and representative government. Kindly separated by Nature and a wide ocean from the exterminating havoc of one quarter of the globe; too high-minded to endure the degradations of the others; possessing a chosen country, with room enough for our descendants to the hundredth and thousandth generation; entertaining a due sense of our equal rights to the use of our own faculties, to the acquisitions of our industry, to honor and confidence from our fellow-citizens, resulting, not from birth, but from our actions and their sense of them; enlightened by a benign religion, professed, indeed, and practised in various forms, yet all of them including honesty, truth, temperance, gratitude, and the love of man; acknowledging and adoring an overruling Providence, which by all its dispensations proves that it delights in the happiness of man here and his greater happiness hereafter; with all these blessings, what more is necessary to make us a happy and prosperous people? Still one thing more, fellow-citizens—a wise and frugal government, which shall restrain men from injuring one another, which shall leave them otherwise free to regulate their own pursuits of industry and improvement, and shall not take from the mouth of labor the bread it has earned. This is the sum of good government, and this is necessary to close the circle of our felicities

OPINION is something with which the government has no business to meddle; it is quite beyond its legitimate province. Millions of innocent men, women and children, since the introduction of Christianity, have been tortured, fined, burnt, imprisoned; yet we have not advanced one inch toward uniformity. Let us reflect that the earth is inhabited by thousands of millions of people; that these profess probably a thousand different systems of religion; that ours is but one of that thousand; that if there be but one right, and ours that one, we should wish to see the nine hundred and ninety-nine wandering sects gathered into the fold of truth. But against such we can not effect this by force. Reason and persuasion are the only practicable instruments. For these, free inquiry must be indulged; and how can we wish others to indulge it, while we refuse it ourselves?

It is vain for commonsense to urge that nothing can produce but nothing; that it is an idle dream to believe in a philosopher's stone which is to turn everything into gold, and to redeem man from the original sentence of his Maker, " in the sweat of his brow shall he eat his bread."

VERY man and every body of men on earth possess the right of self-government. They receive it with their being from the hand of Nature. Individuals exercise it by their single will; collections of men by that of their majority; for the law of the majority is the natural law of every society of men

Nor are we acting for ourselves alone, but for the whole human race. The event of our experiment is to show whether man can be trusted with self-government. The eyes of suffering humanity are fixed on us with anxiety as their only hope; and on such a theater, for such a cause, we must suppress all smaller passions and local considerations. The leaders of Federalism say that man can not be trusted with his own government. We must do no act which shall replace them in the direction of the experiment. We must not, by any departure from principle, disgust the mass of our fellow-citizens who have confided to us this interesting cause

If we move in mass, be it ever so circuitously, we shall obtain our object; but if we break into squads, every one pursuing the path he thinks most direct, we become an easy conquest to those who can now barely hold us in check.

I repeat again, and most emphatically, that we ought not to schismatize on either man or measures. Principles alone can justify that.

I have never conceived that having been in public life requires me to belie my sentiments, or to conceal them.

⸺

When great evils happen, I am in the habit of looking out for what good may arise from them as consolation to us; and Providence has in fact so established the order of things as that most evils are the means of producing some good

⸺

HE spirit of the times may alter, will alter. Our rulers will become corrupt, our people careless. A single zealot may become persecutor, and better men be his victims. It can never be too often repeated, that the time for fixing every essential right, on a legal basis, is while our rulers are honest, and ourselves united. From the conclusion of this war (of the Revolution) we shall be going down hill. It will not then be necessary to resort every moment to the people for support. They will be forgotten, therefore, and their rights disregarded. They will forget themselves, but in the sole faculty of making money, and will never think of uniting to effect a due respect for their rights. The shackles, therefore, which shall not be knocked off at the conclusion of the war, will remain on us long, will be made heavier and heavier, till our rights shall revive or expire in a convulsion

⸺

In a government bottomed on the will of all, the life and liberty of every individual citizen becomes interesting to all

⸺

HERE are two subjects which I shall claim a right to further as long as I have breath: the public education and the subdivision of the counties into wards (townships). I consider the continuance of Republican government as absolutely hanging on these two hooks

Where every man is a sharer in the direction of his

ward republic or of some of the higher ones, and feels
that he is a participator in the government of affairs,
not merely at an election one day in the year, but
every day; when there shall not be a man in the State
who will not be a member of some one of its councils,
great or small, he will let the heart be torn out of
his body sooner than his power be wrested from him
by a Cæsar or a Bonaparte

The last hope of human liberty in this world rests
on us. We ought, for so dear a State, to sacrifice every
attachment, every enmity

I am not among those who fear the people. They,
and not the rich, are our dependence for continued
freedom. And to preserve their independence, we
must not let our rulers load us with perpetual debt.
We must make our election between *economy and
liberty* or *profusion and servitude*

The information of the people at large can alone
make them the safe, as they are the sole, depository
of our religious and political freedom

By the God that made me, I will cease to exist before
I yield to a connection on such terms as the British
Parliament propose

HE greatest of all reformers of the depraved
religion of His own country was Jesus of Naza-
reth
Abstracting what is really His from the rubbish in
which it is buried, easily distinguished by its luster
from the dross of His biographers, and as separable
from that as the diamond from the dunghill, we have
the outlines of a system of the most sublime morality
which has fallen from the lips of man; outlines which
it is lamentable He did not fill up. Epictetus and

Epicurus give laws for governing ourselves, Jesus a supplement of the duties and charities we owe to others

It is impossible not to be sensible that we are acting for all mankind; that circumstances denied to others, but indulged to us, have imposed on us the duty of proving what is the degree of freedom and self-government in which a society may venture to have its individual members

A government held together by the bands of reason only, requires much compromise of opinion; that things even salutary should not be crammed down the throats of dissenting brethren

There is a debt of service due from every man to his country, proportioned to the bounties which Nature and Fortune have measured to him

Opinion and the just maintenance of it shall never be a crime in my view, nor bring injury on the individual

I never yet saw a native American begging in the streets or highways

That government is best which governs least

Honesty is the first chapter of the book of wisdom.

INSTEAD of embarrassing commerce under piles of regulating laws, duties and prohibitions, could it be relieved of all its shackles in all parts of the world, could every country be employed in producing that which Nature has best fitted it to produce, and each be free to exchange with others mutual surpluses for mutual wants, the greatest mass possible would then be produced of those things which contribute to human life and human happiness; the numbers of mankind would be increased, and their condition bettered

---

Our people will remain virtuous so long as agriculture is our principal object, which will be the case while there remain vacant lands in America.

When we get piled on one another in large cities, as in Europe, we shall go to eating each other as they do there

---

It is indeed an animating thought that, while we are securing the rights of ourselves and our posterity, we are pointing out the way to struggling nations who wish, like us, to emerge from their tyrannies also. Heaven help their struggles and lead them, as it has done us, triumphantly through them

---

No government can be maintained without the principle of fear as well as of duty. Good men will obey the last, but bad ones the former only

---

My creed has been formed on unsheathing the sword at Lexington

---

To inform the minds of the people and to follow their will is the chief duty of those placed at their head.

I deem no government safe which is under the vassalage of any self-constituted authorities, or any other authority than that of the nation, or its regular functionaries

---

AS to the calumny of Atheism, I am so broken to calumnies of every kind, from every department of government, Executive, Legislative and Judiciary, and from every minion of theirs holding office or seeking it, that I entirely disregard it. It has been so impossible to contradict all their lies, that I am determined to contradict none; for while I should be engaged with one, they would publish twenty new ones

Had the doctrines of Jesus been preached always as pure as they came from His lips, the whole civilized world would now have been Christian.

To the corruptions of Christianity I am indeed opposed; but not to the genuine precepts of Jesus Himself; I am a Christian in the only sense He wished any one to be; sincerely attached to His doctrines in preference to all others; ascribing to Himself every human excellence; and believing He never claimed any other

Convinced that the Republican is the only form of government which is not eternally at open or secret war with the rights of mankind, my prayers and efforts shall be cordially distributed to the support of that we have so happily established

THE GOSPEL ACCORDING TO
THOMAS PAINE

When it shall be said in any country in the world, "My poor are happy; neither ignorance nor distress is to be found among them; my jails are empty of prisoners, my streets of beggars; the aged are not in want, the taxes are not oppressive; the rational world is my friend, because I am a friend of its happiness "—when these things can be said, then may that country boast of its constitution and its government.

HESE are the times that try men's souls. The Summer soldier and the sunshine patriot will, in this crisis, shrink from the service of his country; but he that stands it *now*, deserves the love and thanks of man and woman. Tyranny, like Hell, is not easily conquered; yet we have this consolation with us, that the harder the conflict, the more glorious the triumph. What we obtain too cheap, we esteem too lightly : 't is dearness only that gives everything its value.

Heaven knows how to put a proper price upon its goods; and it would be strange indeed, if so celestial an article as *Freedom* should not be highly rated. Britain, with an army to enforce her tyranny, has declared that she has a right not only to tax, but " to bind us in all cases whatsoever," and if being bound in that manner is not slavery, then is there not such a thing as slavery on earth. Even the expression is impious, for so unlimited a power can belong only to God

CAN not help being sometimes surprised at the complimentary references which I have seen and heard made to ancient histories and transactions. The wisdom, civil governments, and sense of honor of the States of Greece and Rome are frequently held up as objects of excellence and imitation. Mankind have lived to very little purpose if, at this period of the world, they must go two or three thousand years back for lessons and examples. We do great injustice to ourselves by placing them in such superior line. We have no just authority for it, neither can we tell why it is that we should suppose ourselves inferior. Could the mist of antiquity be cleared away, and men and things be viewed as they really were, it is more than probable that they would admire us, rather than we them. America has surmounted a greater variety and combination of difficulties than, I believe, ever fell to the share of any one people, in the same space of time, and has replenished the world with more useful knowledge and sounder maxims of civil government than were ever produced in any age before

ONCE felt all that kind of anger, which a man ought to feel, against the mean principles that are held by the Tories: a noted one, who kept a tavern at Amboy, was standing at his door, with as pretty a child in his hand, about eight or nine years old, as I ever saw, and after speaking his mind as freely as he thought prudent, finished with this unfatherly expression, " Well, give me peace in my day." Not a man lives on the continent but fully believes that a separation must some time or other finally take place, and a generous parent should have said, " If there must be trouble, let it be in my day, that my child may have peace "; and this single reflection, well applied, is sufficient to awaken every man to duty

HAVE as little superstition in me as any man living, but my secret opinion has ever been, and still is, that God Almighty will not give up a people to military destruction, or leave them unsupportedly to perish, who have so earnestly and repeatedly sought to avoid the calamities of war, by every decent method which wisdom could invent Neither have I so much of the Infidel in me, as to suppose that He has relinquished the government of the world, and given us up to the care of devils

It is, I think, exceedingly easy to define what ought to be understood by national honor; for that which is the best character for an individual is the best character for a nation ; and wherever the latter exceeds or falls beneath the former, there is a departure from the line of true greatness

It is the madness of folly to expect mercy from those who have refused to do justice; and even mercy, where conquest is the object, is only a trick of war.

Nothing hurts the affections both of parents and children so much as living too closely connected, and keeping up the distinction too long

Like men in a state of intoxication, you forget that the rest of the world have eyes, and that the same stupidity which conceals you from yourselves exposes you to their satire and contempt

HE Grecians and Romans were strongly possessed of the spirit of liberty, but not the principle, for at the time that they were determined not to be slaves themselves, they employed their power to enslave the rest of mankind. But this distinguished era is blotted by no one misanthropical vice

As extraordinary power ought not to be lodged in the hands of any individual, so ought there to be no appropriations of public money to any person beyond what his services in a State may be worth

Government on the old system is an assumption of power, for the aggrandizement of itself; on the new, a delegation of power, for the common benefit of society

Instead of referring to musty records and moldy parchments to prove that the rights of the living are lost, " renounced and abdicated forever," by those

who are now no more, **M. De Lafayette** applies to
the living world and emphatically says, " Call to
mind the sentiments which Nature has engraved in
the heart of every citizen, and which take a new force
when they are solemnly recognized by all : For a nation
to love liberty, it is sufficient that she knows it ; and
to be free, it is sufficient that she wills it."

HE error of those who reason by precedents
drawn from antiquity, respecting the rights
of man, is that they do not go far enough
into antiquity. They do not go the whole
way. They stop in some of the intermediate stages of
a hundred or a thousand years, and produce what was
then done as a rule for the present day. This is no
authority at all
If we travel still further into antiquity, we shall find
a directly contrary opinion and practise prevailing,
and, if antiquity is to be authority, a thousand such
authorities may be produced, successively contra-
dicting each other ; but if we proceed on, we shall at
last come out right ; we shall come to the time when
man came from the hand of his Maker. What was he
then ? Man. Man was his high and only title, and a
higher can not be given him.
    We have now arrived at the origin of man and at
the origin of his rights. As to the manner in which the
world has been governed from that day to this, it
is no further any concern of ours than to make a proper
use of the errors or the improvements which the history of it presents. Those who lived a hundred or a
thousand years ago were then moderns as we are now.
They had their ancients, and those ancients had others,
and we also shall be ancients in our turn
If the mere name of antiquity is to govern in the affairs
of life, the people who are to live a hundred or a thousand years hence may as well take us for a precedent,
as we make a precedent of those who lived a hundred

or a thousand years ago. The fact is, that portions of antiquity, by proving everything, establish nothing. It is authority against authority all the way, till we come to the divine origin of the rights of man, at the Creation. Here our inquiries find a resting-place, and our reason finds a home.

If a dispute about the rights of man had arisen at a distance of a hundred years from the Creation, it is to this source of authority they must have referred, and it is to the same source of authority that we must now refer

THOUGH I mean not to touch upon any sectarian principle of religion, yet it may be worth observing that the genealogy of Christ is traced to Adam. Why, then, not trace the rights of man to the creation of man? I will answer the question. Because there have been upstart governments, thrusting themselves between, and presumptuously working to unmake man

If any generation of men ever possessed the right of dictating the mode by which the world should be governed forever, it was the first generation that existed; and if that generation did it not, no succeeding generation can show any authority for doing it nor can set any up

The illuminating and divine principle of the equal rights of man (for it has its origin from the Maker of man) relates not only to the living individuals, but to generations of men succeeding each other. Every generation is equal in rights to the generation which preceded it, by the same rule that every individual is born equal in rights with his contemporary

It is also to be observed that all the religions known in the world are founded, so far as they relate to man, on the unity of man, as being all of one degree

Whether in Heaven or in Hell, or in whatever state man may be supposed to exist hereafter, the good and the bad are the only distinctions. Nay, even the laws of government are obliged to slide into this principle, by making degrees to consist in crimes, and not in persons

It is one of the greatest of all truths, and of the highest advantage to cultivate. By considering man in this light, and by instructing him to consider himself in this light, it places him in close connection with all his duties, whether to his Creator or to the Creation, of which he is a part; and it is only when he forgets his origin, or, to use a more fashionable phrase, his birth and family, that he becomes dissolute

It is not among the least of the evils of the present existing governments in all parts of Europe, that man, considered as man, is thrown back to a vast distance from his Maker, and the artificial chasm filled up by a succession of barriers, or a sort of turn-pike gates, through which he has to pass

I T is a perversion of terms to say that a charter gives rights. It operates by a contrary effect, that of taking rights away. Rights are inherently in all the inhabitants; but charters, by annulling these rights in the majority, leave the right, by exclusion, in the hands of a few. If charters were constructed so as to express in direct terms " that every inhabitant who is not a member of a corporation shall not exercise the right of voting," such charters would in the face be charters, not of rights, but of exclusion. The effect is the same under the form they now stand; and the only persons on whom they operate, are the persons whom they exclude

A S war is the system of government on the old construction, the animosity which nations reciprocally entertain is nothing more than what the policy of their governments excites to keep up the spirit of the system. Each government accuses the other of perfidy, intrigue, ambition, as a means of heating the imagination of their respective nations, and increasing them to hostilities. Man is not the enemy of man but through the medium of a false system of government. Instead, therefore, of exclaiming against the ambition of kings, the exclamation should be directed against the principle of such governments; and instead of seeking to reform the individual, the wisdom of a nation should apply itself to reform the system

⎯⎯

MAN did not enter into society to become worse than he was before, nor to have fewer rights than he had before, but to have those rights better secured. His natural rights are the foundation of all his civil rights. But in order to pursue this distinction with more precision, it is necessary to make the different qualities of natural and civil rights.

A few words will explain this. Natural rights are those which appertain to man in right of his existence. Of this kind are all the intellectual rights, or rights of the mind, and also all those rights of acting as an individual for his own comfort and happiness, which are not injurious to the natural rights of others. Civil rights are those which appertain to man in right of his being a member of society

⎯⎯

THE natural rights which man retains are all those in which the power to execute is as perfect in the individual as the right itself. Among this class, as is before mentioned, are all the intellectual rights, or rights of the mind: consequently, religion is one of those rights The natural rights which are not retained, are all those in which, though the right is perfect in the individual, the power to execute them is defective. They answer not his purpose. A man, by natural right, has a right to judge in his own cause; and so far as the right of the mind is concerned, he never surrenders it: but what availeth him it to judge, if he has not power to redress? He therefore deposits his right in the common stock of society, and takes the arm of society, of which he is a part, in preference and in addition to his own. Society grants him nothing. Every man is proprietor in society, and draws on the capital as a matter of right. From these premises, two or three certain conclusions will follow:

First, That every civil right grows out of a natural right, or, in other words, is a natural right exchanged.

Secondly, That civil power, properly considered as such, is made up of the aggregate of that class of the natural rights of man, which becomes defective in the individual in point of power, and answers not his purpose, but when collected to a focus becomes competent to the purpose of every one.

Thirdly, That the power produced from the aggregate of natural rights, imperfect in power in the individual, can not be applied to invade the natural rights which are retained in the individual, and in which the power to execute is as perfect as the right itself

We have now in a few words traced man from a natural individual to a member of society, and shown, or endeavored to show, the quality of the natural rights retained, and those which are exchanged for civil rights. Let us now apply those principles to governments

In casting our eyes over the world, it is extremely easy to distinguish the governments which have arisen out of society, or out of the social compact, from those which have not: but to place this in a clearer light than what a single glance will afford, it will be proper to take a review of the several sources from which the governments have arisen, and on which they have been founded

They may all be comprehended under three heads: first, superstition; secondly, power; thirdly, the com-

mon interests of society, and the common rights of
man

The first was a government of priestcraft, the second
of conquerors, and the third of reason.

When a set of artful men pretended, through the
medium of oracles, to hold intercourse with the Deity,
as familiarly as they now march up the backstairs
in European courts, the world was completely under
the government of superstition. The oracles were
consulted, and whatever they were made to say,
became the law; and this sort of government lasted
as long as this sort of superstition lasted

After these a race of conquerors arose, whose government, like that of William the Conqueror, was founded
in power, and the sword assumed the name of a
scepter. Governments thus established last as long
as the power to support them lasts; but that they
might avail themselves of every engine in their favor,
they united fraud to force, and set up an idol which
they called Divine Right, and which, in imitation
of the Pope, who affects to be spiritual and temporal,
and in contradiction to the founder of the Christian
religion, twisted itself afterwards into an idol of
another shape, called Church and State. The key
of Saint Peter and the key of the Treasury became
quartered on one another, and the wondering, cheated
multitude worshiped the invention

HEN I contemplate the natural dignity of man;
when I feel for the honor and happiness of its
character, I become irritated at the attempt to govern
mankind by force and fraud, as if they were all knaves
and fools, and can scarcely avoid disgust at those
who are thus imposed upon

A constitution is not the act of a government, but
of a people constituting a government; and government without a constitution is power without a right.

❡ All power exercised over a nation must have some beginning. It must be either delegated or assumed. There are no other sources. All delegated power is trust, and all assumed power is usurpation. Time does not alter the nature and quality of either

⎯

I T has been thought a considerable advance towards establishing the principles of freedom to say, that government is a compact between those who govern and those who are governed : but this can not be true, because it is putting the effect before the cause ; for as man must have existed before governments existed, there necessarily was a time when governments did not exist, and consequently there could originally exist no governors to form such a compact with

The fact therefore must be that the individuals themselves, each in his own personal and sovereign right, entered into a compact with each other to produce a government : and this is the only mode in which governments have a right to arise, and the only principle on which they have a right to exist.

❡ To possess ourselves of a clear idea of what government is, or ought to be, we must trace it to its origin. In doing this, we shall easily discover that governments must have arisen, either out of the people or over the people

Governments arise, either out of the people or over the people. The English government is one of those which arose out of a conquest, and not out of society, and consequently it arose over the people ; and though it has been much modified from the opportunity of circumstances since the time of William the Conqueror, the country has never yet regenerated itself, and is therefore without a constitution

⎯

Those who expect to reap the blessings of freedom must, like men, undergo the fatigues of supporting it.

WHEN all the governments of Europe shall be established on the representative system, nations will become acquainted, and the animosities and prejudices fomented by the intrigues and artifice of courts will cease. The oppressed soldier will become a freeman; and the tortured sailor, no longer dragged through the streets like a felon, will pursue his mercantile voyage in safety. It would be better that nations would continue the pay of their soldiers during their lives, and give them their discharge and restore them to freedom and their friends, and cease recruiting, than retain such multitudes at the same expense, in a condition useless to society and to themselves

FOR myself, I fully and conscientiously believe that it is the will of the Almighty that there should be a diversity of religious opinions among us: it affords a larger field for our Christian kindness. Were we all of one way of thinking, our religious dispositions would want matter for probation, and on this liberal principle I look on the various denominations among us to be like children of the same family, differing only in what is called their Christian names

Conquest and defeat are each of the same price

Independence is my happiness, and I view things as they are, without regard to place or person; my country is the world, and my religion is to do good

I DO not believe that any two men, on what are called doctrinal points, think alike who think at all. It is only those who have not thought that appear to agree. It is in this case as with what is called the British Constitution; it has been taken for granted to be good, and encomiums have supplied the place of proof. But when the

nation comes to examine into its principles and the
abuses it admits, it will be found to have more defects
than I have hitherto pointed out

As to what are called national religions, we may,
with as much propriety, talk of national gods. It is
either political craft or the remains of the pagan
system, when every nation had its separate and
particular deity.

Who, then, art thou, vain dust and ashes! by whatever name thou art called, whether a king, a bishop,
a church or a State, a parliament or anything else,
that obtrudest thine insignificance between the soul
of man and his Maker? Mind thine own concerns.
If he believes not as thou believest, it is a proof that
thou believest not as he believeth, and there is no
earthly power can determine between you

With respect to what are called denominations of
religion, if every one is left to judge of his own religion,
there is no such thing as a religion that is wrong;
but if they are to judge of each other's religion, there
is no such thing as a religion that is right; and therefore, all the world is right, or all the world is wrong.

But with respect to religion itself, without regard
to names, and as directing itself from the universal
family of mankind to the divine object of all ador-
ation, it is man bringing to his Maker the fruits of
his heart; and though these fruits may differ from
each other, like the fruits of the earth, the grateful
tribute of every one is accepted

THE duty of man is not a wilderness of turnpike-
gates, through which he is to pass by tickets
from one to the other. It is plain and simple, and
consists of but two points: his duty to God, which
every man must feel; and with respect to his neighbor,
to do as he would be done by. If those to whom power
is delegated do well, they will be respected; if not,
they will be despised; and with regard to those to

whom no power is delegated, but who assume it, the rational world can know nothing of them

I love the man that can smile in trouble, that can gather strength from distress, and grow brave by reflection. 'T is the business of little minds to shrink, but he whose heart is firm, and whose conscience approves his conduct, will pursue his principles unto death

As reforms, or revolutions—call them which you please—extend themselves among nations, those nations will form connections and conventions; and when a few are thus confederated, the progress will be rapid, till despotism and corrupt government be totally expelled, at least out of two quarters of the world, Europe and America

IF we suppose a large family of children who on any particular day, or particular occasion, make it a custom to present to their parents some token of their affection and gratitude, each of them would make a different offering, and most probably in a different manner

Some would pay their congratulations in themes of verse and prose, by some little devices, as their genius dictated, or according to what they thought would please; and, perhaps, the least of all, not able to do any of those things, would ramble into the garden, or the field, and gather what it thought the prettiest flower it could find, though, perhaps, it might be but a simple weed. The parents would be more gratified by such a variety than if the whole of them had acted on a concerted plan, and each had made exactly the same offering

This would have the cold appearance of contrivance, or the harsh one of control. But of all unwelcome things, nothing would more afflict the parents than to know that the whole of them had afterwards gotten together by the ears, boys and girls, fighting, reviling and abusing each other about which was the best or the worst present

Had it not been for America, there had been no such thing as freedom left throughout the whole universe

As to religion, I hold it to be the indispensable duty of all governments to protect all conscientious professors thereof, and I know of no other business which government hath to do therewith

HEN it shall be said in any country in the world, " My poor are happy; neither ignorance nor distress is to be found among them; my jails are empty of prisoners, my streets of beggars; the aged are not in want, the taxes are not oppressive; the rational world is my friend, because I am a friend of its happiness "—when these things can be said, then may that country boast of its constitution and its government. Within the space of a few years we have seen two revolutions, those of America and France. In the former, the contest was long and the conflict severe; in the latter, the nation acted with such a consolidated impulse that having no foreign enemy to contend with, the revolution was complete in power the moment it appeared From both these instances it is evident that the greatest forces that can be brought into the field of revolutions are reason and common interest. Where these can have the opportunity of acting, opposition dies with fear, or crumbles away by conviction. It is a great standing which they have now universally obtained; and we may hereafter hope to see revolutions, or changes in governments, produced with the same quiet operation by which any measure, determinable by reason and discussion, is accomplished

When a nation changes its opinion and habits of thinking, it is no longer to be governed as before; but it would not only be wrong, but bad policy, to attempt by force what ought to be accomplished by reason. Rebellion consists in forcibly opposing the general will of a nation, whether by a party or by a government. There ought, therefore, to be in every nation a method of occasionally ascertaining the state of public opinion with respect to government.

ADMITTING that any annual sum—say, for instance, one thousand pounds—is necessary or sufficient for the support of a family, consequently the second thousand is of the nature of a luxury, the third still more so, and by proceeding on, we shall at last arrive at a sum that may not improperly be called a prohibitable luxury. It would be impolitic to set bounds to property acquired by industry, and therefore it is right to place the prohibition beyond the probable acquisition to which industry can extend; but there ought to be a limit to property, or the accumulation of it by bequest. It should pass in some other line

I know not why any plant or herb of the field should be a greater luxury in one country than in another, but an overgrown estate in either is a luxury at all times, and, as such, is the proper object of taxation.

AS to the offices of which any civil government may be composed, it matters but little by what names they are described. In the routine of business, as before observed, whether a man be styled a president, a king, an emperor, a senator, or anything else, it is impossible that any service he can perform, can merit from a nation more

than ten thousand pounds a year; and as no man
should be paid beyond his services, so every man
of a proper heart will not accept more

Public money ought to be touched with the most
scrupulous consciousness of honor. It is not the
product of riches only, but of the hard earnings
of labor and poverty. It is drawn even from the
bitterness of want and misery. Not a beggar passes,
or perishes in the streets, whose mite is not in that
mass

HE Crown signifies a nominal office of a
million sterling a year, the business of
which consists in receiving the money.
Whether the person be wise or foolish,
sane or insane, a native or a foreigner, matters
not. Every ministry acts upon the same idea that
Mr. Burke writes; namely, that the people must
be hoodwinked and held in superstitious ignorance
by some bugbear or other; and what is called the
Crown answers this purpose, and therefore it answers
all the purposes to be expected from it. This is more
than can be said of the other two branches

The hazard to which this office is exposed in all
countries is not from anything that can happen to
the man, but from what may happen to the nation
—the danger of its coming to its senses.

It has been customary to call the Crown the
executive power, and the custom has continued,
though the reason has ceased

It was called the executive, because the person whom
it signifies used, formerly, to sit in the character of
a judge, in administering or executing the laws. The
tribunals were then a part of the court. The power,
therefore, which is now called the judicial is what
was called the executive; and, consequently, one or
the other of the terms is redundant, and one of the
offices useless. When we speak of the Crown, now,

it means nothing; it signifies neither a judge nor a general; besides which, it is the laws that govern, and not the man. The old terms are kept up, and give an appearance of consequence to empty forms; and the only effect they have is that of increasing expenses.

⌒

I T is difficult to discover what is meant by the landed interest, if it does not mean a combination of aristocratical landholders, opposing their own pecuniary interest to that of the farmer, and every branch of trade, commerce and manufacture. In all other respects, it is the only interest that needs no special protection. It enjoys the general protection of the world

Every individual, high or low, is interested in the fruits of the earth; men, women and children, of all ages and degrees, will turn out to assist the farmer, rather than that a harvest should not be got in; and they will not act thus by any other property. It is the only one for which the common prayer of mankind is put up, and the only one that can never fail from the want of means. It is the interest, not of the policy, but of the existence of man, and when it ceases, he must cease to be

No other interest in a nation stands on the same united support. Commerce, manufactures, arts, sciences and everything else, compared with this, are supported but in parts. Their prosperity or their decay has not the same universal influence. When the valleys laugh and sing, it is not the farmer only, but all creation that rejoices. It is a prosperity that excludes all envy; and this can not be said of anything else

⌒

W HAT is called the House of Peers is constituted on a ground very similar to that against which there is a law in other cases. It amounts to a combination of persons in one common interest. No reason can be given why a house of legislation should be composed entirely of men whose occupation consists in letting landed property, than why it should be composed of those who hire, or of brewers, or bakers, or any other separate class of men

HEN, in countries that are called civilized, we see age going to the workhouse, and youth to the gallows, something must be wrong in the system of government. It would seem, by the exterior appearance of such countries, that all was happiness ; but there lies hidden from the eye of common observation, a mass of wretchedness that has scarcely any other chance than to expire in poverty or infamy. Its entrance into life is marked with the presage of its fate ; and until this is remedied, it is in vain to punish.

Civil government does not consist in executions ; but in making that provision for the instruction of youth, and the support of age, as to exclude, as much as possible, profligacy from the one, and despair from the other. Instead of this, the resources of a country are lavished upon kings, upon courts, upon hirelings, impostors, and prostitutes ; and even the poor themselves, with all their wants upon them, are compelled to support the fraud that oppresses them
Why is it that scarcely any are executed but the poor? The fact is a proof, among other things, of a wretchedness in their condition. Bred up without morals, and cast upon the world without any prospect, they are the exposed sacrifice of vice and legal barbarity. The millions that are superfluously wasted upon governments are more than sufficient to reform those evils, and to benefit the condition of every man in the nation, not included within the purlieus of a court.

Suspicion is the companion of mean souls, and the bane of all good society

THE idea of having navies for the protection of commerce is delusive. It is putting the means of destruction for the means of protection. Commerce needs no other protection than the reciprocal interest which every nation feels in supporting it—it is common stock—it exists by a balance of advantages to all; and the only interruption it meets is from the present uncivilized state of governments, and which it is its common interest to reform

EVERY history of the Creation, and every traditionary account, whether from the lettered or the unlettered world, however they may vary in their opinion or belief of certain particulars, all agree in establishing one point: the unity of man; by which I mean that men are all of one degree, and consequently, that all men are born equal, and with equal natural rights, in the same manner as if posterity had been continued by creation instead of generation, the latter being only the mode by which the former is carried forward; and consequently, every child born into the world must be considered as deriving its existence from God. The world is as new to him as it was to the first man that existed, and his natural right in it is of the same kind

There can be no such thing as a nation flourishing alone in commerce; she can only participate; and the destruction of it in any part must necessarily affect all. When, therefore, governments are at war, the attack is made upon the common stock of commerce, and the consequence is the same as if each had attacked his own

CONSTITUTION is not a thing in name only, but in fact. It has not an ideal, but a real existence; and wherever it can not be produced in a visible form, there is none. A constitution is a thing antecedent to a government, and a government is only the creature of a constitution. The constitution of a country is not the act of its government, but of the people constituting a government

The prosperity of any commercial nation is regulated by the prosperity of the rest. If they are poor, she can not be rich ; and her condition, be it what it may, is an index of the height of the commercial tide in other nations

Revolutions have for their object, a change in the moral condition of governments, and with this change the burden of public taxes will lessen, and civilization will be left to the enjoyment of that abundance, of which it is now deprived

Man acquires a knowledge of his rights by attending justly to his interest, and discovers in the event that the strength and powers of despotism consist wholly in the fear of resisting it, and that in order " to be free," it is sufficient that he will it

He who takes Nature for his guide is not easily beaten out of his argument

IT requires but a very small glance of thought to perceive that, although laws made in one generation often continue in force through succeeding generations, yet they continue to derive their force from the consent of the living. A law not repealed continues in force, not because it can not be repealed, but because it is *not* repealed, and the non-repealing passes for consent.

Immortal power is not a human right, and therefore can not be a right of Parliament.

The Parliament of Sixteen Hundred Eighty-eight might as well have passed an act to have authorized

themselves to live forever as to make their authority
to live forever. All therefore that can be said of them
is, that they are a formality of words, of as much
import as if those who used them had addressed a
congratulation to themselves, and in the Oriental style
of antiquity had said, O Parliament, live forever!

⁌ The circumstances of the world are continually
changing, and the opinions of men change also; and
as government is for the living and not for the dead,
it is the living only that has any right in it. That which
may be thought right and found convenient in one
age may be thought wrong and found inconvenient
in another. In such cases, who is to decide—the living,
or the dead?

NORMAL government makes but a small part of
civilized life; and when even the best that human
wisdom can devise is established, it is a thing more in
name and idea than in fact. It is to the great and
fundamental principles of society and civilization—
to the common usage universally consented to, and
mutually and reciprocally maintained—to the unceas-
ing circulation of interest, which, passing through its
million channels, invigorates the whole mass of civilized man—it is to these things, infinitely more than
to anything which even the best instituted government can perform, that the safety and prosperity
of the individual and of the whole depends
The more perfect civilization is, the less occasion has
if for government, because the more does it regulate
its own affairs, and govern itself; but so contrary
is the practise of old governments to the reason of
the case, that the expenses of them increase in the
proportion they ought to diminish. It is but few
general laws that civilized life requires, and those of
such common usefulness that, whether they are
enforced by the forms of government or not, the
effect will be nearly the same. If we consider what
the principles are that first condense men into society,

and what the motives that regulate their mutual intercourse afterwards, we shall find, by the time we arrive at what we call government, that nearly the whole of the business is performed by the natural operation of the parts upon each other

Man, with respect to all those matters, is more a creature of consistency than he is aware, or that governments would wish him to believe. All the great laws of society are laws of Nature. Those of trade and commerce, whether with respect to the intercourse of individuals, or of nations, are laws of mutual and reciprocal interest. They are followed and obeyed because it is the interest of the parties so to do, and not on account of any formal laws their governments may impose or interpose

Conquest and tyranny, at some early period, dispossessed man of his rights, and he is now recovering them

It is impossible to make wisdom hereditary

All religions are in their nature mild and benign, and united with principles of morality. They could not have made proselytes at first, by professing anything that was vicious, cruel, persecuting or immoral. Like everything else, they had their beginning; and they proceeded by persuasion, exhortation and example

HE French Constitution says there shall be no titles; and of consequence, all that class of equivocal generation, which in some countries is called " aristocracy," and in others " nobility," is done away, and the peer is exalted into man

Titles are but nicknames, and every nickname is a title. The thing is perfectly harmless in itself, but it marks a sort of foppery in the human character which degrades it. It renders man diminutive in things which are great, and the counterfeit of woman in things which are little. It talks about its fine blue riband like a girl, and shows its new garter like a child. A certain writer of some antiquity says, " When I was a child, I thought as a child : but when I became a man, I put away childish things."

It is, properly, from the elevated mind of France, that the folly of titles has been abolished. It has outgrown the baby-clothes of count and duke, and breeched itself in manhood. France has not leveled, it has exalted. It has put down the dwarf to set up the man. The insignificance of a senseless word like duke, count or earl has ceased to please. Even those who possessed them have disowned the gibberish, and as they outgrew the rickets have despised the rattle

The genuine mind of man, thirsting for its native home, society, contemns the gewgaws that separate him from it. Titles are like circles drawn by a magician's wand, to contract the sphere of man's felicity. He lives immured within the Bastile of a word, and surveys at a distance the envied life of man.

Is it then any wonder that titles should fall in France? Is it not a greater wonder that they should be kept up anywhere? What are they? What is their worth, and what is their amount? When we think or speak of a judge or a general, we associate with it the ideas of office and character ; we think of gravity in the one, and bravery in the other ; but when we use a word merely as a title, no ideas associate with it.

THROUGH all the vocabulary of Adam, there is no such an animal as a duke or a count ; neither can we connect any idea to the words. Whether they mean strength or weakness, wisdom or folly, a child or a man, or a rider or a horse, is all equivocal. What respect then can be paid to that which describes nothing and which means nothing? Imagination has given figure and character to centaurs, satyrs, and down to all the fairy tribe; but titles baffle even the powers of fancy, and are a chimerical nondescript. But this is not all. If a whole country is disposed to hold them in contempt, all their value is gone and none will own them. It is common opinion only that makes them anything or nothing or worse than nothing. There is no occasion to take titles away, for they take themselves away when society concurs to ridicule them. This species of imaginary consequence has visibly declined in every part of Europe, and it hastens to its exit as the world of reason continues to rise

HE patriots of France have discovered, in good time, that rank and dignity in society must take a new ground. The old one has fallen through. It must now take the substantial ground of character, instead of the chimerical ground of titles; and they have brought their titles to the altar and made of them a burnt-offering to Reason.

That, then, which is called aristocracy in some countries, and nobility in others, arose out of the governments founded upon conquest. It was originally a military order, for the purpose of supporting military government (for such were all governments founded in conquest); and to keep up a succession of this order for the purpose for which it was established, all the younger branches of those families were disinherited, and the law of primogenitureship set up

The nature and character of aristocracy shows itself to us in this law. It is a law against every law of Nature and Nature herself calls for its destruction. Establish family justice and aristocracy falls. By the aristocratical law of primogenitureship, in a family of six children, five are exposed. Aristocracy has never more than one child. The rest are begotten to be devoured. They are thrown to the cannibal for prey, and the natural parent himself prepares the unnatural repast.

As everything which is out of Nature in man affects, more or less, the interest of society, so does this. All the children which the aristocracy disowns (which are all, except the eldest) are, in general, cast like orphans on a parish to be provided for by the public, but at a greater charge. Unnecessary offices and places in governments and courts are created at the expense of the public, to maintain them.

With what kind of parental reflections can the father or mother contemplate their younger offspring? By nature they are children, and by marriage they are heirs; but by aristocracy they are bastards and orphans. They are the flesh and blood of their parents in one line, and nothing akin to them in the other. To restore, therefore, parents to their children, and children to their parents—relations to each other and man to society—and to exterminate the monster, aristocracy, root and branch—the French Constitution has destroyed the law of Primogenitureship. Here then lies the monster; and Mr. Burke, if he pleases, may write its epitaph

VOLTAIRE has remarked that King William never appeared to full advantage but in difficulties and in action; the same remark may be made on General Washington, for the character fits him. There is a natural firmness in some minds which can not be unlocked by trifles, but which, when unlocked, discovers a cabinet of fortitude; and I reckon it among those kinds of public blessings, which we do not immediately see, that God hath blessed him with uninterrupted health, and given him a mind that can even flourish upon care

Whatever the form or constitution of government may be, it ought to have no other object than the general happiness

When the ability in any nation to buy is destroyed, it equally involves the seller. Could the government of England destroy the commerce of all other nations, she would most effectually ruin her own

A body of men holding themselves accountable to nobody ought not to be trusted by anybody

A firm bargain and a right reckoning make long friends.

The sublime and the ridiculous are often so nearly related that it is difficult to class them separately. One step below the sublime makes the ridiculous, and one step above the ridiculous makes the sublime again

Poverty is a thing created by that which is called civilized life

Nature seems sometimes to laugh at mankind, by giving them so many fools for kings; at other times, she punishes their folly by giving them tyrants

A republican government hath more true grandeur in it than a kingly one. On the part of the public it is more consistent with freemen to appoint their rulers than to have them born; and on the part of those who preside, it is far nobler to be a ruler by the choice of the people, than a king by the chance of birth. Every honest delegate is more than a monarch. Disorders will unavoidably happen in all States, but monarchical governments are the most subject thereto, because the balance hangs uneven.

The balance of power is the scale of peace. The same balance would be preserved were all the world destitute of arms, for all would be alike; but since some will not, others dare not lay them aside

THE GOSPEL ACCORDING TO
ABRAHAM LINCOLN

I insist that if there is anything which it is the duty of the whole people never to entrust to any hands but their own, that thing is the preservation and perpetuity of their own liberties and institutions.

FOURSCORE and seven years ago our fathers brought forth on this continent a new nation, conceived in liberty, and dedicated to the proposition that all men are created equal

Now we are engaged in a great civil war, testing whether that nation, or any nation so conceived and so dedicated, can long endure. We are met on a great battlefield of that war. We have come to dedicate a portion of that field as a final resting-place for those who here gave their lives that that nation might live. It is altogether fitting and proper that we should do this

But, in a larger sense, we can not dedicate—we can not consecrate—we can not hallow—this ground. The brave men, living and dead, who struggled here, have consecrated it far above our poor power to add or detract. The world will little note nor long remember what we say here, but it can never forget what they did here. It is for us, the living, rather, to be dedicated here to the unfinished work which they who fought here have thus far so nobly advanced. It is rather for us to be here dedicated to the great task remaining before us—that from these honored dead we take increased devotion to that cause for which they gave the last full measure of devotion; that we here highly resolve that these dead shall not have died in vain; that this nation, under God, shall have a new birth of freedom; and that government of the people, by the people, for the people, shall not perish from the earth.—*Address at the Dedication of the Gettysburg National Cemetery, November 19, '63.*

WITH malice toward none; with charity for all; with firmness in the right, as God gives us to see the right, let us strive on to finish the work we are in; to bind up the nation's wounds; to care for him who shall have borne the battle, and for his widow, and his orphan—to do all which may achieve and cherish a just and lasting peace among ourselves, and with all nations

---

THUS let bygones be bygones: let past differences as nothing be; and with steady eye on the real issue, let us reinaugurate the good old " central ideas " of the Republic. We can do it. The human heart is with us; God is with us. We shall again be able not to declare that " all States as States are equal," nor yet that " all citizens as citizens are equal," but to renew the broader, better declaration, including both these and much more, that " all men are created equal."

WHAT an ignorance of human nature does it exhibit to ask or expect a whole community to rise up and labor for the temporal happiness of others, after themselves shall be consigned to the dust, a majority of which community take no pains whatever to secure their own eternal welfare at no more distant day? Great distance in either time or space has wonderful power to lull and render quiescent the human mind. Pleasures to be enjoyed, or pains to be endured, after we shall be dead and gone, are but little regarded even in our own cases, and much less in the cases of others. Still, in addition to this, there is something so ludicrous in promises of good or threats of evil a great way off as to render the whole subject with which they are connected, easily turned into ridicule

---

PROPERTY is the fruit of labor; property is desirable, is a positive good in the world. That some should be rich shows that others may become rich, and hence is just encouragement to industry and enterprise. Let not him who is houseless pull down the house of another, but let him work diligently and build one for himself, thus by example assuring that his own shall be safe from violence when built

Few can be induced to labor exclusively for posterity ; and none will do it enthusiastically. Posterity has done nothing for us; and theorize on it as we may, practically we shall do very little for it, unless we are made to think we are at the same time doing something for ourselves

I never encourage deceit, and falsehood, especially if you have got a bad memory, is the worst enemy a fellow can have. The fact is, truth is your truest friend, no matter what the circumstances are

POLITICIANS who have interests aside from the interest of the people, are—that is, the most of them are, taken as a mass—at least one long step removed from honest men. I say this with the greater freedom because, being a politician myself, none can regard it as personal

It is better only sometimes to be right than at all times to be wrong

OUR progress in degeneracy appears to me to be pretty rapid. As a nation we began by declaring that " all men are created equal." We now practically read it " all men are created equal, except negroes." When the Know-Nothings get control, it will read, " All men are created equal, except negroes and foreigners and Catholics." When it comes to this, I shall prefer emigrating to some country where they make no pretense of loving liberty—to Russia, for instance, where despotism can be taken pure, and without the base alloy of hypocrisy

HE subject presented in the memorial is one upon which I have thought much for weeks past, and I may even say for months. I am approached with the most opposite opinions and advice, and that by religious men who are equally certain that they represent the divine will. I am sure that either the one or the other class is mistaken in that belief, and perhaps in some respects both. I hope it will not be irreverent for me to say that if it is probable that God would reveal His will to others on a point so connected with my duty, it might be supposed He would reveal it directly to me; for, unless I am more deceived in myself than I often am, it is my earnest desire to know the will of Providence in this matter. And if I can learn what it is, I will do it. —*Reply to a Committee From the Religious Denominations of Chicago, Asking the President to Issue a Proclamation of Emancipation.*

Important principles may and must be inflexible

ENERAL : I have placed you at the head of the Army of the Potomac. Of course I have done this upon what appear to me to be sufficient reasons, and yet I think it best for you to know that there are some things in regard to which I am not quite satisfied with you. I believe you to be a brave and skilful soldier, which of course I like. I also believe you do not mix politics with your profession, in which you are right. You have confidence in yourself, which is a valuable if not an indispensable quality. You are ambitious, which, within reasonable bounds, does good rather than harm; but I think that during General Burnside's command of the army you have taken counsel of your ambition and thwarted him as much as you could, in which you did a great wrong to the country and to a most meritorious and honorable brother officer.

❧ I have heard, in such a way as to believe it, of your recently saying that both the army and the government needed a dictator ⚘ ⚘

Of course it was not for this, but in spite of it, that I have given you the command. Only those generals who gain successes can set up dictatorships.

❧ What I now ask of you is military success, and I will risk the dictatorship. The government will support you to the utmost of its ability, which is neither more nor less than it has done and will do for all commanders ⚘ ⚘

I much fear that the spirit you have aided to infuse into the army, of criticizing their commander and withholding confidence from him, will now turn upon you. I shall assist you as far as I can to put it down ⚘ ⚘ Neither you nor Napoleon, if he were alive again, could get any good out of an army while such a spirit prevails in it.

❧ And now beware of rashness : beware of rashness, but with energy and sleepless vigilance go forward and give us victories.

—Letter to General J. Hooker ⚘ ⚘

D EAR SIR: Yours of the Twenty-third is received, and I am constrained to say it is difficult to answer so ugly a letter in good temper. I am, as you intimate, losing much of the great confidence I placed in you, not from any act or omission of yours touching the public service, up to the time you were sent to Leavenworth, but from the flood of grumbling despatches and letters I have seen from you since ⚘ ⚘

I knew you were being ordered to Leavenworth at the time it was done; and I aver that with as tender a regard for your honor and your sensibilities as I had for my own, it never occurred to me that you were being " humiliated, insulted and disgraced ! " nor have I, up to this day, heard an intimation that you have been wronged, coming from any one but yourself. No one has blamed you for the retrograde movement from Springfield, nor for the information you gave General Cameron; and this you could readily understand if it were not for your unwarranted assumption that the ordering you to Leavenworth must necessarily have been done as a punishment for some fault

I thought then, and think yet, the position assigned to you is as responsible, and as honorable, as that assigned to Buell—I know that General McClellan expected more important results from it.

My impression is that at the time you were assigned to the new Western Department, it had not been determined to replace General Sherman in Kentucky; but of this I am not certain, because the idea that a command in Kentucky was very desirable, and one in the farther West undesirable, had never occurred to me

You constantly speak of being placed in command of only three thousand. Now tell me, is this not mere impatience? Have you not known all the while that you are to command four or five times that many?

I have been, and am sincerely your friend; and if, as such, I dare to make a suggestion, I would say you are adopting the best possible way to ruin yourself. " Act well your part, there all the honor lies." He who does something at the head of one Regiment will eclipse him who does nothing at the head of a hundred.—*Letter to Major-General Hunter*

Y DEAR SIR : I have just assisted the Secretary of War in framing part of a despatch to you relating to army corps, which despatch of course will have reached you before this will. I wish to say a few words to you privately on this subject. I ordered the army-corps organization not only on the unanimous opinion of the twelve generals whom you had selected and assigned as generals of division, but also on the unanimous opinion of every military man I could get an opinion from (and every modern military book), yourself only excepted. Of course I did not on my own judgment pretend to understand the subject

I now think it indispensable for you to know how your struggle against it is received in quarters which we can not entirely disregard. It is looked upon as merely an effort to pamper one or two pets and to persecute and degrade their supposed rivals

I have had no word from Sumner, Heintzelman or Keyes. The commanders of these corps are of course the three highest officers with you, but I am constantly told that you have no consultation or communication with them; that you consult and communicate with nobody but General Fitz-John Porter and perhaps General Franklin. I do not say these complaints are true or just, but at all events it is proper you should know of their existence. Do the commanders of corps disobey your orders in anything?

When you relieved General Hamilton of his command the other day, you thereby lost the confidence of at least one of your best friends in the Senate

And here let me say, not as applicable to you personally, that Senators and Representatives speak of me in their places as they please without question, and that officers of the army must cease addressing insulting letters to them for taking no greater liberty with them

But to return. Are you strong enough—are you strong enough, even with my help—to set your foot upon the necks of Sumner, Heintzelman and Keyes all at once? This is a practical and very serious question for you

The success of your army and the cause of the country are the same, and of course I only desire the good of the cause.—*Letter to General G. B. McClellan*

K. McCLURE, *Philadelphia:* Do we gain any-thing by opening one leak to stop another? Do we gain anything by quieting one clamor merely to open another, and probably a larger one?

MY DEAR SIR: The lady bearer of this says she has two sons who want to work. Set them at it if possible. Wanting to work is so rare a want that it should be encouraged.—*Note to Major Ramsey.*

DEAR MADAM: I have been shown in the files of the War Department a statement of the Adju-tant-General of Massachusetts that you are the mother of five sons who have died gloriously on the field of battle. I feel how weak and fruitless must be any words of mine which should attempt to beguile you from the grief of a loss so overwhelming. But I can not refrain from tendering to you the consolation that may be found in the thanks of the republic they died to save. I pray that our Heavenly Father may assuage the anguish of your bereavement, and leave you only the cherished memory of the loved and lost, and the solemn pride that must be yours to have laid so costly a sacrifice upon the altar of freedom —*Letter to Mrs. Bixby, of Boston, Massachusetts.*

It is difficult to make a man miserable while he feels he is worthy of himself and claims kindred to the great God who made him

---

War does not admit of holidays

THE way for a young man to rise is to improve himself every way he can, never suspecting that anybody wishes to hinder him. Allow me to assure you that suspicion and jealousy never did help any man in any situation. There may sometimes be ungenerous attempts to keep a young man down;

and they will succeed, too, if he allows his mind to be diverted from its true channel to brood over the attempted injury. Cast about, and see if this feeling has not injured every person you have ever known to fall into it

The dogmas of the quiet past are inadequate to the stormy present. The occasion is piled high with difficulty, and we must rise with the occasion. As our case is new, so we must think anew and act anew.

I am in no boastful mood. I shall not do more than I can, and I shall do all I can, to save the government, which is my sworn duty as well as my personal inclination. I shall do nothing in malice. What I deal with is too vast for malicious dealing

I can not fly from my thoughts—my solicitude for this great country follows me wherever I go. I do not think it is personal vanity or ambition, though I am not free from these infirmities

The loss of enemies does not compensate us for the loss of friends

We better know there is fire whence we see much smoke rising than we could know it by one or two witnesses swearing to it. The witnesses may commit perjury, but the smoke can not

Will springs from the two elements of moral sense and self-interest

A universal feeling, whether well or ill founded, can not be safely disregarded

In law it is good policy never to plead what you need not, lest you oblige yourself to prove what you can not.

IF you intend to go to work, there is no better place than right where you are; if you do not intend to go to work, you can not get along anywhere. Squirming and crawling about from place to place can do no good

---

THERE is not, of necessity, any such thing as the free hired laborer being fixed to that condition of life. Many independent men everywhere in these States, a few years back in their lives, were hired laborers. The prudent, penniless beginner in the world labors for wages awhile, saves a surplus with which to buy tools or land for himself, then labors on his own account another while, and at length hires another new beginner to help him. This is the just and generous and prosperous system which opens the way to all—gives hope to all, and consequent energy and progress and improvement of condition to all. No men living are more worthy to be trusted than those who toil up from poverty —none less inclined to take or touch aught which they have not honestly earned

---

We see it, and to us it appears like principle, and the best sort of principle at that: the principle of allowing the people to do as they please with their own business

---

WHILE I remain in my present position I shall not attempt to retract or modify the Emancipation Proclamation, nor shall I return to slavery any person who is free by the terms of that Proclamation, or by any of the acts of Congress.

If the people should, by whatever mode or means, make it an executive duty to re-enslave such persons, another, and not I, must be their instrument to perform it

In stating a single condition of peace, I mean simply

to say that the war will cease on the part of the government whenever it shall have ceased upon the part of those who began it

THE true rule, in determining to embrace or reject anything, is not whether it have any evil in it, but whether it have more of evil than of good. There are few things wholly evil or wholly good. Almost everything, especially of government policy, is an inseparable compound of the two, so that our best judgment of the preponderance between them is continually demanded

I am always for the man who wishes to work

The strongest bond of human sympathy, outside of the family relation, should be one uniting all working people, of all nations, and tongues, and kindreds

THE legitimate object of government is to do for a community of people whatever they need to have done, but can not do at all, or can not do so well, for themselves, in their separate and individual capacities. In all that the people can individually do as well for themselves, government ought not to interfere. The desirable things which the individuals of a people can not do, or can not well do, for themselves, fall into two classes: those which have relation to wrongs, and those which have not. Each of these branches off into an infinite variety of subdivisions
The first—that in relation to wrongs—embraces all crimes, misdemeanors and non-performance of contracts. The other embraces all which, in its nature, and without wrong, requires combined action, as public roads and highways, public schools, charities, pauperism, orphanage, estates of the deceased, and the machinery of government itself.

❧ From this it appears that if all men were just, there still would be some, though not so much, need of government ❧ ❧

━━

Stand with anybody that stands right. Stand with him while he is right, and part with him when he goes wrong ❧ ❧

━━

I TAKE it that it is best for all to leave each man free to acquire property as fast as he can. Some will get wealthy. I don't believe in a law to prevent a man getting rich; it would do more harm than good. So while we do not propose any war upon capital, we do wish to allow the humblest man an equal chance to get rich with everybody else. When one starts poor, as most do in the race of life, free society is such that he knows he can better his condition; he knows that there is no fixed condition of labor for his whole life. I am not ashamed to confess that twenty-five years ago I was a hired laborer, mauling rails, at work on a flatboat—just what might happen to any poor man's son. I want every man to have a chance—and I believe a black man is entitled to it—in which he can better his condition—when he may look forward and hope to be a hired laborer this year and the next, work for himself afterward, and finally to hire men to work for him. That is the true system ❧ ❧

━━

No man is good enough to govern another man without that other's consent ❧ ❧

━━

IT is true, as has been said by the President of the Senate, that very great responsibility rests upon me in the position to which the votes of the American people have called me. I am deeply sensible of that weighty responsibility. I can not but know what you all know, that without a

name, perhaps without a reason why I should have
a name, there has fallen upon me a task such as did
not rest even upon the Father of his Country; and
so feeling, I can turn and look for that support without
which it will be impossible for me to perform that
great task. I turn, then, and look to the American
people, and to that God who has never forsaken them.
Allusion has been made to the interest felt in relation
to the policy of the new administration. In this I
have received from some a degree of credit for having
kept silence, and from others some deprecation. I still
think that I was right

In the varying and repeatedly shifting scenes of the
present, and without a precedent which could enable
me to judge by the past, it has seemed fitting that
before speaking upon the difficulties of the country I
should have gained a view of the whole field, being
at liberty to modify and change the course of policy
as future events may make a change necessary.

I have not maintained silence from any want of
real anxiety. It is a good thing that there is no more
than anxiety, for there is nothing going wrong. It is
a consoling circumstance that when we look out there
is nothing that really hurts anybody. We entertain
different views upon political questions, but nobody
is suffering anything. This is a most consoling circumstance, and from it we may conclude that all we want
is time, patience, and a reliance on that God who has
never forsaken this people.

Address to the Legislature of Ohio.

O other occupation opens so wide a field
for the profitable and agreeable combination
of labor with cultivated thought, as agriculture. I know nothing so pleasant to the
mind as the discovery of anything that is at once new
and valuable—nothing that so lightens and sweetens
toil as the hopeful pursuit of such discovery. And

how vast and varied a field is agriculture for such discovery! The mind, already trained to thought in the country school, or higher school, can not fail to find there an exhaustless source of enjoyment. Every blade of grass is a study; and to produce two where there was but one is both a profit and a pleasure. And not grass alone, but soil, seeds and seasons—hedges, ditches and fences—draining, droughts and irrigation—plowing, hoeing and harrowing—reaping, mowing and threshing—saving crops, pests of crops, diseases of crops, and what will prevent or cure them—implements, utensils and machines, their relative merits and how to improve them—hogs, horses and cattle—sheep, goats and poultry—trees, shrubs, fruits, plants and flowers—the thousand things of which these are specimens—each a world of study within itself

You can fool all the people some of the time and some of the people all the time, but you can not fool all the people all of the time

I believe each individual is naturally entitled to do as he pleases with himself and the fruit of his labor, so far as it in no wise interferes with any other man's rights

Consciences differ in different individuals

I AM glad I made the late race. It gave me a hearing on the great and durable question of the age, which I could have had in no other way; and though I now sink out of view, and shall be forgotten, I believe I have made some marks which will tell for the cause of civil liberty long after I am gone

Gold is good in its place, but living, brave, patriotic men are better than gold

It is said an Eastern monarch once charged his wise men to invent him a sentence to be ever in view, and which should be true and appropriate in all times and situations. They presented him the words, " And this, too, shall pass away."

INASMUCH as most good things are produced by labor, it follows that all such things of right belong to those whose labor has produced them. But it has so happened, in all ages of the world, that some have labored, and others have without labor enjoyed a large proportion of the fruits. This is wrong and should not continue. To secure to each laborer the whole product of his labor as nearly as possible, is a worthy subject of any good government

In this age and in this country, public sentiment is everything. With it nothing can fail ; against it nothing can succeed

The plainest print can not be read through a gold eagle

All I ask for the negro is that if you do not like him, let him alone. If God gave him but little, that little let him enjoy

Unless among those deficient in intellect, everybody you trade with makes something

If you make a bad bargain, hug it all the tighter

The better part of one's life consists of his friendships.

I say "try" ; if we never try, we shall never succeed

Every blade of grass is a study ; and to produce two where there was but one is both a profit and a pleasure.

There is no grievance that is a fit object of redress by mob law

---

The leading rule for the lawyer, as for the man of every other calling, is diligence. Leave nothing for tomorrow which can be done today

---

It is better only sometimes to be right than at all times to be wrong

---

Towering genius disdains a beaten path

Discourage litigation. Persuade your neighbor to compromise whenever you can. As a peacemaker the lawyer has a superior opportunity of being a good man. There will still be business enough

---

The race gave me a hearing on the great and durable question of the age, which I could have had in no other way; and though I now sink out of view, and shall be forgotten, I believe I have made some marks which will tell for the cause of civil liberty long after I am gone

THE GOSPEL ACCORDING TO
WALT WHITMAN

I swear I see what is better than to tell the best,
It is always to leave the best untold

LOVER divine and perfect Comrade,
Waiting content, invisible yet, but certain,
Be thou my God

Thou, thou, the Ideal Man,
Fair, able, beautiful, content and loving.
Complete in body and dilate in spirit,
Be thou my God

O Death (for Life has served its turn),
Opener and usher to the heavenly mansion,
Be thou my God

Aught, aught of mightiest, best I see, conceive or
know,
(To break the stagnant tie — thee, thee to free, O
Soul),
Be thou my God

All great ideas, the races' aspirations,
All heroisms, deeds of rapt enthusiasts,
Be ye my Gods

Or Time and Space,
Or shape of Earth divine and wondrous,
Or some fair shape I viewing, worship,
Or lustrous orb of sun or star by night,
Be ye my Gods

AFOOT and light-hearted I take to the open road,
Healthy, free, the world before me,
The long brown path before me leading wherever I
choose.
Henceforth I ask not good fortune, I myself am good
fortune,

Henceforth I whimper no more, postpone no more, need nothing,

Done with indoor complaints, libraries, querulous criticisms,

Strong and content I travel the open road

HIS day before dawn I ascended a hill and look'd at the crowded heaven,

And I said to my spirit, " When we become the enfolders of those orbs, and the pleasure and knowledge of everything in them, shall we be fill'd and satisfied then? "

And my spirit said, " No, we but level that lift to pass and continue beyond."

PASSING stranger! you do not know how longingly I look upon you,

You must be he I was seeking, or she I was seeking (it comes to me as of a dream),

I have somewhere surely lived a life of joy with you,

All is recall'd as we flit by each other, fluid, affectionate, chaste, matured,

You grew up with me, were a boy with me or a girl with me,

I ate with you and slept with you, your body has become not yours only nor left my body mine only,

You give me the pleasure of your eyes, face, flesh, as we pass, you take of my beard, breast, hands, in return,

I am not to speak to you, I am to think of you when I sit alone or wake at night alone,

I am to wait, I do not doubt I am to meet you again,

I am to see to it that I do not lose you

THINK I could turn and live with animals, they are so placid and self-contain'd,

I stand and look at them long and long

They do not sweat and whine about their condition,
They do not lie awake in the dark and weep for their
        sins,
They do not make me sick discussing their duty to God,
Not one is dissatisfied, not one is demented with the
        mania of owning things,
Not one kneels to another, nor to his kind that lived
        thousands of years ago,
Not one is respectable or unhappy over the whole
        earth

ERE mankind murderous or jealous upon you,
        my brother, my sister?
I am sorry for you, they are not murderous or jealous
        upon me,
All has been gentle with me, I keep no account with
        lamentation,
(What have I to do with lamentation?)

I am an acme of things accomplish'd, and I am
encloser of things to be

HAVE said that the soul is not more than
        the body,
    And I have said that the body is not more
        than the soul,
And nothing, not God, is greater to one than one's
        self is,
And whoever walks a furlong without sympathy
        walks to his own funeral drest in his shroud,
And I or you pocketless of a dime may purchase the
        pick of the earth,
And to glance with an eye or show a bean in its pod
        confounds the learning of all times,
And there is no trade or employment but the young
        man following it may become a hero,
And there is no object so soft but it makes a hub
        for the wheel'd universe,

And I say to any man or woman, Let your soul stand
    cool and composed before a million universes.
And I say to mankind, Be not curious about God,
For I who am curious about each am not curious
    about God,
(No array of terms can say how much I am at peace
    about God and about death)

I hear and behold God in every object, yet understand
    God not in the least,
Nor do I understand who there can be more wonderful
    than myself

Why should I wish to see God better than this day?
I see something of God each hour of the twenty-four,
    and each moment then,
In the faces of men and women I see God, and in my
    own face in the glass

There is that in me—I do not know what it is—but
I know it is in me

AND the hints about old men and mothers, and
    the offspring taken soon out of their laps.
What do you think has become of the young
    and old men?
And what do you think has become of the women
    and children?

They are alive and well somewhere,
The smallest sprout shows there is really no death,
And if ever there was it led forward life, and does
    not wait at the end to arrest it,
And ceas'd the moment life appear'd

All goes forward and outward, nothing collapses,
And to die is different from what any one supposed,
    and luckier

I FIND letters from God dropt in the street,
    and every one is sign'd by God's name,
And I leave them where they are, for I know that
    wheresoe'er I go,
Others will punctually come for ever and ever

I TOO pass from the night,
    I stay awhile away O night, but I return to you
    again and love you

Why should I be afraid to trust myself to you?
I am not afraid, I have been well brought forward
    by you,
I love the rich, running day, but I do not desert her
    in whom I lay so long,
I know not how I came of you, and I know not where
    I go with you, but I know I came well and
    shall go well

I will stop only a time with the night, and rise betimes,
I will duly pass the day O my mother, and duly
    return to you

DAREST thou now O soul,
    Walk out with me toward the unknown
    region,
    Where neither ground is for the feet nor any
    path to follow?

No map there, nor guide,
Nor voice sounding, nor touch of human hand,
Nor face with blooming flesh, nor lips, nor eyes,
    are in that land

I know it not, O soul,
Nor dost thou, all is a blank before us,
All waits undreamed of in that region, that inaccessible
    land

Till when the ties loosen,
All but the ties eternal, Time and Space,
Nor darkness, gravitation, sense, nor any bounds
     bounding us

Then we burst forth, we float,
In Time and Space, O Soul, prepared for them
Equal, equipt at last, (O joy! O fruit of all!) them
     to fulfil, O Soul!

I KNOW I am deathless,
     I know this orbit of mine can not be swept
     by a carpenter's compass,
     I know I shall not pass like a child's carlacue
     cut with a burnt stick at night

I know I am august,
I do not trouble my spirit to vindicate itself or be
     understood,
I see that the elementary laws never apologize (I
     reckon I behave no prouder than the level
     I plant my house by, after all)

I exist as I am, that is enough,
If no other in the world be aware I sit content
And if each and all be aware I sit content

One world is aware and by far the largest to me, and
     that is myself,
And whether I come to my own today or in ten thou-
     sand or ten million years,
I can cheerfully take it now, or with equal cheerful-
     ness I can wait.
My foothold is tenon'd and mortis'd in granite,
I laugh at what you call dissolution,
And I know the amplitude of time

Whoever you are! claim your own at any hazard!

THE earth, that is sufficient,
I do not want the constellations any nearer,
I know they are very well where they are,
I know they suffice for those who belong to them

Still here I carry my old delicious burdens,
I carry them, men and women, I carry them with
    me wherever I go,
I swear it is impossible for me to get rid of them,
I am fill'd with them, and I will fill them in return.

WHEN lilacs last in the dooryard bloom'd,
    And the great star early droop'd in the
        Western sky in the night,
        I mourn'd, and yet shall mourn with ever-
        returning Spring

Ever-returning Spring, trinity sure to me you bring,
Lilac blooming perennial and drooping star in the
    West,
And thought of him I love

O POWERFUL Western fallen star!
    O shades of night—O moody, tearful night!
O great star disappeared—O the black murk that
    hides the star!
O cruel hands that hold me powerless—O helpless
    soul of me!
O harsh surrounding cloud that will not free my soul!

IN the dooryard fronting an old farmhouse near
    the whitewash'd palings,
Stands the lilac-bush tall-growing with heart-shaped
    leaves of rich green,
With many a pointed blossom rising delicate, with
    the perfume strong I love,
With every leaf a miracle—and from this bush in
    the dooryard,

With delicate-color'd blossoms and heart-shaped
      leaves of rich green,
A sprig with its flower I break

IN the swamp in secluded recesses,
      A shy and hidden bird is warbling a song

Solitary the thrush,
The hermit withdrawn to himself, avoiding the settle-
      ments,
Sings by himself a song

Song of the bleeding throat,
Death's outlet song of life (for well dear brother I know,
If thou wast not granted to sing thou would'st surely
      die)

OVER the breast of the Spring, the land, amid
      cities,
Amid lanes and through old woods, where lately the
      violets peep'd from the ground, spotting the
      gray debris,
Amid the grass in the fields each side of the lanes,
      passing the endless grass,
Passing the yellow-spear'd wheat, every grain from
      its shroud in the dark-brown fields uprisen,
Passing the apple-tree blows of white and pink in
      the orchards,
Carrying a corpse to where it shall rest in the grave,
Night and day journeys a coffin

COFFIN that passes through lanes and streets,
      Through day and night with the great cloud
      darkening the land,
With the pomp of the inloop'd flags with the cities
      draped in black,
With the show of the States themselves as of crape-
      veil'd women standing,

With processions long and winding and the flambeaus
    of the night,
With the countless torches lit, with the silent sea
    of faces and the unbared heads,
With the waiting depot, the arriving coffin, and the
    somber faces,
With dirges through the night, with the thousand
    voices rising strong and solemn,
With all the mournful voices of the dirges pour'd
    around the coffin,
The dim-lit churches and the shuddering organs—
    where amid these you journey,
With the tolling, tolling bells' perpetual clang,
Here, coffin that slowly passes,
I give you my sprig of lilac

NOR for you, for one alone,
    Blossoms and branches green to coffins all I bring,
For fresh as the morning, thus would I chant a song
    for you O sane and sacred death

All over bouquets of roses,
O death, I cover you over with roses and early lilies,
But mostly and now the lilac that blooms the first,
Copious I break, I break the sprigs from the bushes,
With loaded arms I come, pouring for you,
For you and the coffins all of you O death

O WESTERN orb sailing the heaven
    Now I know what you must have meant as a
    month since I walk'd,
As I walk'd in silence the transparent shadowy night,
As I saw you had something to tell as you bent to
    me night after night,
As you droop'd from the sky low down as if to my
    side (while the other stars all look'd on),
As we wandered together the solemn night (for some-
    thing I know not what kept me from sleep),

As the night advanced, and I saw on the rim of the
　　　West how full you were of woe,
As I stood on the rising ground in the breeze in the
　　　cool transparent night,
As I watch'd where you pass'd and was lost in the
　　　netherward black of the night,
As my soul in its trouble dissatisfied sank, as where
　　　you sad orb,
Concluded, dropt in the night, and was gone

ING on there in the swamp,
　　　O singer bashful and tender, I hear your notes,
　　　I hear your call,
I hear, I come presently, I understand you,
But a moment I linger, for the lustrous star has
　　　detain'd me,
The star my departing comrade holds and detains me.

OUTH, large, lusty, loving—youth full of grace,
　　　force, fascination,
Do you know that Old Age may come after you with
　　　equal grace, force, fascination?

Day full-blown and splendid—day of the immense
　　　sun, action, ambition, laughter,
The Night follows close with millions of suns, and
　　　sleep and restoring darkness

O those who 've failed, in aspiration vast,
　　　To unnam'd soldiers fallen in front on the lead,
To calm, devoted engineers—to over-ardent travelers
　　　—to pilots on their ships,
To many a lofty song and picture without recognition
　　　—I 'd rear a laurel-cover'd monument.
High, high above the rest—To all cut off before their
　　　time,
Possess'd by some strange spirit of fire,
Quench'd by an early death

CAPTAIN! my Captain! our fearful trip is
                    done,
            The ship has weather'd every rack, the prize
                    we sought is won,
The port is near, the bells I hear, the people all
            exulting,
While follow eyes the steady keel, the vessel grim
            and daring;
            But O heart! heart! heart!
                    O the bleeding drops of red,
                        Where on the deck my Captain lies,
                            Fallen cold and dead.

O Captain! my Captain! rise up and hear the
            bells;
Rise up—for you the flag is flung—for you the bugle
            trills,
For you bouquets and ribbon'd wreaths—for you the
            shores a-crowding,
For you they call, the swaying mass, their eager faces
            turning;
            Here Captain! dear father!
                This arm beneath your head!
                    It is some dream that on the deck,
                        You 've fallen cold and dead.

My Captain does not answer, his lips are pale and
            still,
My father does not feel my arm, he has no pulse nor
            will,
The ship is anchor'd safe and sound, its voyage closed
            and done,
From fearful trip the victor ship comes in with object
            won;
            Exult O shores, and ring O bells!
                But I with mournful tread,
                    Walk the deck my Captain lies,
                        Fallen cold and dead.

GONIES are one of my changes of garments,
   I do not ask the wounded person how he feels,
I myself become the wounded person

HE soul is always beautiful,
   The universe is duly in order, everything is in
      its place,
What has arrived is in its place and what waits shall
      be in its place

TRANGER, if you passing meet me and desire
      to speak to me, why should you not speak
      to me?
And why should I not speak to you?

HY, who makes much of a miracle?
      As to me I know of nothing else but miracles,
      Whether I walk the streets of Manhattan,
         Or dart my sight over the roofs of houses
            toward the sky,
Or wade with naked feet along the beach just in the
      edge of the water,
Or stand under trees in the woods,
Or talk by day with any one I love, or sleep in the
      bed at night with any one I love,
Or sit at table at dinner with the rest,
Or look at strangers opposite me riding in the car,
Or watch honeybees busy around the hive of a Sum-
      mer forenoon,
Or animals feeding in the fields,
Or birds, or the wonderfulness of insects in the air,
Or the wonderfulness of the sundown, or of stars
      shining so quiet and bright,
Or the exquisite delicate thin curve of the new moon
      in Spring;
These with the rest, one and all, are to me miracles,
The whole referring, yet each distinct and in its
      place

To me every hour of the light and dark is a miracle,
Every cubic inch of space is a miracle,
Every square yard of the surface of the earth is spread
      with the same,
Every foot of the interior swarms with the same.
To me the sea is a continual miracle,
The fishes that swim—the rocks—the motions of the
      waves—the ships with men in them,
What stranger miracles are there?

POETS to come! orators, singers, musicians to
      come!
Not today is to justify me and answer what I am for,
But you, a new brood, native, athletic, continental,
      greater than before known,
Arouse! for you must justify me

I myself but write one or two indicative words for
      the future,
I but advance a moment only to wheel and hurry
      back in the darkness.
I am a man who, sauntering along without fully
      stopping, turns a casual look upon you and
      then averts his face,
Leaving it to you to prove and define it,
Expecting the main things from you

COME lovely and soothing death,
      Undulate round the world, serenely arriving,
            arriving,
      In the day, in the night, to all, to each,
Sooner or later delicate death

Prais'd be the fathomless universe,
For life and joy, and for objects and knowledge
      curious,
And for love, sweet love—but praise! praise! praise!
For the sure-enwinding arms of cool enfolding death.

Dark mother always gliding near with soft feet,
Have none chanted for thee a chant of fullest welcome?
Then I chant it for thee, I glorify thee above all,
I bring thee a song that when thou must indeed come,
      come unfalteringly

Approach, strong deliveress,
When it is so, when thou hast taken them I joyously
      sing the dead,
Lost in the loving floating ocean of thee,
Laved in the flood of thy bliss O death

From me to thee glad serenades,
Dances for thee I propose saluting thee, adornments
      and feastings for thee,
And the sights of the open landscape and the high
      spread sky are fitting,
And life and the fields, and the huge and thoughtful
      night

The night in silence under many a star,
The ocean shore and the husky whispering wave
      whose voice I know,
And the soul turning to thee O vast and well-veil'd
      death,
And the body gratefully nestling close to thee

Over the tree-tops I float thee a song,
Over the rising and sinking waves, over the myriad
      fields and the prairies wide,
Over the dense-pack'd cities all and the teeming
      wharves and ways,
I float this carol with joy, with joy to thee O death

SAIL forth—steer for the deep waters only,
    Reckless O soul, exploring, I with thee, and thou
      with me,
For we are bound where mariner has not yet dared to go,

And we will risk the ship, ourselves and all

O my brave soul!
O farther, farther sail!
O daring joy, but safe! are they not all the seas of
     God?
O farther, farther, farther sail

S I watched the plowman plowing,
    Or the sower sowing in the fields, or the harvester
     harvesting,
I saw there too, O life and death, your analogies;
(Life, life is the tillage, and Death is the harvest
     according)

They go! they go! I know that they go, but I know
     not where they go,
But I know that they go toward the best — toward
     something great

A child said, *What is the grass?* fetching it to me
     with full hands;
How could I answer the child? I do not know what
     it is any more than he

All truths wait in all things: They neither hasten
their own delivery nor resist it

I know I have the best of time and space, and was
never measured and never will be measured.

          Do I contradict myself?
          Very well then I contradict myself,
          (I am large, I contain multitudes).

Produce great Persons, the rest follows

Come forward O my soul, and let the rest retire

LIVING always, always dying !
 O the burials of me past and present,
O me while I stride ahead, material, visible, imperious
  as ever ;
O me, what I was for years, now dead (I lament not,
  I am content) ;
O to disengage myself from those corpses of me,
  which I turn and look at where I cast them,
To pass on (O living ! always living !), and leave the
  corpses behind

NOT from successful love alone,
 Nor wealth, nor honor'd middle age, nor victories
  of politics or war ;
But as life wanes, and all the turbulent passions
  calm,
As gorgeous, vapory, silent hues cover the evening
  sky,
As softness, fulness, rest, suffuse the flame, like
  freshier, balmier air,
As the days take on a mellower light, and the apple
  at lasts hangs really finish'd and indolent-ripe
  on the tree,
Then for the teeming quietest, happiest days of all !
The brooding and blissful halcyon days !

THE GOSPEL ACCORDING TO
ROBERT INGERSOLL

We need no myths, no miracles, no gods, no devils.

BY this time the whole world should know that the real bible has not yet been written, but is being written, and that it will never be finished until the race begins its downward march, or ceases to exist

The real bible is not the work of inspired men, nor prophets, nor apostles, nor evangelists, nor of Christs. Every man who finds a fact adds, as it were, a word to this great book. It is not attested by prophecy, by miracles or signs. It makes no appeal to faith, to ignorance, to credulity or fear. It has no punishment for unbelief, and no reward for hypocrisy. It appeals to man in the name of demonstration. It has nothing to conceal. It has no fear of being read, of being contradicted, of being investigated and understood. It does not pretend to be holy, or sacred; it simply claims to be true. It challenges the scrutiny of all, and implores every reader to verify every line for himself. It is incapable of being blasphemed. This book appeals to all the surroundings of man. Each thing that exists testifies of its perfection. The earth, with its heart of fire and crowns of snow; with its forests and plains, its rocks and seas; with its every wave and cloud; with its every leaf and bud and flower, confirms its every word, and the solemn stars, shining in the infinite abysses, are the eternal witnesses of its truth.

IF we abandon myth and miracle, if we discard the supernatural and the scheme of redemption, how are we to civilize the world?

Is falsehood a reforming power? Is credulity the mother of virtue? Is there any saving grace in the impossible and absurd? Did wisdom perish with the dead? Must the civilized accept the religion of savages?

If we wish to reform the world we must rely on truth, on fact, on reason. We must teach men that they are good or bad for themselves, that others can not be good or bad for them, that they can not be charged with the crimes, or credited with the virtues, of others. We must discard the doctrine of the atonement, because it is absurd and immoral. We are not accountable for the sins of " Adam," and the virtues of Christ can not be transferred to us. There can be no vicarious virtue, no vicarious vice. Why should the sufferings of the innocent atone for the crimes of the guilty?

According to the doctrine of the atonement, right and wrong do not exist in the nature of things, but in the arbitrary will of the Infinite. This is a subversion of all ideas of justice and mercy.

An act is good, bad or indifferent, according to its consequences. No power can step between an act and its natural consequences. A governor may pardon the criminal, but the natural consequences of the crime remain untouched. A god may forgive, but the consequences of the act forgiven are still the same. We must teach the world that the consequences of a bad action can not be avoided, that they are the invisible police, the unseen avengers, that accept no gifts, hear no prayers, that no cunning can deceive.

We do not need the forgiveness of gods, but of ourselves and the ones we injure. Restitution without repentance is far better than repentance without restitution

We know nothing of any god who rewards, punishes or forgives.

We must teach our fellow-men that honor comes from within, not from without, that honor must be earned, that it is not alms, that even an infinite God could not enrich the beggar's palm with the gem of honor

Teach them also that happiness is the bud, the blossom and the fruit of good and noble actions, that it is not the gift of any god; that it must be earned by man—must be deserved

In this world of ours there is no magic, no sleight-of-hand, by which consequences can be made to punish the good and reward the bad.

¶ Teach men not to sacrifice this world for some other, but to turn their attention to the natural, to the affairs of this life. Teach them that theology has no known foundation, that it was born of ignorance and fear, that it has hardened the heart, polluted the imagination and made fiends of men

Theology is not for this world. It is no part of real religion. It has nothing to do with goodness or virtue. Religion does not consist in worshiping gods, but in adding to the well-being, the happiness, of man. No human being knows whether any god exists or not, and all that has been said and written about " our god " or the gods of other people has no known fact for a foundation. Words without thoughts, clouds without rain

Let us put theology out of religion

Let us develop the brain, civilize the heart, and give wings to the imagination

HAPPINESS is the true end and aim of life. It is the task of intelligence to ascertain the conditions of happiness, and when found, the truly wise will live in accordance with them. By happiness is meant not simply the joy of eating and drinking—the gratification of the appetite—but good, well-being, in the highest and noblest forms. The joy that springs from obligations discharged, from duty done, from generous acts, from being true to the ideal, from a perception of the beautiful in Nature, art and conduct. The happiness that is born of and gives birth to poetry and music, that follows the gratification of the highest wants. Happiness is the result of all that is really right and sane

ORTHODOXY dies hard, and its defenders tell us that this fact shows that it is of divine origin. Judaism dies hard. It has lived several thousand years longer than Christianity. The religion of Mohammed dies hard. Buddhism dies hard. Why do all these religions die hard? Because intelligence increases slowly

RELIGION is supposed to consist in a discharge of the duties we owe to God. In other words, we are taught that God is exceedingly anxious that we should believe a certain thing. For my part, I do not believe that there is any infinite being to whom we owe anything. The reason I say this is, we can not owe any duty to any being who requires nothing— to any being that we can not possibly help, to any being whose happiness we can not increase. If God is infinite, we can neither give, nor can He receive anything. Anything that we do or fail to do, can not, in the slightest degree, affect an infinite God ; consequently, no relations can exist between the finite and the Infinite, if by relations is meant mutual duties and obligations
Some tell us that it is the desire of God that we should worship Him. What for? Why does He desire worship? Others tell us that we should sacrifice something to Him. What for? Is He in want? Can we assist Him? Is He unhappy? Is He in trouble? Does He need human sympathy? We can not assist the Infinite, but we can assist our fellow-men

WHENEVER a man believes that he has the exact truth from God, there is in that man no spirit of compromise. He has not the modesty born of the imperfections of human nature ; he has the arrogance

of theological certainty and the tyranny born of
ignorant assurance. Believing himself to be the slave
of God, he imitates his master, and of all tyrants the
worst is a slave in power

When a man really believes that it is necessary to do
a certain thing to be happy forever, or that a certain
belief is necessary to insure eternal joy, there is in
that man no spirit of concession. He divides the whole
world into saints and sinners, into believers and
unbelievers, into God's sheep and Devil's goats, into
people who will be glorified and people who will be
damned

NOW and then some one says that the religion of
his father and mother is good enough for him,
and wonders why anybody should desire a better.
Surely we are not bound to follow our parents in
religion, any more than in politics, science or art.
China has been petrified by the worship of ancestors.
If our parents had been satisfied with the religion of
theirs, we would be still less advanced than we are.
If we are, in any way, bound by the belief of our
fathers, the doctrine will hold good back to the first
people who had a religion; and if this doctrine is true,
we ought now to be believers in that first religion.
In other words, we would all be barbarians! You can
not show real respect to your parents by perpetuating
their errors. Good fathers and mothers wish their
children to advance, to overcome obstacles which
baffled them, and to correct the errors of their education. If you wish to reflect credit upon your parents,
accomplish more than they did, solve problems that
they could not understand, and build better than they
knew. To sacrifice your manhood upon the grave of
your father is an honor to neither. Why should a son
who has examined a subject throw away his reason
and adopt the views of his mother? Is not such a
course dishonorable to both?

We must remember that this " ancestor " argument is as old at least as the second generation of men. that it has served no purpose except to enslave mankind, and results mostly from the fact that acquiescence is easier than investigation. This argument pushed to its logical conclusion would prevent the advance of all people whose parents were not freethinkers

Let us forget that we are Baptists, Methodists, Catholics, Presbyterians or Freethinkers, and remember only that we are men and women. After all, man and woman are the highest possible titles. All other names belittle us, and show that we have consented to wear the collar of authority—that we are followers.

N infinite God ought to be able to protect Himself, without going in partership with State Legislatures. Certainly He ought not so to act that laws become necessary to keep Him from being laughed at. No one thinks of protecting Shakespeare from ridicule, by the threat of fine and imprisonment. It strikes me that God might write a book that would not necessarily excite the laughter of His children. In fact, I think it would be safe to say that a real God could produce a work that would excite the admiration of mankind. Surely politicians could be better employed than in passing laws to protect the literary reputation of the Jewish God

LL laws for the purpose of making man worship God are born of the same spirit that kindled the fires of the *auto da fe*, and lovingly built the dungeons of the Inquisition. All laws defining and punishing blasphemy—making it a crime to give your honest ideas about the Bible, or to laugh at the ignorance of the ancient Jews, or to enjoy yourself on the Sabbath, or to give your opinion of Jehovah—were passed by impudent bigots, and should be at once repealed by honest men

CHE Sciences are not sectarian. People do not persecute each other on account of disagreements in mathematics. Families are not divided about botany, and astronomy does not even tend to make a man hate his father and mother.

It is what people do not know, that they persecute each other about. Science will bring, not a sword, but peace

Just as long as religion has control of the schools, Science will be an outcast. Let us free our institutions of learning. Let us dedicate them to the science of eternal truth. Let us tell every teacher to ascertain all the facts he can—to give us light, to follow Nature, no matter where she leads; to be infinitely true to himself and us; to feel that he is without a chain, except the obligation to be honest; that he is bound by no books, by no creed, neither by the sayings of the dead nor of the living; that he is asked to look with his own eyes, to reason for himself without fear, to investigate in every possible direction, and to bring us the fruit of all his work

AS we become civilized, more and more liberty will be accorded to these men, until finally ministers will give their best and highest thoughts. The congregations will finally get tired of hearing about the patriarchs and saints, the miracles and wonders, and will insist upon knowing something about the men and women of our day, and the accomplishments and discoveries of our time. They will finally insist upon knowing how to escape the evils of this world, instead of the next. They will ask light upon the enigmas of this life. They will wish to know what we shall do with our criminals, instead of what God will do with His—how we shall do away with beggary and want—with crime and misery—with prostitution, disease and famine—with tyranny in all its cruel forms—with prisons and scaffolds, and how we shall reward the honest workers, and fill the world with happy homes! These are the problems for the pulpits and congregations of an enlightened future. If Science can not finally answer these questions, it is a vain and worthless thing ✒ ✒

CAN there be Methodist mathematics, Catholic astronomy, Presbyterian geology, Baptist biology or Episcopal botany? Why, then, should a sectarian college exist? Only that which somebody knows should be taught in our schools. We should not collect taxes to pay people for guessing. The common school is the bread of life for the people, and it should not be touched by the withering hand of superstition.

❧ Our country will never be filled with great institutions of learning until there is an absolute divorce between Church and School. As long as the mutilated records of a barbarous people are placed by priest and professor above the reason of mankind, we shall reap but little benefit from church and school.

❧ Instead of dismissing professors for finding something out, let us rather discharge those who do not. Let each teacher understand that investigation is not dangerous to him ; that his bread is safe, no matter how much truth he may discover ; that his salary will not be reduced, just because he finds that the ancient Jews did not know the entire history of the world ✒ ✒

The pulpit should not be a pillory. Congregations should allow the minister a little liberty. They should, at least, permit him to tell the truth ✒ ✒

It is my desire to free the schools. When a professor in a college finds a fact, he should make it known, even if it is inconsistent with something Moses said.

I WANT to do what little I can to make my country truly free, to broaden the intellectual horizon of our people, to destroy the prejudices born of ignorance and fear, to do away with the blind worship of the ignoble past, with the idea that all the great and good are dead, that the living are totally depraved, that all pleasures are sins, that sighs and groans are alone pleasing to God, that thought is dangerous, that intellectual courage is a crime, that cowardice is a virtue, that a certain belief is necessary to secure salvation, that to carry a cross in this world will give us a palm in the next, and that we must allow some priest to be the pilot of our souls

Until every soul is freely permitted to investigate every book, every creed, and dogma for itself, the world can not be free. Mankind will be enslaved until there is mental grandeur enough to allow each man to have his thought and say. This earth will be a paradise when men can, upon all these questions, differ, and yet grasp each other's hands as friends. It is amazing to me that a difference of opinion upon subjects that we know nothing with certainty about, should make us hate, persecute and despise each other. Why a difference of opinion upon predestination, or the Trinity, should make people imprison and burn each other seems beyond the comprehension of man; and yet in all countries where Christians have existed, they have destroyed each other to the exact extent of their power. Why should a believer in God hate an atheist? Surely the atheist has not injured God, and surely he is human, capable of joy and pain, and entitled to all the rights of man. Would it not be far better to treat this atheist, at least, as well as he treats us?

Christians tell me that they love their enemies, and yet all I ask is—not that they love their enemies, not that they love their friends even, but that they treat those who differ from them, with simple fairness. We do not wish to be forgiven, but we wish Christians to so act that we will not have to forgive them *• *• If all will admit that all have an equal right to think, then the question is forever solved; but as long as organized and powerful churches, pretending to hold the keys of Heaven and Hell, denounce every person as an outcast and criminal who thinks for himself and denies their authority, the world will be filled with hatred and suffering. To hate man and worship God seems to be the sum of all the creeds *• *•

That which has happened in most countries has happened in ours. When a religion is founded, the educated, the powerful—that is to say, the priests and nobles—tell the ignorant and superstitious—that is to say, the people—that the religion of their country was given to their fathers by God Himself; that it is the only true religion; that all others were conceived in falsehood and brought forth in fraud. and that all who believe in the true religion will be happy forever, while all others will burn in Hell. For the purpose of governing the people—that is to say, for the purpose of being supported by the people —the priests and nobles declare this religion to be sacred, and that whoever adds to, or takes from it, will be burned here by man, and hereafter by God. The result of this is, that the priests and nobles will not allow the people to change; and when, after a time, the priests, having intellectually advanced, wish to take a step in the direction of progress, the people will not allow them to change. At first, the rabble are enslaved by the priests, and afterwards the rabble become the masters.

❡ One of the first things I wish to do, is to free the orthodox clergy. I am a great friend of theirs, and in spite of all they may say against me, I am going to do them a great and lasting service. Upon their necks are visible the marks of the collar, and upon

their backs, those of the lash. They are not allowed
to read and think for themselves. They are taught
like parrots, and the best are those who repeat, with
the fewest mistakes, the sentences they have been
taught. They sit like owls upon some dead limb of
the tree of knowledge, and hoot the same old hoots
that have been hooted for eighteen hundred years.
Their congregations are not grand enough, nor
sufficiently civilized, to be willing that the poor
preachers shall think for themselves. They are not
employed for that purpose. Investigation is regarded
as a dangerous experiment, and the ministers are
warned that none of that kind of work will be toler-
ated. They are notified to stand by the old creed,
and to avoid all original thought, as a mortal pesti-
lence. Every minister is employed like an attorney—
either for plaintiff or defendant—and he is expected
to be true to his client. If he changes his mind, he is
regarded as a deserter, and denounced, hated and
slandered accordingly.

Every orthodox clergyman agrees not to change.
He contracts not to find new facts, and makes a
bargain that he will deny them if he does. Such is
the position of a Protestant minister in this Nineteenth Century. His condition excites my pity; and
to better it, I am going to do what little I can.

Some of the clergy have the independence to break
away, and the intellect to maintain themselves as
free men, but the most are compelled to submit to
the dictation of the orthodox and the dead. They are
not employed to give their thoughts, but simply to
repeat the ideas of others. They are not expected to
give even the doubts that may suggest themselves,
but are required to walk in the narrow, verdureless
path trodden by the ignorance of the past. The forests
and fields on either side are nothing to them. They
must not even look at the purple hills, nor pause to
hear the babble of the brooks. They must remain in

the dusty road where the guide-boards are. They must confine themselves to the " fall of man," the expulsion from the garden, the " scheme of salvation," the " second birth," the atonement, the happiness of the redeemed, and the misery of the lost. They must be careful not to express any new ideas upon these great questions. It is much safer for them to quote from the works of the dead. The more vividly they describe the sufferings of the unregenerate, of those who attended theaters and balls, and drank wine in summer-gardens on the Sabbath day, and laughed at priests, the better ministers they are supposed to be. They must show that misery fits the good for Heaven, while happiness prepares the bad for Hell; that the wicked get all their good things in this life, and the good all their evil; that in this world God punishes the people He loves, and in the next, the ones He hates; that happiness makes us bad here, but not in Heaven; that pain makes us good here, but not in Hell. No matter how absurd these things may appear to the carnal mind, they must be preached and they must be believed. If they were reasonable, there would be no virtue in believing. Even the publicans and sinners believe reasonable things. To believe without evidence, or in spite of it, is accounted as righteousness to the sincere and humble Christian.

The ministers are in duty bound to denounce all intellectual pride, and show that we are never quite so dear to God as when we admit that we are poor, corrupt and idiotic worms; that we never should have been born; that we ought to be damned without the least delay; that we are so infamous that we like to enjoy ourselves; that we love our wives and children better than our God; that we are generous only because we are vile; that we are honest from the meanest motives, and that sometimes we have fallen so low that we have had doubts about the inspiration of the Jewish Scriptures. In short, they are expected to denounce all pleasant paths and rustling trees, to curse the grass and flowers, and glorify the dust and weeds. They are expected to malign the wicked people in the green and happy fields, who sit and laugh beside the gurgling springs or climb the hills and wander as they will. They are expected to point out the dangers of freedom, the safety of implicit obedience, and to show the wickedness of philosophy, the goodness of faith, the immorality of science and the purity of ignorance

Now and then a few pious people discover some young man of a religious turn of mind and a consumptive habit of body, not quite sickly enough to die, nor healthy enough to be wicked. The idea occurs to them that he would make a good orthodox minister. They take up a contribution and send the young man to some theological school, where he can be taught to repeat a creed and despise reason.

Should it turn out that the young man had some mind of his own, and, after graduating, should change his opinions and preach a different doctrine from that taught in the school, every man who contributed a dollar towards his education would feel that he had been robbed, and would denounce him as a dishonest and ungrateful wretch

AS long as woman regards the Bible as the charter of her rights, she will be the slave of man. The Bible was not written by a woman. Within its lids there is nothing but humiliation and shame for her. She is regarded as the property of man. She is made to ask forgiveness for becoming a mother. She is as much below her husband as her husband is below Christ. She is not allowed to speak. The gospel is too pure to be spoken by her polluted lips. Woman should learn in silence

In the Bible will be found no description of a civilized home. The free mother surrounded by free and loving children, adored by a free man, her husband, was unknown to the inspired writers of the Bible. They did not believe in the democracy of the home—in the republicanism of the fireside ⋙ ⋙

These inspired gentlemen knew nothing of the rights of children. They were the advocates of brute force— the disciples of the lash. They knew nothing of human rights. Their doctrines have brutalized the homes of millions, and filled the eyes of infancy with tears ⋙ ⋙

Let us free ourselves from the tyranny of a book, from the slavery of dead ignorance, from the aristocracy of the air.

❡ There has never been upon the earth a generation of free men and women. It is not yet time to write a creed. Wait until the chains are broken—until dungeons are not regarded as temples. Wait until solemnity is not mistaken for wisdom—until mental cowardice ceases to be known as reverence. Wait until the living are considered the equals of the dead —until the cradle takes precedence of the coffin. Wait until what we know can be spoken without regard to what others may believe. Wait until teachers take the place of preachers—until followers become investigators. Wait until the world is free before you write a creed ⋙ ⋙

In this creed there will be but one word—Liberty!

MEN should be liberated from the aristocracy of the air. Every chain of superstition should be broken. The rights of men and women should be equal and sacred—marriage should be a perfect partnership—children should be governed by kindness—every family should be a republic—every fireside a democracy ⋙ ⋙

I believe in the fireside. I believe in the democracy of home. I believe in the republicanism of the family. I believe in liberty, equality and love ⋙ ⋙

IF women have been slaves, what shall I say of children; of the little children in alleys and sub-cellars; the little children who turn pale when they hear their father's footsteps; little children who run away when they only hear their names called by the lips of a mother; little children—the children of poverty, the children of crime, the children of brutality, wherever they are—flotsam and jetsam upon the wild, mad sea of life—my heart goes out to them, one and all.

I tell you, the children have the same rights that we have, and we ought to treat them as though they were human beings. They should be reared with love, with kindness, with tenderness, and not with brutality. That is my idea of children.
When your little child tells a lie, do not rush at him as though the world were about to go into bankruptcy. Be honest with him. A tyrant father will have liars for his children; do you know that? A lie is born of tyranny upon the one hand and weakness upon the other, and when you rush at a poor little boy with a club in your hand, of course he lies.

I thank thee, Mother Nature, that thou hast put ingenuity enough in the brain of a child, when attacked by a brutal parent, to throw up a little breastwork in the shape of a lie.
When one of your children tells a lie, be honest with him; tell him that you have told hundreds of them yourself. Tell him it is not the best way; that you have tried it. Tell him as the man did in Maine when his boy left home, " John, honesty is the best policy; I have tried both." Be honest with him. Suppose a man as much larger than you as you are larger than a child five years old, should come at you with a liberty-pole in his hand, and in a voice of thunder shout, " Who broke that plate? " There is not a solitary one of you who would not swear you never saw it, or that it was cracked when you got it. Why

not be honest with these children? Just imagine a
man who deals in stocks whipping his boy for putting
false rumors afloat! Think of a lawyer beating his
own flesh and blood for evading the truth when he
makes half of his own living that way! Think of a
minister punishing his child for not telling all he
thinks! Just think of it!

⁋ When your child commits a wrong, take it in your
arms; let it feel your heart beat against its heart;
let the child know that you really and truly and
sincerely love it. Yet some Christians, good Christians, when a child commits a fault, drive it from
the door and say, " Never do you darken this house
again." Think of that! And then these same people
will get down on their knees and ask God to take
care of the child they have driven from home. I will
never ask God to take care of my children unless I
am doing my level best in that same direction 🙢 🙢

Life should not be treated as a solemn matter. I like
to see the children at table, and hear each one telling
of the wonderful things he has seen and heard. I like
to hear the clatter of knives and forks and spoons
mingling with their happy voices. I had rather hear
it than any opera that was ever put upon the boards.
Let the children have liberty. Be honest and fair with
them; be just; be tender; and they will make you
rich in love and joy 🙢 🙢

HE laugh of a child will make the holiest day
more sacred still. Strike with hand of fire, O
weird musician, thy harp strung with Apollo's golden
hair; fill the vast cathedral aisles with symphonies
sweet and dim, deft toucher of the organ keys; blow,
bugler, blow, until thy silver notes do touch and kiss
the moonlit waves, and charm the lovers wandering
'mid the vine-clad hills. But know, your sweetest
strains are discords all, compared with childhood's

happy laugh—the laugh that fills the eyes with light
and every heart with joy. O rippling river of laughter,
thou art the blessed boundary-line between the beasts
and men; and every wayward wave of thine doth
drown some fretful fiend of care. O laughter, rose-
lipped daughter of Joy, there are dimples enough in
thy cheeks to catch and glorify all the tears of grief.

T is not necessary to be great to be happy; it
is not necessary to be rich to be just and generous
and to have a heart filled with divine affection. No
matter whether you are rich or poor, treat your wife
as though she were a splendid flower, and she will
fill your life with perfume and with joy
And do you know, it is a splendid thing to think that
the woman you really love will never grow old to you.
Through the wrinkles of time, through the mask of
years, if you really love her, you will always see the
face you have loved and won. And a woman that really
loves a man does not see that he grows old; he is not
decrepit to her; he does not tremble; he is not old;
she always sees the same gallant gentleman who won
her hand and heart. I like to think of it in that way;
I like to think that love is eternal. And to love in that
way and then go down the hill of life together, and as
you go down, hear, perhaps, the laughter of grand-
children, while the birds of love and joy sing once
more in the leafless branches of the tree of age

REASON, Observation and Experience—the Holy
Trinity of Science—have taught us that happiness is the only good; that the time to be happy is
now, and the way to be happy is to make others so.
This is enough for us. In this belief we are content
to live and die. If by any possibility the existence
of a power superior to, and independent of, Nature
shall be demonstrated, there will then be time enough
to kneel. Until then, let us stand erect

OR ages, a deadly conflict has been waged between a few brave men and women of thought and genius upon the one side, and the great ignorant religious mass on the other. This is the war between Science and Faith. The few have appealed to reason, to honor, to law, to freedom, to the known, and to happiness here in this world. The many have appealed to prejudice, to fear, to miracle, to slavery, to the unknown, and to misery hereafter. The few have said," Think ! " The many have said, " Believe ! "

Man must learn to rely upon himself. Reading Bibles will not protect him from the blasts of Winter; but houses, fires and clothing will. To prevent famine, one plow is worth a million sermons

AN should cease to expect aid from on high. By this time he should know that Heaven has no ear to hear, and no hand to help. The present is the necessary child of all the past. There has been no chance, and there can be no interference

If abuses are destroyed, man must destroy them. If slaves are freed, man must free them. If new truths are discovered, man must discover them. If the naked are clothed; if the hungry are fed; if justice is done; if labor is rewarded; if superstition has been driven from the mind; if the defenseless are protected, and if the right finally triumphs, all must be the work of man. The grand victories of the future must be won by man, and by man alone

Give me the storm and tempest of thought and action, rather than the dead calm of ignorance and faith!

Banish me from Eden when you will; but first let me eat of the fruit of the tree of knowledge!

Beyond Nature man can not go even in thought—

above Nature he can not rise—below Nature he can not fall

Salvation through slavery is worthless. Salvation from slavery is inestimable

Heresy is what the minority believe

When a fact can be demonstrated, force is unnecessary; when it can not be demonstrated, an appeal to force is infamous. In the presence of the unknown, all have an equal right to think

ALL that is good in our civilization is the result of commerce, climate, soil, geographical position, industry, invention, discovery, art and science. The church has been the enemy of progress, for the reason that it has endeavored to prevent man from thinking for himself. To prevent thought is to prevent all advancement except in the direction of faith

Virtue is a subordination of the passions to the intellect. It is to act in accordance with your highest convictions. It does not consist in believing, but in doing.

FOR the vagaries of the clouds the Infidels propose to substitute the realities of earth; for superstition, the splendid demonstrations and achievements of science; and for theological tyranny, the chainless liberty of thought We do not say that we have discovered all; that our doctrines are the all in all of truth. We know of no end to the development of man. We can not unravel the infinite complications of matter and force. The history of one monad is as unknown as that of the universe; one drop of water is as wonderful as all the seas; one leaf, as all the forests; and one grain of sand as all the stars

We are not endeavoring to chain the future, but to free the present. We are not forging fetters for our children, but we are breaking those our fathers made for us. We are the advocates of inquiry, of investigation and thought. This, of itself, is an admission that we are not perfectly satisfied with all our conclusions. Philosophy has not the egotism of faith. While superstition builds walls and creates obstructions, science opens all the highways of thought. We do not pretend to have circumnavigated everything and to have solved all difficulties; but we do believe that it is better to love men than to fear gods; that it is grander and nobler to think and investigate for yourself than to repeat a creed. We are satisfied that there can be but little liberty on Earth while men worship a tyrant in Heaven. We do not expect to accomplish everything in our day; but we want to do what good we can, and to render all the service possible in the holy cause of human progress. We know that doing away with gods and supernatural persons and powers is not an end. It is a means to an end, the real end being the happiness of man

Felling forests is not the end of agriculture. Driving pirates from the sea is not all there is of commerce.

We are laying the foundations of the grand temple of the future—not the temple of all the gods, but of all the people—wherein with appropriate rites will be celebrated the Religion of Humanity

⊂⊃

EVERY wrong in some way tends to abolish itself. It is hard to make a lie stand always. A lie will not fit a fact. It will only fit another lie made for the purpose. The life of a lie is simply a question of time. Nothing but Truth is immortal

⊂⊃

There are real crimes enough without creating artificial ones. All progress in legislation has for centuries consisted in repealing the laws of the ghosts

The first great step towards progress is, for man to cease to be the slave of man; the second, to cease to be the slave of the monsters of his own creation—of the ghosts and phantoms of the air

Religion has not civilized man—man has civilized religion. God improves as man advances

Fear paralyzes the brain. Progress is born of courage. Fear believes—courage doubts. Fear falls upon the earth and prays—courage stands erect and thinks. Fear retreats—courage advances. Fear is barbarism—courage is civilization. Fear believes in witchcraft, in devils and in ghosts. Fear is religion—courage is science

IN the republic of mind, one is a majority. There, all are monarchs, and all are equals. The tyranny of a majority even is unknown. Each one is crowned, sceptered and throned. Upon every brow is the tiara, and around every form is the imperial purple. Only those are good citizens who express their honest thoughts, and those who persecute for opinion's sake are the only traitors. There, nothing is considered infamous except an appeal to brute force, and nothing sacred but love, liberty and joy

I THANK the inventors, the discoverers, the thinkers. I thank Columbus and Magellan. I thank Galileo, and Copernicus, and Kepler, and Descartes, and Newton, and Laplace. I thank Locke, and Hume, and Bacon, and Shakespeare, and Kant, and Fichte, and Leibnitz, and Goethe. I thank Fulton, and Watts, and Volta, and Galvini, and Franklin, and Morse, who made lightning the messenger of man. I thank Humboldt, the Shakespeare of science. I thank Crompton and Arkwright, from whose brains leaped the looms and spindles that clothed the world. I thank Luther for protesting against the abuses of the Church, and I denounce him because he was the enemy of liberty. I thank Calvin for writing a book in favor of religious freedom, and I abhor him because he burned Servetus. I thank Knox for resisting Episcopal persecution, and I hate him because he persecuted in his turn. I thank the Puritans for saying, " Resistance to tyrants is obedience to God," and yet I am compelled to say that they were tyrants themselves. I thank Thomas Paine because he was a believer in liberty, and because he did as much to make my country free as any other human being. I thank Voltaire, that great man who, for half a century, was the intellectual emperor of Europe, and who, from his throne at the foot of the Alps, pointed the finger of scorn at every hypocrite in Christendom. I thank Darwin, Haeckel and Buechner, Spencer, Tyndall and Huxley, Draper, Lecky and Buckle

I thank the inventors, the discoverers, the thinkers, the scientists, the explorers. I thank the honest millions who have toiled.

❡ I thank the brave men with brave thoughts. They are the Atlases upon whose broad and mighty shoulders rests the grand fabric of civilization. They are the men who have broken, and are still breaking, the chains of Superstition. They are the Titans who carried Olympus by assault, and who will soon stand victors upon Sinai's crags

We are beginning to learn that to exchange a mistake for the truth—a superstition for a fact—to ascertain the real—is to progress

Happiness is the only possible good, and all that tends to the happiness of man is right, and is of value. All that tends to develop the bodies and minds of men; all that gives us better houses, better clothes, better food, better pictures, grander music, better heads, better hearts; all that renders us more intellectual and more loving, nearer just; that makes us better husbands and wives, better children, better citizens—all these things combined produce what I call Progress.

I DO not pretend to tell what all the truth is. I do not pretend to have fathomed the abyss, nor to have floated on outstretched wings level with the dim heights of thought. I simply plead for freedom. I denounce the cruelties and horrors of slavery. I ask for light and air for the souls of men. I say, take off those chains—break those manacles—free those limbs—release that brain! I plead for the right to think, to reason, to investigate. I ask that the future may be enriched with the honest thoughts of men. I implore every human being to be a soldier in the army of progress

I will not invade the rights of others. You have no right to erect your tollgate upon the highways of thought. You have no right to leap from the hedges of superstition, and strike down the pioneers of the human race. You have no right to sacrifice the liberties of man upon the altars of ghosts. Believe what you may; preach what you desire; have all the forms and ceremonies you please; exercise your liberty in your own way, but extend to all others the same right

MAN has found that he must give liberty to others in order to have it himself. He has found that a master is also a slave—that a tyrant is himself a serf. He has found that governments should be founded and administered by man and for man; that the rights of all are equal; that the powers that be are not ordained by God; that woman is at least the equal of man; that men existed before books; that religion is one of the phases of thought through which the world is passing; that all creeds were made by man; that everything is natural; that a miracle is an impossibility; that we know nothing of origin and

destiny; that concerning the unknown we are all
equally ignorant; that the pew has the right to contradict what the pulpit asserts; that man is responsible
only to himself and those he injures, and that all have
a right to think

TRUE religion must be free. Without perfect
liberty of the mind there can be no true religion.
Without liberty the brain is a dungeon—the mind a
convict. The slave may bow and cringe and crawl,
but he can not adore, he can not love
True religion is the perfume of a free and grateful
heart. True religion is a subordination of the passions
to the perceptions of the intellect. True religion is not
a theory—it is a practise. It is not a creed—it is life.
A theory that is afraid of investigation is undeserv-
ing of a place in the human mind

MAN advances only as he overcomes the obstructions of Nature, and this can be done only by
labor and by thought. Labor is the foundation of all.
Without labor, and without great labor, progress is
impossible. The progress of the world depends upon
the men who walk in the fresh furrows and through
the rustling corn; upon those who sow and reap; upon
those whose faces are radiant with the glare of furnace
fires; upon the delvers in mines, and the workers
in shops; upon those who give to the Winter air the
ringing music of the ax; upon those who battle with
the boisterous billows of the sea; upon the inventors
and discoverers; upon the brave thinkers

Why should we sacrifice a real world that we have,
for one we know not of?

As far as I am concerned, I wish to be out on the high
seas. I wish to take my chances with wind and wave
and star. And I had rather go down in the glory and

grandeur of the storm, than to rot in any orthodox harbor whatever

There is no slavery but ignorance. Liberty is the child of intelligence

This is my doctrine: Give every other human being every right you claim for yourself. Keep your mind open to the influences of Nature. Receive new thoughts with hospitality. Let us advance

The man who does not do his own thinking is a slave, and is a traitor to himself and to his fellow-men

NEARLY every religion has accounted for the devilment in this world by the crime of woman. What a gallant thing that is! And if it is true, I had rather live with the woman I love in a world full of trouble, than to live in Heaven with nobody but men

I read in a book—and I will say now that I can not give the exact language, as my memory does not retain the words, but I can give the substance—I read in a book that the Supreme Being concluded to make a world and one man; that He took some nothing and made a world and one man, and put this man in a garden. In a little while He noticed that the man got lonesome; that he wandered around as if he were waiting for a train. There was nothing to interest him: no news; no papers; no politics; no policy; and, as the Devil had not yet made his appearance, there was no chance for reconciliation—not even for civil-service reform. Well, he wandered about the garden in this condition, until finally the Supreme Being made up His mind to make him a companion.

Having used up all the nothing He originally took in making the world and one man, He had to take a part of the man to start a woman with. So He caused a sleep to fall upon this man—now, understand me, I do not say this story is true. After the sleep fell upon this man, the Supreme Being took a rib, or as the French would call it, a cutlet, out of this man, and from that He made a woman. And considering the amount of raw material used, I look upon it as the most successful job ever performed. Well, after He got the woman done, she was brought to the man— not to see how she liked him, but to see how he liked her. He liked her, and they started housekeeping; and they were told of certain things they might do and of one thing they could not do—and of course they did it. I would have done it in fifteen minutes, and I know it. There would n't have been an apple on that tree half an hour from date, and the limbs would have been full of clubs ✦✦

And then they were turned out of the park and extra policemen were put on to keep them from getting back.
❧ Devilment commenced. The mumps, and the measles, and the whooping-cough, and the scarlet fever started in their race for man. They began to have the toothache, roses began to have thorns, snakes began to have poisoned teeth, and people began to divide about religion and politics, and the world has been full of trouble from that day to this.

❧ Nearly all of the religions of this world account for the existence of evil by such a story as that! ✦✦

I READ in another book what appeared to be an account of the same transaction. It was written about four thousand years before the other. All commentators agree that the one that was written last was the original, and that the one that was written first was copied from the one that was written last. But I would advise you all not to allow your creed to be disturbed by a little matter of four or five thousand years. In this other story, Brahma made up his mind to make the world and a man and a woman. He made the world, and he made the man and then the woman,

and put them on the Island of Ceylon. According
to the account, it was the most beautiful island of
which man can conceive. Such birds, such songs,
such flowers and such verdure! And the branches
of the trees were so arranged that when the wind
swept through them every tree was a thousand
Eolian harps

Brahma, when he put them there, said, " Let them
have a period of courtship, for it is my desire and will
that true love should forever precede marriage."
When I read that, it was so much more beautiful
and lofty than the other, that I said to myself, " If
either one of these stories turns out to be true, I hope
it will be this one."

Then they had their courtship, with the nightingale
singing, and the stars shining, and the flowers blooming, and they fell in love. Imagine that courtship!
No prospective fathers or mothers in law; no prying
and gossiping neighbors; nobody to say, " Young
man, how do you expect to support her? " Nothing
of that kind. They were married by the Supreme
Brahma, and he said to them, " Remain here; you
must never leave this island." Well, after a little
while, the man—and his name was Adami, and the
woman's name was Heva—said to Heva, " I believe
I 'll look about a little." He went to the Northern
extremity of the island, where there was a little
narrow neck of land connecting it with the mainland,
and the Devil, who is always playing pranks with us,
produced a mirage, and when he looked over to the
mainland, such hills and vales, such dells and dales,
such mountains crowned with snow, such cataracts
clad in bows of glory did he see there, that he went
back and told Heva, " The country over there is a
thousand times better than this; let us migrate."
She, like every other woman that ever lived, said,
" Let well enough alone; we have all we want; let us
stay here." But he said, " No, let us go "; so she

followed him and when they came to this narrow neck of land, he took her on his back like a gentleman and carried her over. But the moment they got over they heard a crash, and looking back, discovered that this narrow neck of land had fallen into the sea. The mirage had disappeared, and there was naught but rocks and sand; and then the Supreme Brahma cursed them both to the lowest hell.

Then it was that the man spoke—and I have liked him ever since for it—" Curse me, but curse not her; it was not her fault, it was mine."

That's the kind of man to start a world with! The Supreme Brahma said," I will save her, but not thee." And then she spoke out of her fulness of love, out of a heart in which there was love enough to make all her daughters rich in holy affection, and said, " If thou wilt not spare him, spare neither me; I do not wish to live without him; I love him." Then the Supreme Brahma said—and I have liked him ever since I read it—" I will spare you both and watch over you and your children forever."

<hr>

As man develops, he places a greater value upon his own rights. Liberty becomes a grander and diviner thing. As he values his own rights, he begins to value the rights of others. And when all men give to all others all the rights they claim for themselves, this world will be civilized

<hr>

LIBERTY, float not forever in the far horizon —remain not forever in the dream of the enthusiast, the philanthropist and poet, but come and make thy home among the children of men!

I know not what discoveries, what inventions, what thoughts may leap from the brain of the world. I know not what garments of glory may be woven by the years to come. I can not dream of the victories to be won upon the fields of thought; but I do know

that, coming from the infinite sea of the future, there
will never touch this " bank and shoal of time " a
richer gift, a rarer blessing, than liberty for man,
for woman and for child

LITTLE while ago, I stood by the grave
of the old Napoleon—a magnificent tomb of
gilt and gold, fit almost for a deity dead—
and gazed upon the sarcophagus of rare and
priceless marble, where rest at last the ashes of that
restless man. I leaned over the balustrade and thought
about the career of the greatest soldier of the modern
world
I saw him walking upon the banks of the Seine,
contemplating suicide. I saw him at Toulon—I saw
him putting down the mob in the streets of Paris—
I saw him at the head of the army of Italy—I saw
him crossing the bridge of Lodi, with the tricolor in
his hand—I saw him in Egypt in the shadows of the
Pyramids—I saw him conquer the Alps and mingle
the eagles of France with the eagles of the crags. I
saw him at Marengo—at Ulm and Austerlitz. I saw
him in Russia, where the infantry of the snow and
the cavalry of the wild blasts scattered his legions
like Winter's withered leaves. I saw him at Leipsic
in defeat and disaster—driven by a million bayonets
back upon Paris—clutched like a wild beast—banished to Elba. I saw him escape and retake an empire
by the force of his genius. I saw him upon the frightful
field of Waterloo, where Chance and Fate combined
to wreck the fortunes of their former king. And I
saw him at Saint Helena, with his hands crossed behind
him, gazing out upon the sad and solemn sea
I thought of the orphans and widows he had made—
of the tears that had been shed for his glory, and of
the only woman who ever loved him, pushed from
his heart by the cold hand of ambition. And I said
I would rather have been a French peasant and worn

wooden shoes. I would rather have lived in a hut with a vine growing over the door, and the grapes growing purple in the kisses of the Autumn sun. I would rather have been that poor peasant with my loving wife by my side, knitting as the day died out of the sky—with my children upon my knees and their arms about me—I would rather have been that man and gone down to the tongueless silence of the dreamless dust, than to have been that imperial impersonation of force and murder, known as " Napoleon the Great."

Y Creed is to love justice, to long for the right, to love mercy, to pity the suffering, to assist the weak, to forget wrongs and remember benefits —to love the truth, to be sincere, to utter honest words, to love liberty, to wage relentless war against slavery in all its forms, to love wife and child and friend, to make a happy home, to love the beautiful in art, in Nature, to cultivate the mind, to be familiar with the mighty thoughts that genius has expressed, the noble deeds of all the world, to cultivate courage and cheerfulness, to make others happy, to fill life with the splendor of generous acts, the warmth of loving words, to discard error, to destroy prejudice, to receive new truths with gladness, to cultivate hope, to see the calm beyond the storm, the dawn before the night, to do the best that can be done and then —to be resigned

Let us develop the brain, civilize the heart, and give wings to the imagination

The road is short to anything we fear

A good deed is the best prayer

Intellectual freedom is only the right to be honest.

THE GOSPEL ACCORDING TO
RALPH W. EMERSON

Cast the bantling on the rocks,
Suckle him with the she-wolf's teat;
Wintered with the hawk and fox,
Power and speed be hands and feet.

I READ the other day some verses written by an eminent painter which were original and not conventional. Always the soul hears an admonition in such lines, let the subject be what it may. The sentiment they instil is of more value than any thought they may contain. To believe your own thought, to believe that what is true for you in your private heart is true for all men —that is genius.

Speak your latent conviction and it shall be the universal sense; for always the inmost becomes the outmost—and our first thought is rendered back to us by the trumpets of the Last Judgment. Familiar as the voice of the mind is to each, the highest merit we ascribe to Moses, Plato and Milton is that they set at naught books and traditions, and spoke not what men, but what they, thought. A man should learn to detect and watch that gleam of light which flashes across his mind from within, more than the luster of the firmament of bards and sages. Yet he dismisses without notice his thought, because it is his.

In every work of genius we recognize our own rejected thoughts: they come back to us with a certain alienated majesty. Great works of art have no more affecting lesson for us than this. They teach us to abide by our spontaneous impression with good-humored inflexibility then most when the whole cry of voices is on the other side. Else, tomorrow a stranger will say with masterly good sense precisely what we have thought and felt all the time, and we shall be forced to take with shame our own opinion from another.

There is a time in every man's education when he arrives at the conviction that envy is ignorance;

that imitation is suicide; that he must take himself for better, for worse, as his portion; that though the wide universe is full of good, no kernel of nourishing corn can come to him but through his toil bestowed on that plot of ground which is given to him to till. The power which resides in him is new in Nature, and none but he knows what that is which he can do, nor does he know until he has tried.

❡ Not for nothing one face, one character, one fact makes much impression on him, and another none. It is not without pre-established harmony, this sculpture in the memory. The eye was placed where one ray should fall, that it might testify of that particular ray. Bravely let him speak the utmost syllable of his confession. We but half-express ourselves, and are ashamed of that divine idea which each of us represents. It may be safely trusted as proportionate and of good issues, so it be faithfully imparted, but God will not have His work made manifest by cowards. It needs a divine man to exhibit anything divine. A man is relieved and gay when he has put his heart into his work and done his best; but what he has said or done otherwise shall give him no peace. It is a deliverance which does not deliver. In the attempt his genius deserts him; no muse befriends; no invention, no hope ❦ ❦

⌒

We crave a sense of reality, though it come in strokes of pain ❦ ❦

⌒

TRUST thyself: every heart vibrates to that iron string. Accept the place the divine Providence has found for you, the society of your contemporaries, the connection of events. Great men have always done so, and confided themselves childlike to the genius of their age, betraying their perception that the Eternal was stirring at their heart, working through their hands, predominating in all their being. And we are now men, and must accept in the highest mind the same transcendent destiny ; and not pinched in a corner, not cowards fleeing before a revolution, but redeemers and benefactors, pious aspirants to be noble clay, plastic under the Almighty effort, let us advance and advance on Chaos and the Dark.

¶ What pretty oracles Nature yields us on this text in the face and behavior of children, babes and even brutes. That divided and rebel mind, that distrust of a sentiment because our arithmetic has computed the strength and means opposed to our purpose, these have not. Their mind being whole, their eye is as yet unconquered, and when we look in their faces, we are disconcerted ·• ·•

Infancy conforms to nobody; all conform to it; so that one babe commonly makes four or five out of the adults who prattle and play to it. So God has armed youth and puberty and manhood no less with its own piquancy and charm, and made it enviable and gracious and its claims not to be put by, if it will stand by itself ·• ·•

Do not think the youth has no force because he can not speak to you and me. Hark ! in the next room, who spoke so clear and emphatic? Good Heaven ! it is he ! it is that very lump of bashfulness and phlegm which for weeks has done nothing but eat when you were by, that now rolls out these words like bellstrokes. It seems he knows how to speak to his contemporaries. Bashful or bold, then, he will know how to make us seniors very unnecessary.

¶ The nonchalance of boys who are sure of a dinner, and would disdain as much as a lord to do or say aught to conciliate one, is the healthy attitude of human nature. How is a boy the master of society ! Independent, irresponsible, looking out from his corner on such people and facts as pass by, he tries and sentences them on their merits, in the swift summary way of boys, as good, bad, interesting, silly, eloquent, troublesome. He cumbers himself never about consequences, about interests; he gives an independent, genuine verdict. You must court him; he does not court you. But the man is, as it were, clapped into jail by his consciousness. As soon as he has once acted or spoken with eclat, he is a committed person, watched by the sympathy or the hatred of hundreds whose affections must now enter into his account

There is no Lethe for this. Ah, that he could pass again into his neutral, godlike independence! Who can thus lose all pledge, and having observed, observe again from the same unaffected, unbiased, unbribable, unaffrighted innocence, must always be formidable, must always engage the poet's and the man's regards. Of such an immortal youth the force would be felt. He would utter opinions on all passing affairs, which being seen to be not private but necessary, would sink like darts into the ear of men, and put them in fear

These are the voices which we hear in solitude, but they grow faint and inaudible as we enter into the world. Society everywhere is in conspiracy against the manhood of every one of its members. Society is a joint-stock company in which the members agree, for the better securing of his bread to each shareholder, to surrender the liberty and culture of the eater. The virtue in most request is conformity. Self-reliance is its aversion. It loves not realities and creators, but names and customs

We can drive a stone upward for a moment into the air, but it is yet true that all stones will forever fall; and whatever instances can be quoted of unpunished theft, or of a lie which somebody credited, justice must prevail, and it is the privilege of truth to make itself believed

HOSO would be a man must be a noncon-
formist. He who would gather immortal
palms must not be hindered by the name
. of goodness, but must explore if it be goodness. Nothing is at last sacred but the integrity of
our own mind. Absolve you to yourself, and you shall
have the suffrage of the world

I remember an answer which when quite young I
was prompted to make to a valued adviser who was
wont to importune me with the dear old doctrines
of the church. On my saying,"What have I to do with
the sacredness of traditions, if I live wholly from
within? " my friend suggested," But these impulses
may be from below, not from above." I replied, " They
do not seem to me to be such ; but if I am the Devil's
child, I will live then from the Devil."

No law can be sacred to me but that of my nature.

Good and bad are but names very readily trans-
ferable to that or this : the only right is what is after
my constitution ; the only wrong what is against it.
A man is to carry himself in the presence of all opposition as if everything were titular and ephemeral
but he. I am ashamed to think how easily we capitu-
late to badges and names, to large societies and dead
institutions

Every decent and well-spoken individual affects and
sways me more than is right. I ought to go upright,
and vital, and speak the rude truth in all ways. If
malice and vanity wear the coat of philanthropy,
shall that pass? If an angry bigot assumes this bounti-
ful cause of Abolition, and comes to me with his last
news of the Barbadoes, why should I not say to him :
" Go love thy infant; love thy wood-chopper; be
good-natured and modest; have that grace; and
never varnish your hard, uncharitable ambition with
this incredible tenderness for black folks a thousand
miles off. Thy love afar is spite at home." Rough and
graceless would be such greeting, but truth is hand-

somer than the affectation of love. Your goodness
must have some edge to it—else it is none
The doctrine of hatred must be preached as the
counteraction of the doctrine of love when that pules
and whines. I shun father and mother and wife and
brother, when my genius calls me. I would write on
the lintels of the doorpost, *Whim*. I hope it is somewhat better than whim at last, but we can not spend
the day in explanation. Expect me not to show cause
why I seek or why I exclude company
Then again, do not tell me, as a good man did today,
of my obligation to put all poor men in good situations.
Are they *my* poor? I tell thee, thou foolish philanthropist, that I grudge the dollar, the dime, the cent, I
give to such men as do not belong to me and to whom
I do not belong. There is a class of persons to whom
by all spiritual affinity I am bought and sold; for
them I will go to prison, if need be; but your miscel-
laneous popular charities; the education at college
of fools; the building of meetinghouses to the vain
end to which many now stand; alms to sots; and the
thousandfold Relief Societies—though I confess with
shame I sometimes succumb and give the dollar,
it is a wicked dollar which by and by I shall have
the manhood to withhold

We have seen many counterfeits, but we are born
believers in great men

VIRTUES are in the popular estimate rather
the exception than the rule. There is the
man *and* his virtues. Men do what is called
a good action, as some piece of courage or
charity, much as they would pay a fine in expiation
of daily non-appearance on parade. Their works are
done as an apology or extenuation of their living in
the world—as invalids and the insane pay a high
board. Their virtues are penances. I do not wish to

expiate, but to live. My life is not an apology, but a
life. It is for itself and not for a spectacle. I much
prefer that it should be of a lower strain, so it be
genuine and equal, than that it should be glittering
and unsteady. I wish it to be sound and sweet, and
not to need diet and bleeding. My life should be
unique; it should be an alms, a conquest, a medicine.
I ask primary evidence that you are a man, and refuse
this appeal from the man to his actions. I know that
for myself it makes no difference whether I do or
forbear those actions which are reckoned excellent.
I can not consent to pay for a privilege where I have
intrinsic right. Few and mean as my gifts may be, I
actually am, and do not need for my own assurance or
the assurance of my fellows any secondary testimony.

What must I do is all that concerns me, not what
the people think. This rule, equally arduous in actual
and in intellectual life, may serve for the whole distinction between greatness and meanness. It is the
harder, because you will always find those who think
they know what is your duty better than you know it.
It is easy in the world to live after the world's opinion;
it is easy in solitude to live after our own; but the
great man is he who in the midst of the crowd keeps
with perfect sweetness the independence of solitude.

A divine person is the prophecy of the mind; a friend
is the hope of the heart. Our beatitude waits for the
fulfilment of these two in one

THE objection to conforming to usages that
have become dead to you is that it scatters
your force. It loses your time and blurs the
impression of your character. If you maintain a dead church, contribute to a dead Bible Society,
vote with a great party either for the Government or
against it, spread your table like base housekeepers—
under all these screens, I have difficulty to detect the

precise man you are. And of course, so much force is withdrawn from your proper life. But do your thing, and I shall know you. Do your work, and you shall reinforce yourself. A man must consider what a blindman's-buff is this game of conformity. If I know your sect, I anticipate your argument. I hear a preacher announce for his text and topic the expediency of one of the institutions of his church. Do I not know beforehand that not possibly can he say a new and spontaneous word? Do I not know that with all this ostentation of examining the grounds of the institution he will do no such thing? Do I not know that he is pledged to himself not to look but at one side, the permitted side—not as a man, but as a parish minister? He is a retained attorney, and these airs of the bench are the emptiest affectation. Well, most men have bound their eyes with one or another handkerchief, and attached themselves to some one of these communities of opinion. This conformity makes them not false in a few particulars, authors of a few lies, but false in all particulars. Their every truth is not quite true. Their two is not the real two, their four not the real four; so that every word they say chagrins us, and we know not where to begin to set them right. Meantime Nature is not slow to equip us in the prison-uniform of the party to which we adhere. We come to wear one cut of face and figure, and acquire by degrees the gentlest asinine expression.

There is a mortifying experience in particular, which does not fail to wreak itself also in the general history; I mean, " the foolish face of praise," the forced smile which we put on in company where we do not feel at ease in answer to conversation which does not interest us. The muscles, not spontaneously moved, but moved by a low usurping wilfulness, grow tight about the outline of the face and make the most disagreeable sensation, a sensation of rebuke and warning which no brave young man will suffer twice.

FOR nonconformity the world whips you with its displeasure. And therefore a man must know how to estimate a sour face. The bystanders look askance on him in the public street or in the friend's parlor. If this aversation had its origin in contempt and resistance like his own, he might well go home with a sad countenance; but the sour faces of the multitude, like their sweet faces, have no deep cause—disguise no god, but are put on and off as the wind blows and a newspaper directs.

❡ Yet is the discontent of the multitude more formidable than that of the senate and the college. It is easy enough for a firm man who knows the world to brook the rage of the cultured classes. Their rage is decorous and prudent, for they are timid, as being very vulnerable themselves. But when to their feminine rage the indignation of the people is added, when the ignorant and the poor are aroused, when the unintelligent brute force that lies at the bottom of society is made to growl and mow, it needs the habit of magnanimity and religion to treat it godlike as a trifle of no concernment

The other terror that scares us from self-trust is our consistency: a reverence for our past act or word, because the eyes of others have no other data for computing our orbit than our past acts, and we are loath to disappoint them

But why should you keep your head over your shoulder? Why drag about this monstrous corpse of your memory, lest you contradict somewhat you have stated in this or that public place? Suppose you should contradict yourself; what then? It seems to be a rule of wisdom never to rely on your memory alone, scarcely even in acts of pure memory, but to bring the past for judgment into the thousand-eyed present, and live ever in a new day. Trust your emotion. In your metaphysics you have denied personality to the Deity; yet when the devout motions of the soul

come, yield to them heart and life, though they should
clothe God with shape and color. Leave your theory,
as Joseph his coat in the hand of the harlot, and flee.

⊂⊃

He who confronts the gods, without any misgiving,
knows Heaven

⊂⊃

FOOLISH consistency is the hobgoblin of
little minds, adored by little statesmen and
philosophers and divines. With consistency
a great soul has simply nothing to do. He
may as well concern himself with his shadow on the
wall. Out upon your guarded lips! Sew them up with
packthread, do. Else, if you would be a man, speak
what you think today in words as hard as cannon-
balls, and tomorrow speak what tomorrow thinks
in hard words again, though it contradict everything
you said today. Ah, then, exclaim the aged ladies,
you shall be sure to be misunderstood! Misunderstood! It is a right fool's word. Is it so bad then to
be misunderstood? Pythagoras was misunderstood,
and Socrates, and Jesus, and Luther, and Copernicus,
and Galileo, and Newton, and every pure and wise
spirit that ever took flesh. To be great is to be misunderstood

I suppose no man can violate his nature. All the
sallies of his will are rounded in by the law of his being,
as the inequalities of Andes and Himmaleh are insignificant in the curve of the sphere. Nor does it matter
how you gauge and try him. A character is like an
acrostic or Alexandrian stanza: read it forward,
backward or across, it still spells the same thing.
In this pleasing contrite wood-life which God allows
me, let me record day by day my honest thought
without prospect or retrospect, and, I can not doubt,
it will be found symmetrical, though I mean it not
and see it not. My book should smell of pines and
resound with the hum of insects. The swallow over

my window should interweave that thread or straw
he carries in his bill into my web also. We pass for
what we are. Character teaches above our wills.
Men imagine that they communicate their virtue
or vice only by overt actions, and do not see that
virtue or vice emit a breath every moment
Fear never but you shall be consistent in whatever
variety of actions, so they be each honest and natural
in their hour. For of one will, the actions will be
harmonious, however unlike they seem. These varieties are lost sight of when seen at a little distance,
at a little height of thought. One tendency unites
them all. The voyage of the best ship is a zigzag
line of a hundred tacks. This is only microscopic
criticism. See the line from a sufficient distance,
and it straightens itself to the average tendency.
Your genuine action will explain itself and will explain
your other genuine actions. Your conformity explains
nothing. Act singly, and what you have already done
singly will justify you now

If I quake, what matters it what I quake at?

GREATNESS always appeals to the future.
If I can be great enough to do right now
and scorn eyes, I must have done so much
right before as to defend me now. Be it how
it will, do right now. Always scorn appearances, and
you always may. The force of character is cumulative.
All the foregone days of virtue work their health into
this. What makes the majesty of the heroes of the
senate and the field, which so fills the imagination?
The consciousness of a train of great days and victories behind. There they all stand and shed a united
light on the advancing actor. He is attended as by a
visible escort of angels to every man's eye. That is it
which throws thunder into Chatham's voice, and
dignity into Washington's port, and America into

Adams' eye. Honor is venerable to us because it is no ephemeris. It is always ancient worship. We worship it today, because it is not of today. We love it and pay it homage, because it is not a trap for our love and homage, but is self-dependent, self-derived, and therefore of an old immaculate pedigree, even if shown in a young person ⁂ ⁂

I hope in these days we have heard the last of conformity and consistency. Let the words be gazetted and ridiculous henceforward. Instead of the gong for dinner, let us hear a whistle from the Spartan fife. Let us bow and apologize never more.

❡ A great man is coming to eat at my house. I do not wish to please him: I wish that he should wish to please me. I will stand here for humanity, and though I would make it kind, I would make it true. Let us affront and reprimand the smooth mediocrity and squalid contentment of the times, and hurl in the face of custom, and trade, and office, the fact which is the upshot of all history, that there is a great responsible Thinker and Actor moving wherever moves a man; that a true man belongs to no other time or place, but is the center of things. Where he is, there is Nature. He measures you, and all men, and all events. You are constrained to accept his standard ⁂ ⁂

Ordinarily, everybody in society reminds us of somewhat else or of some other person. Character, reality, reminds you of nothing else; it takes place of the whole creation. The man must be so much that he must make all circumstances indifferent—put all means into the shade. This all great men are and do.

❡ Every true man is a cause, a country and an age; requires infinite spaces and numbers and time fully to accomplish his thought—and posterity seem to follow his steps as a procession. A man Cæsar is born, and for ages after we have a Roman Empire. Christ is born, and millions of minds so grow and cleave to

His genius that He is confounded with virtue and
the possible of man. An institution is the lengthened
shadow of one man ; as, the Reformation, of Luther ;
Quakerism, of Fox ; Methodism, of Wesley ; Abolition,
of Clarkson. Scipio, Milton called " the height of
Rome " ; and all history resolves itself very easily
into the biography of a few stout and earnest persons.

What a man most wishes is to be lifted to some higher
platform, that he may see beyond his present fear the
transalpine good, so that his fear, his coldness, his
custom may be broken up like fragments of ice, melted
and carried away in the great stream of good-will.

LET a man then know his worth, and keep
things under his feet. Let him not peep or
steal, or skulk up and down with the air of
a charity-boy, a bastard or an interloper, in
the world which exists for him. But the man in the
street, finding no worth in himself which corresponds
to the force which built a tower or sculptured a
marble god, feels poor when he looks on these. To
him, a palace, a statue or a costly book have an alien
and forbidding air, much like a gay equipage, and
seem to say like that, " Who are you, sir ! " Yet they
all are his, suitors for his notice, petitioners to his
faculties that they will come out and take possession.
The picture waits for my verdict : it is not to command
me, but I am to settle its claims to praise
That popular fable of the sot who was picked up dead-
drunk in the street, carried to the duke's house,
washed and dressed and laid in the duke's bed, and,
on his waking, treated with all obsequious ceremony
like the duke, and assured that he had been insane—
owes its popularity to the fact that it symbolizes so
well the state of man, who is in the world a sort of
sot, but now and then wakes up, exercises his reason,
and finds himself a true prince

UR reading is mendicant and sycophantic. In history, our imagination makes fools of us, plays us false. Kingdom and lordship, power and estate, are a gaudier vocabulary than private John and Edward in a small house and common day's work : but the things of life are the same to both : the sum total of both is the same. Why all this deference to Alfred, and Scanderbeg, and Gustavus? Suppose they were virtuous: did they wear out virtue? As great a stake depends on your private act today as followed their public and renowned steps. When private men shall act with vast views, the luster will be transferred from the actions of kings to those of gentlemen

The world has indeed been instructed by its kings, who have so magnetized the eyes of nations. It has been taught by this colossal symbol the mutual reverence that is due from man to man. The joyful loyalty with which men have everywhere suffered the king, the noble, or the great proprietor to walk among them by a law of his own, make his own scale of men and things, and reverse theirs, pay for benefits not with money but with honor, and represent the Law in his person, was the hieroglyphic by which they obscurely signified their consciousness of their own right and comeliness, the right of every man

The magnetism which all original action exerts is explained when we inquire the reason of self-trust. Who is the Trustee? What is the aboriginal Self, on which a universal reliance may be grounded? What is the nature and power of that science-baffling star, without parallax, without calculable elements, which shoots a ray of beauty even into trivial and impure actions, if the least mark of independence appear? The inquiry leads us to that source, at once the essence of genius, the essence of virtue, the essence of life, which we call Spontaneity or Instinct. We denote

this primary wisdom as Intuition, whilst all later
teachings are tuitions

In that deep force, the last fact behind which analysis
can not go, all things find their common origin. For
the sense of being which in calm hours rises, we know
not how, in the soul, is not diverse from things, from
space, from light, from time, from man, but one with
them, and proceedeth obviously from the same source
whence their life and being proceedeth. We first share
the life by which things exist, and afterwards see them
as appearances in Nature, and forget that we have
shared their cause

Here is the fountain of action and the fountain of
thought. Here are the lungs of that inspiration which
giveth man wisdom, of that inspiration of man which
can not be denied without impiety and atheism. We
lie in the lap of immense intelligence, which makes
us organs of its activity and receivers of its truth.
When we discern justice, when we discern truth, we
do nothing of ourselves, but allow a passage to its
beams. If we ask whence this comes, if we seek to
pry into the soul that causes—all metaphysics, all
philosophy is at fault. Its presence or its absence is
all we can affirm

The reward of a thing well done is to have done it

VERY man discerns between the voluntary
acts of his mind and his involuntary perceptions. And to his involuntary perceptions
he knows a perfect respect is due. He may
err in the expression of them, but he knows that these
things are so, like day and night, not to be disputed.
All my wilful actions and acquisitions are but roving;
the most trivial reverie, the faintest native emotion,
are domestic and divine

Thoughtless people contradict as readily the statement of perceptions as of opinions, or rather much

more readily; for they do not distinguish between perception and notion. They fancy that I choose to see this or that thing. But perception is not whimsical, but fatal. If I see a trait, my children will see it after me, and in course of time all mankind—although it may chance that no one has seen it before me. For my perception of it is, indeed, as much a fact as is the sun

The relations of the soul to the divine spirit are so pure that it is profane to seek to interpose helps. It must be that when God speaketh He should communicate not one thing, but all things; should fill the world with His voice; should scatter forth light, Nature, time, souls, from the center of the present thought; and new date and new create the whole. Whenever a mind is simple, and receives a divine wisdom, then old things pass away: means, teachers, texts, temples, fall; it lives now, and absorbs past and future into the present hour. All things are made sacred by relation to it—one thing as much as another. All things are dissolved to their center by their cause, and in the universal miracle petty and particular miracles disappear

This is and must be. If, therefore, a man claims to know and speak of God, and carries you backward to the phraseology of some old moldered nation in another country, in another world, believe him not. Is the acorn better than the oak which is its fulness and completion? Is the parent better than the child into whom he has cast his ripened being? Whence then this worship of the past?

¶ The centuries are conspirators against the sanity and majesty of the soul. Time and space are but physiological colors which the eye maketh, but the soul is light; where it is, is day; where it was, is night; and history is an impertinence and an injury, if it be anything more than a cheerful apologue or parable of my being and becoming

AN is timid and apologetic. He is no longer upright. He dares not say, " I think," " I am," but quotes some saint or sage. He is ashamed before the blade of grass or the blowing rose. These roses under my window make no reference to former roses or to better ones; they are for what they are; they exist with God today. There is no time to them. There is simply the rose; it is perfect in every moment of its existence. Before a leaf-bud has burst, its whole life acts; in the full-blown flower, there is no more; in the leafless root, there is no less. Its nature is satisfied, and it satisfies Nature, in all moments alike. There is no time to it.

But man postpones or remembers; he does not live in the present, but with reverted eye laments the past, or, heedless of the riches that surround him, stands on tiptoe to foresee the future. He can not be happy and strong until he, too, lives with Nature in the present, above time

This should be plain enough. You see what strong intellects dare not yet hear God Himself, unless He speak the phraseology of I know not what David, or Jeremiah, or Paul. We shall not always set so great a price on a few texts, on a few lives. We are like children who repeat by rote the sentences of grandames and tutors, and as they grow older, of the men of talents and character they chance to see, painfully recollecting the exact words they spoke; afterwards, when they come into the point of view which those had who uttered these sayings, they understand them, and are willing to let the words go; for, at any time, they can use words as good, when occasion comes. So was it with us, so will it be, if we proceed. If we live truly, we shall see truly.

It is as easy for the strong man to be strong, as it is for the weak to be weak. When we have new perception, we shall gladly disburden the memory of its hoarded treasures as old rubbish. When a man lives with God, his voice shall be as sweet as the murmur of the brook and the rustle of the corn

I believe it is the conviction of the purest men that the net amount of man and man does not much vary.

ND now at last the highest truth on this subject remains unsaid—probably can not be said—for all that we say is the far-off remembering of the intuition. That thought, by what I can now nearest approach to say it, is this: When good is near you, when you have life in yourself, it is not by any known or appointed way; you shall not discern the footprints of any other; you shall not see the face of man; you shall not hear any name: the way, the thought, the good shall be wholly strange and new. It shall exclude all other being. You take the way from man, not to man. All persons that ever existed are its fugitive ministers. There shall be no fear in it. Fear and hope are alike beneath it. It asks nothing

There is somewhat low even in hope. We are then in vision. There is nothing that can be called gratitude nor properly joy. The soul is raised over passion. It seeth identity and eternal causation. It is a perceiving that Truth and Right are. Hence it becomes a Tranquillity out of the knowing that all things go well. Vast spaces of Nature; the Atlantic Ocean, the South Sea; vast intervals of time, years, centuries, are of no account

This which I think and feel, underlay that former state of life and circumstances, as it does underlie my present, and will always all circumstance, and what is called life, and what is called death

Life only avails, not the having lived. Power ceases in the instant of repose; it resides in the moment of transition from a past to a new state; in the shooting of the gulf; in the darting to an aim. This one fact

the world hates, that the soul *becomes;* for, that
forever degrades the past ; turns all riches to poverty ;
all reputation to a shame ; confounds the saint with
the rogue ; shoves Jesus and Judas equally aside.
Why then do we prate of self-reliance? Inasmuch
as the soul is present, there will be power not confident
but agent

To talk of reliance is a poor external way of speaking.
Speak rather of that which relies, because it works
and is. Who has more soul than I masters me, though
he should not raise his finger. Round him I must
evolve by the gravitation of spirits ; who has less, I
rule with like facility. We fancy it rhetoric when we
speak of eminent virtue. We do not yet see that virtue
is Height, and that a man or a company of men, plastic
and permeable to principles, by the law of Nature
must overpower and ride all cities, nations, kings,
rich men, poets, who are not

Since we are all so stupid, what benefit that there
should be two stupidities !

HIS is the ultimate fact which we so quickly
reach on this, as on every topic, the resolution
of all into the ever-blessed *One.* Virtue is
the governor, the creator, the reality. All
things real are so by so much of virtue as they contain.
Hardship, husbandry, hunting, whaling, war, elo-
quence, personal weight, are somewhat, and engage
my respect as examples of the soul's presence and
impure action

I see the same law working in Nature for conservation
and growth. The poise of a planet, the bended tree
recovering itself from a strong wind, the vital resources
of every vegetable and animal, are also demonstrations
of the self-sufficing, and therefore self-relying, soul.
All history from its highest to its trivial passages is
the various record of this power. Thus all concen-

trates; let us not rove; let us sit at home with the cause. Let us stun and astonish the intruding rabble of men and books and institutions by a simple declaration of the divine fact. Bid them take the shoes from off their feet, for God is here within. Let our simplicity judge them, and our docility to our own law demonstrate the poverty of Nature and fortune beside our native riches.

But now we are a mob. Man does not stand in awe of man, nor is the soul admonished to stay at home, to put itself in communication with the eternal ocean, but it goes abroad to beg a cup of water of the urns of men. We must go alone. Isolation must precede true society

I like the silent church before the service begins, better than any preaching. How far off, how cool, how chaste the persons look, begirt each one with a precinct or sanctuary. So let us always sit. Why should we assume the faults of our friend, or wife, or father, or child, because they sit around our hearth, or are said to have the same blood? All men have my blood, and I have all men's. Not for that will I adopt their petulance and folly, even to the extent of being ashamed of it. But your isolation must not be mechanical, but spiritual—that is, must be elevation.

At times, the whole world seems to be in conspiracy to importune you with emphatic trifles. Friend, client, child, sickness, fear, want, charity, all knock at once at thy closet-door and say, " Come out unto us." Do not spill thy soul; do not all descend; keep thy state; stay at home in thine own heaven; come not for a moment into their facts, into their hubbub of conflicting appearances, but let in the light of thy law on their confusion. The power men possess to annoy me, I give them by a weak curiosity. No man can come near me but through my act. " What we love that we have, but by desire we bereave ourselves of the love."

IF we can not at once rise to the sanctities of obedience and faith, let us at least resist our temptations, let us enter into the state of war, and wake Thor and Woden, courage and constancy in our Saxon breasts. This is to be done in our smooth times by speaking the truth. Check this lying hospitality and lying affection. Live no longer to the expectation of these deceived and deceiving people with whom we converse. Say to them, O father, O mother, O wife, O brother, O friend, I have lived with you after appearances hitherto. Henceforward I am the truth's ❧ ❧
Be it known unto you that henceforward I obey no law less than the eternal law. I will have no covenants but proximities. I shall endeavor to nourish my parents, to support my family, to be the chaste husband of one wife—but these relations I must fill after a new and unprecedented way. I appeal from your customs. I must be myself ❧ ❧
I can not break myself any longer for you, or you. If you can love me for what I am, we shall be the happier. If you can not, I will still seek to deserve that you should. I must be myself. I will not hide my tastes or aversions. I will so trust that what is deep is holy, that I will do strongly before the sun and moon whatever inly rejoices me, and the heart appoints ❧ ❧
If you are noble, I will love you; if you are not, I will not hurt you and myself by hypocritical attentions. If you are true, but not in the same truth with me, cleave to your companions; I will seek my own. I do this not selfishly, but humbly and truly. It is alike your interest and mine and all men's, however long we have dwelt in lies, to live in truth. Does this sound harsh today? You will soon love what is dictated by your nature as well as mine, and if we follow the truth, it will bring us out safe at last. But so you may give these friends pain. Yes, but I can not sell my liberty and my power, to save their sensibility. Besides, all

persons have their moments of reason when they look out into the region of absolute truth; then will they justify me and do the same thing

Do not be so impatient to set the town right concerning the unfounded pretensions and the false reputation of certain men of standing

HE populace think that your rejection of popular standards is a rejection of all standard, and mere antinomianism; and the bold sensualist will use the name of philosophy to gild his crimes. But the law of consciousness abides. There are two confessionals, in one or the other of which we must be shriven. You may fulfil your round of duties by clearing yourself in the *direct*, or in the *reflex* way. Consider whether you have satisfied your relations to father, mother, cousin, neighbor, town, cat and dog; and whether any of these can upbraid you

But I may also neglect this reflex standard, and absolve me to myself. I have my own stern claims and perfect circle. It denies the name of duty to many offices that are called duties. But if I can discharge its debts, it enables me to dispense with the popular code. If any one imagines that this law is lax, let him keep his commandments one day

And truly it demands something godlike in him who has cast off the common motives of humanity, and has ventured to trust himself for a taskmaster. High be his heart, faithful his will, clear his sight, that he may in good earnest be doctrine, society, law to himself, that a simple purpose may be to him as strong as iron necessity is to others.

If any man consider the present aspects of what is called by distinction *society*, he will see the need of these ethics. The sinew and heart of man seem to be drawn out, and we are become timorous, despond-

ing whimperers. We are afraid of truth, afraid of
fortune, afraid of death, and afraid of each other.
Our age yields no great and perfect persons
We want men and women who shall renovate life
and our social state, but we see that most natures
are insolvent, can not satisfy their own wants, have
an ambition out of all proportion to their practical
force, and so do lean and beg day and night continually. Our housekeeping is mendicant, our arts,
our occupations, our marriages, our religion, we have
not chosen, but society has chosen for us. We are
parlor soldiers. The rugged battle of fate, where
strength is born, we shun

We need not assist the administration of the universe.

IF our young men miscarry in their first
enterprises, they lose all heart. If the young
merchant fails, men say he is *ruined*. If the
finest genius studies at one of our colleges,
and is not installed in an office within one year afterwards in the cities or suburbs of Boston or New York,
it seems to his friends and to himself that he is right
in being disheartened and in complaining the rest
of his life
A sturdy lad from New Hampshire or Vermont, who
in turn tries all the professions, who *teams it, farms
it, peddles*, keeps a school, preaches, edits a newspaper, goes to Congress, buys a township, and so
forth, in successive years, and always, like a cat,
falls on his feet, is worth a hundred of these city dolls.
He walks abreast with his days, and feels no shame
in not " studying a profession," for he does not postpone his life, but lives already. He has not one chance,
but a hundred chances
Let a stoic arise who shall reveal the resources of
man, and tell men they are not leaning willows,
but can and must detach themselves ; that with the

exercise of self-trust, new powers shall appear; that a man is the word made flesh, born to shed healing to the nations, that he should be ashamed of our compassion, and that the moment he acts from himself, tossing the laws, the books, idolatries and customs out of the window—we pity him no more, but thank and revere him—and that teacher shall restore the life of man to splendor, and make his name dear to all History

It is easy to see that a greater self-reliance—a new respect for the divinity in man—must work a revolution in all the offices and relations of men; in their religion; in their education; in their pursuits; their modes of living; their association; in their property; in their speculative views

In what prayers do men allow themselves! That which they call a holy office is not so much as brave and manly. Prayer looks abroad and asks for some foreign addition to come through some foreign virtue, and loses itself in endless mazes of natural and supernatural, and mediatorial and miraculous. Prayer that craves a particular commodity—anything less than all good—is vicious. Prayer is the contemplation of the facts of life from the highest point of view. It is the soliloquy of a beholding and jubilant soul. It is the spirit of God pronouncing His works good

But prayer as a means to effect a private end is theft and meanness. It supposes dualism and not unity in nature and consciousness. As soon as the man is at one with God, he will not beg. He will then see prayer in all action. The prayer of the farmer kneeling in his field to weed it, the prayer of the rower kneeling with the stroke of his oar, are true prayers heard throughout Nature, though for cheap ends. Caratach, in Fletcher's Bonduca, when admonished to inquire the mind of the god Audate, replies,

"His hidden meaning lies in our endeavors;
Our valors are our best gods."

Another sort of false prayers are our regrets. Discontent is the want of self-reliance; it is infirmity of will. Regret calamities, if you can thereby help the sufferer; if not, attend your own work, and already the evil begins to be repaired. Our sympathy is just as base. We come to them who weep foolishly, and sit down and cry for company, instead of imparting to them truth and health in rough electric shocks, putting them once more in communication with the soul. The secret of fortune is joy in our hands

Welcome evermore to gods and men is the self-helping man. For him all doors are flung wide. Him all tongues greet, all honors crown, all eyes follow with desire. Our love goes out to him and embraces him, because he did not need it. We solicitously and apologetically caress and celebrate him, because he held on his way and scorned our disapprobation. The gods love him because men hated him. " To the persevering mortal," said Zoroaster, " the blessed Immortals are swift."

What is it we heartily wish of each other? Is it to be pleased and flattered? No, but to be convicted and exposed, to be shamed out of our nonsense of all kinds, and made men of, instead of ghosts and phantoms

S men's prayers are a disease of the will, so are their creeds a disease of the intellect. They say with those foolish Israelites: " Let not God speak to us, lest we die. Speak thou, speak any man with us, and we will obey." Everywhere I am bereaved of meeting God in my brother, because he has shut his own temple-doors, and recites fables merely of his brother's, or his brother's brother's God

Every new mind is a new classification. If it prove a mind of uncommon activity and power, a Locke, a Lavoisier, a Hutton, a Bentham, a Spurzheim, it imposes its classification on other men, and lo! a new system. In proportion always to the depth of the thought, and so to the number of the objects it touches and brings within reach of the pupil, is his complacency. But chiefly is this apparent in creeds and churches, which are also classifications of some powerful mind acting on the great elemental thought of Duty, and man's relation to the Highest. Such is Calvinism, Quakerism, Swedenborgianism.

¶ The pupil takes the same delight in subordinating everything to the new terminology that a girl does who has just learned botany, in seeing a new earth and new seasons thereby. It will happen for a time, that the pupil will feel a real debt to the teacher— will find his intellectual power has grown by the study of his writings. This will continue until he has exhausted his master's mind

But in all unbalanced minds, the classification is idolized passes for the end, and not for a speedily exhaustible means, so that the walls of the system blend to their eye in the remote horizon with the walls of the universe; the luminaries of heaven seem to them hung on the arch their master built. They can not imagine how you aliens have any right to see— how you can see; " It must be somehow that you stole the light from us."

They do not yet perceive that light, unsystematic, indomitable, will break into any cabin, even into theirs. Let them chirp awhile and call it their own. If they are honest and do well, presently their neat new pinfold will be too strait and low, will crack, will lean, will rot and vanish, and the immortal light, all young and joyful, million-orbed, million-colored, will beam over the universe as on the first morning.

¶ It is for want of self-culture that the idol of Traveling, the idol of Italy, of England, of Egypt, remains for all educated Americans. They who made England, Italy or Greece venerable in the imagination, did so

not by rambling round creation as a moth round a
lamp, but by sticking fast where they were, like an
axis of the earth. In manly hours, we feel that duty
is our place, and that the merry men of circumstance
should follow as they may. The soul is no traveler;
the wise man stays at home with the soul, and when
his necessities, his duties, on any occasion call him
from his house, or into foreign lands, he is at home
still, and is not gadding abroad from himself, and
shall make men sensible, by the expression of his
countenance, that he goes the missionary of wisdom
and virtue, and visits cities and men like a sovereign
and not like an interloper or a valet

I have no churlish objection to the circumnavigation
of the globe for the purposes of art, of study, and
benevolence, so that the man is first domesticated,
or does not go abroad with the hope of finding somewhat greater than he knows. He who travels to be
amused, or to get somewhat which he does not carry,
travels away from himself, and grows old, even in
youth, among old things. In Thebes, in Palmyra,
his will and mind have become old and dilapidated
as they. He carries ruins to ruins

Nothing shall warp me from the belief that every
man is a lover of truth. There is no pure lie, no pure
malignity in Nature

TRAVELING is a fool's paradise. We owe to
our first journeys the discovery that place
is nothing. At home I dream that at Naples,
at Rome, I can be intoxicated with beauty,
and lose my sadness. I pack my trunk, embrace my
friends, embark on the sea, and at last wake up in
Naples, and there beside me is the stern Fact, the
sad self, unrelenting, identical, that I fled from. I
seek the Vatican, and the palaces. I affect to be intoxicated with sights and suggestions, but I am not

intoxicated. My giant goes with me wherever I go.

¶ But the rage of traveling is itself only a symptom of a deeper unsoundness affecting the whole intellectual action. The intellect is vagabond, and the universal system of education fosters restlessness. Our minds travel when our bodies are forced to stay at home. We imitate; and what is imitation but the traveling of the mind? Our houses are built with foreign taste; our shelves are garnished with foreign ornaments; our opinions, our tastes, our whole minds, lean, and follow the Past and the Distant, as the eyes of a maid follow her mistress

The soul created the arts wherever they have flourished. It was in his own mind that the artist sought his model. It was an application of his own thought to the thing to be done and the conditions to be observed. And why need we copy the Doric or the Gothic model? Beauty, convenience, grandeur of thought, and quaint expression are as near to us as to any, and if the American artist will study with hope and love the precise thing to be done by him, considering the climate, the soil, the length of the day, the wants of the people, the habit and form of the government, he will create a house in which all these will find themselves fitted, and taste and sentiment will be satisfied also.

¶ Insist on yourself; never imitate. Your own gift you can present every moment with the cumulative force of a whole life's cultivation; but of the adopted talent of another, you have only an extemporaneous half-possession. That which each can do best, none but his Maker can teach him. No man yet knows what it is, nor can, till that person has exhibited it. Where is the master who could have taught Shakespeare? Where is the master who could have instructed Franklin, or Washington, or Bacon, or Newton? Every great man is a unique. The Scipionism of Scipio is precisely that part he could not borrow.

❡ If anybody will tell me whom the great man imitates in the original crisis when he performs a great act, I will tell him who else than himself can teach him. Shakespeare will never be made by the study of Shakespeare. Do that which is assigned thee, and thou canst not hope too much or dare too much. There is at this moment, there is for me an utterance bare and grand as that of the colossal chisel of Phidias, or the trowel of the Egyptians, or the pen of Moses, of Dante, but different from all these.

❡ Not possibly will the soul, all rich, all eloquent, with thousand-cloven tongue, deign to repeat itself; but if I can hear what these patriarchs say, surely I can reply to them in the same pitch of voice: for the ear and the tongue are two organs of one nature. Dwell up there in the simple and noble regions of thy life, obey thy heart, and thou shalt reproduce the Foreworld again

As our Religion, our Education, our Art look abroad, so does our spirit of society. All men plume themselves on the improvement of society, and no man improves

Society never advances. It recedes as fast on one side as it gains on the other. Its progress is only apparent, like the workers of a treadmill. It undergoes continual changes; it is barbarous, it is civilized, it is Christianized, it is rich, it is scientific; but this change is not amelioration. For everything that is given, something is taken. Society acquires new arts and loses old instincts. What a contrast between the well-clad, reading, writing, thinking American, with a watch, a pencil and a bill of exchange in his pocket, and the naked New Zealander, whose property is a club, a spear, a mat and an undivided twentieth of a shed to sleep under. But compare the health of the two men, and you shall see that his aboriginal strength the white man has lost. If the traveler tell us truly, strike the savage with a broadax, and in a day or two

the flesh shall unite and heal as if you struck the blow
into soft pitch, and the same blow shall send the white
to his grave

⌁

The entertainment of the proposition of depravity
is the last profligacy and profanation. There is no
skepticism, no atheism, but that

⌁

HE civilized man has built a coach, but has
lost the use of his feet. He is supported on
crutches, but loses so much support of
muscle. He has got a fine Geneva watch,
but he has lost the skill to tell the hour by the sun.
A Greenwich nautical almanac he has, and so being
sure of the information when he wants it, the man
in the street does not know a star in the sky. The
solstice he does not observe; the equinox he knows
as little; and the whole bright calendar of the year
is without a dial in his mind.

His notebooks impair his memory; his libraries
overload his wit; the insurance-office increases the
number of accidents; and it may be a question
whether machinery does not encumber; whether we
have not lost by refinement some energy, by a Christianity entrenched in establishments and forms,
some vigor of wild virtue. For every stoic was a
stoic; but in Christendom where is the Christian?

There is no more deviation in the moral standard
than in the standard of height or bulk. No greater
men are now than ever were. A singular equality
may be observed between the great men of the first
and of the last ages; nor can all the science, art,
religion and philosophy of the Nineteenth Century
avail to educate greater men than Plutarch's heroes,
three or four and twenty centuries ago. Not in time
is the race progressive. Phocion, Socrates, Anaxagoras, Diogenes, are great men, but they leave no
class. He who is really of their class will not be called

by their name, but be wholly his own man, and in his turn the founder of a sect.

❡ The arts and inventions of each period are only its costume, and do not invigorate men. The harm of the improved machinery may compensate its good. Hudson and Bering accomplished so much in their fishing-boats as to astonish Parry and Franklin, whose equipment exhausted the resources of science and art. Galileo, with an opera-glass, discovered a more splendid series of facts than any one since. Columbus found the New World in an undecked boat. It is curious to see the periodical disuse and perishing of means and machinery which were introduced with loud laudation a few years or centuries before

The great genius returns to essential man. We reckoned the improvements of the art of war among the triumphs of science, and yet Napoleon conquered Europe by the Bivouac, which consisted of falling back on naked valor, and disencumbering it of all aids. The Emperor held it impossible to make a perfect army, says Las Casas, " without abolishing our arms, magazines, commissaries and carriages, until, in imitation of the Roman custom, the soldier should receive his supply of corn, grind it in his hand-mill, and bake his bread himself."

Men in all ways are better than they seem. They like flattery for the moment, but they know the truth for their own. It is a foolish cowardice which keeps us from trusting them, and speaking to them rude truth.

OCIETY is a wave. The wave moves onward, but the water of which it is composed does not. The same particle does not rise from the valley to the ridge. Its unity is only phenomenal. The persons who make up a nation today, next year die, and their experience with them

And so the reliance on Property, including the reliance
on governments which protect it, is the want of self-
reliance. Men have looked away from themselves
and at things so long that they have come to esteem
what they call the soul's progress, namely, the religious, learned and civil institutions, as guards of
property, and they deprecate assaults on these,
because they feel them to be assaults on property.
They measure their esteem of each other, by what
each has, and not by what each is. But a cultivated
man becomes ashamed of his property, ashamed of
what he has, out of new respect for his being
Especially he hates what he has, if he see that it is
accidental—came to him by inheritance, or gift, or
crime; then he feels that it is not having; it does not
belong to him, has no root in him, and merely lies
there, because no revolution or no robber takes it
away. But that which a man is, does always by necessity acquire, and what the man acquires is permanent
and living property, which does not wait the beck
of rulers, or mobs, or revolutions, or fire, or storm,
or bankruptcies, but perpetually renews itself wherever the man is put.

"Thy lot or portion of life," said the Caliph Ali,
"is seeking after thee; therefore be at rest from
seeking after it." Our dependence on these foreign
goods leads us to our slavish respect for numbers.
The political parties meet in numerous conventions;
the greater the concourse, and with each new uproar
of announcement, The delegation from Essex! The
Democrats from New Hampshire! The Whigs of
Maine! the young patriot feels himself stronger than
before by a new thousand of eyes and arms. In like
manner the reformers summon conventions, and vote
and resolve in multitude. But not so, O friends! will
the God deign to enter and inhabit you, but by a
method precisely the reverse

It is only as a man puts off from himself all external

support and stands alone, that I see him to be strong and to prevail. He is weaker by every recruit to his banner. Is not a man better than a town? Ask nothing of men, and, in the endless mutation, thou only firm column must presently appear the upholder of all that surrounds thee

⊂⊃

This is ever the difference between the wise and the unwise: the latter wonders at what is unusual; the wise man wonders at the usual

⊂⊃

E who knows that power is in the soul, that he is weak only because he has looked for good out of him and elsewhere, and, so perceiving, throws himself unhesitatingly on his thought, instantly rights himself, stands in the erect position, commands his limbs, works miracles; just as a man who stands on his feet is stronger than a man who stands on his head. So use all that is called Fortune. Most men gamble with her, and gain all, and lose all, as her wheel rolls. But do thou leave as unlawful these winnings, and deal with Cause and Effect, the chancellors of God. In the Will, work and acquire, and thou hast chained the wheel of Chance, and shalt always drag her after thee.

A political victory, a rise of rents, the recovery of your sick, or the return of your absent friend, or some other quite external event, raises your spirits, and you think good days are preparing for you. Do not believe it. It can never be so. Nothing can bring you peace but the triumph of principles

⊂⊃

The sign and credentials of the poet are, that he announces that which no man foretold. He is the true and only doctor; he knows and tells; he is the only teller of news, for he was present and privy to the appearances which he describes. He is a beholder of ideas, and an utterer of the necessary and causal

HOSE who are esteemed umpires of taste are often persons who have acquired some knowledge of admired pictures or sculptures, and have an inclination for whatever is elegant; but if you inquire whether they are beautiful souls, and whether their own acts are like fair pictures, you learn that they are selfish and sensual

Homer's words are as costly and as admirable to Homer, as Agamemnon's victories are to Agamemnon.

The man is only half himself, the other half is his expression

> Olympian bards who sung
> Divine ideas below,
> Which always find us young
> And always keep us so

God has not made some beautiful things, but Beauty is the creator of the universe

Nature is as truly beautiful as it is good, or as it is reasonable, and must as such appear, as it must be done, or be known. Words and deeds are quite different modes of the divine energy. Words are also actions, and actions are a kind of words

POETRY was all written before Time was, and whenever we are so finely organized that we can penetrate into that region where the air is music, we hear those primal warblings, and attempt to write them down, but we lose ever and anon a word, or a verse, and substitute something of our own, and thus miswrite the poem. The men of more delicate ear write down these cadences more faithfully, and these transcripts, though imperfect, become the songs of the nations

We know that the secret of the world is profound, but who or what shall be our interpreter, we know not. A mountain ramble, a new style of face, a new person, may put the key into our hands

CRITICISM is infested with a cant of materialism, which assumes that manual skill and activity is the first merit of all men, and disparages such as say and do not, overlooking the fact that some men, namely, poets, are natural sayers, sent into the world to the end of expression, and confounds them with those whose province is action, but who quit it to imitate the sayers

It is not meters, but a meter-making argument, that makes a poem—a thought so passionate and alive that, like the spirit of a plant or an animal, it has an architecture of its own, and adorns Nature with a new thing

The experience of each new age requires a new confession, and the world seems always waiting for its poet

THEOLOGIANS think it a pretty air-castle to talk of the spiritual meaning of a ship or a cloud, of a city or a contract, but they prefer to come again to the solid ground of historical evidence; and even the poets are contented with a civil and conformed manner of living, and to write poems from the fancy. at a safe distance from their own experience

All men live by truth, and stand in need of expression.

Every line we can draw in the sand has expression; and there is no body without its spirit or its genius. All form is an effect of character; all condition, of the quality of the life; all harmony, of health

HE Universe has three children, born at one time, which reappear, under different names, in every system of thought, whether they be called cause, operation and effect; or, more poetically, Jove, Pluto, Neptune; or, theologically, the Father, the Spirit and the Son; but which we will call here, the Knower, the Doer and the Sayer. These stand respectively for the love of truth, for the love of good and for the love of beauty. These three are equal. Each person is that which he is essentially, so that he can not be either surmounted or analyzed, and each of these three has the power of the others latent in him, and his own patent

---

The beautiful rests on the foundations of the necessary. The soul makes the body

---

The Universe is the externization of the soul. Wherever the life is, that bursts into appearance around it.

LL that we call sacred history attests that the birth of a poet is the principal event in chronology. Man, never so often deceived, still watches for the arrival of a brother who can hold him steady to a truth, until he has made it his own

---

All men have the thoughts whereof the universe is the celebration

---

A beauty not explicable is dearer than a beauty which we can see to the end of

---

The people fancy that they hate poetry, and they are all poets and mystics!

The poet alone knows astronomy, chemistry, vegetation and animation, for he does not stop at these facts, but employs them as signs

The poorest experience is rich enough for all the purposes of expressing thought

It is dislocation and detachment from the life of God that makes things ugly

Thought makes everything fit for use

HE vocabulary of an omniscient man would embrace words and images excluded from polite conversation. What would be base, or even obscene, to the obscene, becomes illustrious, spoken in a new connection of thought

Nature has a higher end, in the production of new individuals, than security, namely, *ascension*, or the passage of the soul into higher forms

Milton says, that the lyric poet may drink wine and live generously, but the epic poet, he who shall sing of the gods, and their descent unto men, must drink water out of a wooden bowl. For poetry is not "Devil's wine," but God's wine

Language is fossil poetry

The poet's cheerfulness should be the gift of the sunlight; the air should suffice for his inspiration, and he should be tipsy with water

HE poet knows that he speaks adequately only when he speaks somewhat wildly, or " with the flower of the mind "; not with the intellect, used as an organ, but with the intellect released from all service, and suffered to take its direction from its celestial life; or, as the ancients were wont to express themselves, not with intellect alone, but with the intellect inebriated by nectar

READERS of poetry see the factory-village and the railway, and fancy that the poetry of the landscape is broken up by these, for these works of art are not yet consecrated in their reading; but the poet sees them fall within the great Order not less than the beehive or the spider's geometrical web. Nature adopts them very fast into her vital circles, and the gliding train of cars she loves like her own

We fill the hands and nurseries of our children with all manner of dolls, drums and horses, withdrawing their eyes from the plain face and sufficing objects of Nature, the sun and moon, the animals, the water and stones, which should be their toys

I think nothing is of any value in books, excepting the transcendental and extraordinary

If a man is inflamed and carried away by his thoughts, to that degree that he forgets the authors and the public, and heeds only this one dream, which holds him like an insanity, let me read his paper, and you may have all the arguments and histories and criticism

IT is said, all martyrdoms looked mean when they were suffered. Every ship is a romantic object, except that we sail in. Embark, and the romance quits our vessel, and hangs on every other sail in the horizon. Our life looks trivial, and we shun to record it.

The religions of the world are the ejaculations of a few imaginative men

Every roof is agreeable to the eye, until it is lifted; then we find tragedy and moaning women, and hard-eyed husbands, and deluges of lethe, and the men ask " What 's the news? " as if the old were so bad

I quote another man's saying; unluckily, that other withdraws himself in the same way, and quotes me.

⊂▭▭

So much of our time is preparation, so much is routine, and so much retrospect, that the pith of each man's genius contracts itself to a very few hours

⊂▭▭

NEVER can any advantage be taken of Nature by a trick. The spirit of the world, the great calm presence of the Creator, comes not forth to the sorceries of opium or of wine. The sublime vision comes to the pure and simple soul in a clean and chaste body

⊂▭▭

The only thing grief has taught me is to know how shallow it is

⊂▭▭

People grieve and bemoan themselves, but it is not half so bad with them as they say. There are moods in which we court suffering, in the hope that here, at least, we shall find reality, sharp peaks and edges of truth

⊂▭▭

Nature and books belong to the eyes that see them.

⊂▭▭

A POLITICAL orator wittily compared our party promises to Western roads, which opened stately enough, with planted trees on either side, to tempt the traveler, but soon became narrower and narrower, and ended in a squirrel-track, and ran up a tree. So does culture with us; it ends in headache

⊂▭▭

Into every intelligence there is a door which is never closed, through which the creator passes

⊂▭▭

There are always sunsets, and there is always genius; but only a few hours so serene that we can relish Nature or criticism

In this great society wide-lying around us, a critical analysis would find very few spontaneous actions. It is almost all custom and gross sense. There are even few opinions, and these seem organic in the speakers, and do not disturb the universal necessity.

What opium is instilled into all disaster! It shows formidable as we approach it, but there is at last no rough, rasping friction, but the most slippery sliding surfaces. We fall soft on a thought

The definition of *spiritual* should be, *that which is its own evidence*

Grief, like all the rest, plays about the surface, and never introduces me into the reality, for contact with which we would even pay the costly price of sons and lovers

NOTHING is dead: men feign themselves dead, and endure mock funerals and mournful obituaries, and there they stand looking out of the window, sound and well, in some new and strange disguise

We animate what we can, and we see only what we animate

Was it Boscovich who found out that bodies never come in contact? Well, souls never touch their objects. An innavigable sea washes with silent waves between us and the things we aim at and converse with. Grief, too, will make us idealists

IF we could have any security against moods! If the profoundest prophet could be holden to his words, and the hearer who is ready to sell all and join the crusade could have any certificate that tomorrow the prophet shall not unsay his testimony!

E are students of words : we are shut up in schools, and colleges, and recitation-rooms, for ten or fifteen years, and come out at last with a bag of wind, a memory of words, and do not know a thing.

We can not use our hands, or our legs, or our eyes, or our arms. We do not know an edible root in the woods, we can not tell our course by the stars, nor the hour of the day by the sun

The human spirit is equal to all emergencies, alone, and man is more often injured than helped by the means he uses

No society can ever be so large as one man

The soul lets no man go without some visitations and holy-days of a diviner presence

Shall not the heart which has received so much, trust the Power by which it lives? May it not quit other leadings, and listen to the Soul that has guided it so gently, and taught it so much, secure that the future will be worthy of the past?

I think I have done well, if I have acquired a new word from a good author; and my business with him is to find my own, though it were only to melt him down into an epithet or an image for daily use

S every man at heart wishes the best and not inferior society, wishes to be convicted of his error, and to come to himself, so he wishes that the same healing should not stop in his thought, but should penetrate his will or active power

The man whose part is taken, and who does not wait for society in anything, has a power which society can not choose but feel

We fetch fire and water, run about all day among the shops and markets, and get our clothes and shoes made and mended, and are the victims of these details, and once in a fortnight we arrive perhaps at a rational moment

---

Every man is wanted, and no man is wanted much.

ONCE (say two centuries ago), Latin and Greek had a strict relation to all the science and culture there was in Europe, and the Mathematics had a momentary importance at some era of activity in physical science. These things became stereotyped as *education*, as the manner of men is. But the Good Spirit never cared for the colleges, and though all men and boys were now drilled in Latin, Greek and Mathematics, it had quite left these shells high and dry on the beach, and was now creating and feeding other matters at other ends of the world. But in a hundred high schools and colleges, this warfare against commonsense still goes on

---

Why have only two or three ways of life, and not thousands

Rightly, every man is a channel through which Heaven floweth, and whilst I fancied I was criticizing him, I was censuring or rather terminating my own soul

---

IS there any religion but this: to know that, wherever in the wide desert of being, the holy sentiment we cherish has opened into a flower, it blooms for me? If none sees it, I see it; I am aware, if I alone, of the greatness of the fact. Whilst it blooms, I will keep sabbath or holy time, and suspend my gloom, and my folly and jokes. Nature is indulged by the presence of this guest

What is it men love in Genius, but its infinite hope?

MEN are conservatives when they are least vigorous, or when they are most luxurious. They are
conservatives after dinner, or before taking their
rest; when they are sick, or aged: in the morning,
or when their intellect or their conscience have been
aroused, when they hear music, or when they read
poetry, they are radicals

Let a man fall into the divine circuits, and he is
enlarged

Friends follow the laws of divine necessity; they
gravitate to each other

I do not think the Apollo and the Jove impossible
in flesh and blood. Every trait which the artist
recorded in stone he had seen in life, and better
than his copy

WORK in every hour, paid or unpaid, see only that
thou work, and thou canst not escape the reward:
whether thy work be fine or coarse, planting corn,
or writing epics, so only it be honest work, done to
thine own approbation, it shall earn a reward to the
senses as well as to the thought: no matter how often
defeated, you are born to victory

Obedience to his genius is the only liberating influence.

Some natures are too good to be spoiled by praise,
and wherever the vein of thought reaches down into
the profound, there is no danger from vanity

New actions are the only apologies and explanations
of old ones, which the noble can bear to offer or to
receive

He conquers, because his arrival alters the face of affairs. " O Iole! how did you know that Hercules was a god? " " Because," answered Iole, " I was content the moment my eyes fell on him."

⚬⊃

This is that which we call character—a reserved force which acts directly by presence and without means

⚬⊃

I do not believe in two classes

⚬⊃

EAR to us are those who love us; the swift moments we spend with them are at compensation for a great deal of misery; they enlarge our life—but dearer are those who reject us as unworthy, for they add another life: they build a heaven before us, whereof we had not dreamed, and thereby supply to us new powers out of the recesses of the spirit, and urge us to new and unattempted performances.

⚬⊃

I remember the indignation of an eloquent Methodist at the kind admonitions of a Doctor of Divinity, " My friend, a man can neither be praised nor insulted." But forgive the counsels; they are very natural

⚬⊃

All I know is reception; I am and I have: but I do not get, and when I have decided I had gotten anything, I found I did not

⚬⊃

OCIETY is frivolous, and shreds its day into scraps, its conversation into ceremonies and escapes. But if I go to see an ingenious man, I shall think myself poorly entertained if he give me nimble pieces of benevolence and etiquette; rather he shall stand stoutly in his place, and let me apprehend, if it were only his existence; know that I have encountered a new and positive quality—great refreshment for both of us

E boast our emancipation from many super-stitions; but if we have broken any idols, it is through a transfer of the idolatry. What have I gained, that I no longer immolate a bull to Jove, or to Neptune, or a mouse to Hecate, that I do not tremble before the Eumenides, or the Catholic Purgatory, or the Calvinistic Judgment-Day—if I quake at opinion, the public opinion, as we call it, or at the threat of assault, or contumely, or bad neighbors, or poverty, or mutilation, or at the rumor of revolution, or of murder?

No change of circumstances can repair a defect of character

Feeble souls do not wish to be lovely, but to be loved.

The will of the pure runs down from them into other natures, as water runs down from a higher into a lower vessel. This natural force is no more to be withstood than any other natural force

All things exist in the man tinged with the manners of his soul

A WORD warm from the heart enriches me. I surrender at discretion. How death-cold is literary genius before this fire of life! These are the touches that reanimate my heavy soul, and give it eyes to pierce the dark of Nature

I should think myself very unhappy in my associates, if I could not credit the best things in history

Nothing but itself can copy it

Nature never rhymes her children, nor makes two men alike

The covetousness or the malignity which saddens me, when I ascribe it to society, is my own. I am always environed by myself

It is disgraceful to fly to events for confirmation of our truth and worth

'HE hero is misconceived and misreported: he can not therefore wait to unravel any man's blunders: he is again on his road, adding new powers and honors to his domain, and new claims on your heart, which will bankrupt you, if you have loitered about the old things, and have not kept your relation to him, by adding to your wealth

If we are related, we shall meet

The moment is all, in all noble relations

To fill the hour—that is happiness: to fill the hour, and leave no crevice for a repentance or an approval.

Let us be poised, and wise, and our own, today. Let us treat the men and women well: treat them as if they were real—perhaps they are

If we will take the good we find, asking no questions, we shall have heaping measures

The great gifts are not got by analysis

O not craze yourself with thinking, but go about your business anywhere. Life is not intellectual or critical, but sturdy. Its chief good is for well-mixed people who can enjoy what they find, without question. Nature hates peeping, and our mothers speak her very sense when they say, " Children, eat your victuals, and say no more of it."

TWO persons lately—very young children of the Most High God—have given me occasion for thought. When I explored the source of their sanctity, and charm for the imagination, it seemed as if each answered: " From my non-conformity: I never listened to your people's law, or to what they call their gospel, and wasted my time. I was content with the simple rural poverty of my own: hence this sweetness: my work never reminds you of that—is pure of that."

Everything runs to excess: every good quality is noxious, if unmixed, and, to carry the danger to the edge of ruin, Nature causes each man's peculiarity to superabound

Everything good is on the highway

A man will not be observed in doing that which he can do best. There is a certain magic about his properest action, which stupefies your powers of observation, so that, though it is done before you, you wist not of it. The art of life has a prudency, and will not be exposed

I KNOW nothing which life has to offer so satisfying as the profound good understanding which can subsist, after much exchange of good offices, between two virtuous men, each of whom is sure of himself, and sure of his friend

Nature and literature are subjective phenomena; every evil and every good thing is a shadow which we cast. The street is full of humiliations to the proud.

It is very unhappy, but too late to be helped, the discovery we have made, that we exist. That discovery is called the Fall of Man

A man is a golden impossibility. The line he must walk is a hair's breadth. The wise through excess of wisdom is made a fool

People forget that it is the eye which makes the horizon, and the rounding mind's eye which makes this or that man a type or representative of humanity with the name of hero or saint

The universe is the bride of the soul

CHARACTER wants room; must not be crowded on by persons, nor be judged from glimpses got in the press of affairs or on few occasions. It needs perspective, as a great building. It may not, probably does not, form relations rapidly; and we should not require rash explanation, either on the popular ethics, or on our own, of its action

The soul is not twin-born, but the only begotten, and though revealing itself as child in time, child in appearance, is of a fatal and universal power, admitting no co-life

We believe in ourselves, as we do not believe in others. We permit all things to ourselves, and that which we call sin in others is experiment for us

GOD delights to isolate us every day, and hide from us the past and the future. We would look about us, but with grand politeness He draws down before us an impenetrable screen of purest sky, and another behind us of purest sky; "You will not remember," He seems to say; "and you will not expect." All good conversation, manners and action come from spontaneity, which forgets usages, and makes the moment great. Nature hates calculators; her methods are saltatory and impulsive

UT ah ! presently comes a day, or is it only a half-hour, with its angel-whispering, which discomfits the conclusions of nations and of years! Tomorrow again, everything looks real and angular, the habitual standards are reinstated, commonsense is as rare as genius—is the basis of genius, and experience is hands and feet to every enterprise—and yet, he who should do his business on this understanding would be quickly bankrupt. Power keeps quite another road than the turnpikes of choice and will; namely, the subterranean and invisible tunnels and channels of life

I have learned that I can not dispose of other people's facts; but I possess such a key to my own, as persuades me, against all their denials, that they also have a key to theirs

There is nothing settled in manners, but the laws of behavior yield to the energy of the individual.

All things sooner or later fall into place

A man should not go where he can not carry his whole sphere or society with him—not bodily the whole circle of his friends, but atmospherically

Nature will not spare us the smallest leaf of laurel

HY sickness, they say, and thy puny habit, require that thou do this or avoid that, but know that thy life is a flitting state, a tent for a night, and do thou, sick or well, finish that stint. Thou art sick, but shalt not be worse, and the universe, which holds thee dear, shall be the better

A gentleman never dodges: his eyes look straight forward, and he assures the other party, first of all, that he has been met

What is it that we seek, in so many visits and hospitalities? Is it your draperies, pictures and decorations? Or, do we not insatiably ask, Was a man in the house?

⸺

Everybody we know surrounds himself with a fine house, fine books, conservatory, gardens, equipage, and all manner of toys, as screens to interpose between himself and his guests

⸺

I AM explained without explaining, I am felt without acting, and where I am not. Therefore, all just persons are satisfied with their own praise. They refuse to explain themselves, and are content that new actions should do them that office. They believe that we communicate without speech, and above speech, and that no right action of ours is quite unaffecting to our friends, at whatever distance; for the influence of action is not to be measured by miles

⸺

Elegance comes of no breeding, but of birth

⸺

You can not give anything to a magnanimous person. After you have served him, he at once puts you in debt by his magnanimity

⸺

NO man at last believes that he can be lost, nor that the crime in him is as black as in the felon. Because the intellect qualifies in our own case the moral judgments. For there is no crime to the intellect. That is antinomian or hypernomian, and judges law as well as fact

⸺

The gift, to be true, must be the flowing of the giver unto me, correspondent to my flowing unto him When the waters are at level, then my goods pass to him, and his to me. All his are mine, all mine his.

NATURE, as we know her, is no saint. Her darlings, the great, the strong, the beautiful, are not children of our law, do not come out of the Sunday-School, nor weigh their food, nor punctually keep the commandments. If we will be strong with her strength, we must not harbor such disconsolate consciences, borrowed too from the consciences of other nations

No rent-roll nor army-list can dignify skulking and dissimulation: and the first point of courtesy must always be truth, as really all the forms of good-breeding point that way

A beautiful form is better than a beautiful face; a beautiful behavior is better than a beautiful form: it gives a higher pleasure than statues or pictures; it is the finest of the fine arts

Everything that is called fashion and courtesy humbles itself before the cause and fountain of honor, creator of titles and dignities, namely, the heart of love

It seems as if the day was not wholly profane, in which we have given heed to some natural object.

A sainted soul is always elegant

MAN lives by pulses; our organic movements are such; and the chemical and ethereal agents are undulatory and alternate; and the mind goes antagonizing on, and never prospers but by fits. We thrive by casualties. Our chief experiences have been casual. The most attractive class of people are those who are powerful obliquely, and not by the direct stroke: men of genius, but not yet accredited: one gets the cheer of their light, without paying too great a tax.

The difference between landscape and landscape is small, but there is great difference in the beholders.

───

The expectation of gratitude is mean, and is continually punished by the total insensibility of the obliged person

───

AS the fop contrived to dress his bailiffs in his livery, and make them wait on his guests at table, so the chagrins which the bad heart gives off as bubbles, at once take form as ladies and gentlemen in the street, shopmen or barkeepers in hotels, and threaten or insult whatever is threatenable and insultable in us

───

It is a great happiness to get off without injury and heart-burning, from one who has had the ill luck to be served by you

───

I find that I am not much to you ; you do not need me ; you do not feel me ; then am I thrust out of doors, though you proffer me house and lands

───

A SYMPATHETIC person is placed in the dilemma of a swimmer among drowning men, who all catch at him, and if he give so much as a leg or a finger, they will drown him. They wish to be saved from the mischiefs of their vices, but not from their vices. Charity would be wasted on this poor waiting on the symptoms. A wise and hardy physician will say, *Come out of that*, as the first condition of advice

───

The service a man renders his friend is trivial and selfish, compared with the service he knows his friend stood in readiness to yield to him, alike before he had begun to serve his friend, and now also

───

Manhood first, and then gentleness

HAT *is* rich? Are you rich enough to help any-body? to succor the unfashionable and the eccentric? rich enough to make the Canadian in his wagon, the itinerant with his consul's paper which commends him "to the charitable," the swarthy Italian with his few broken words of English, the lame pauper hunted by overseers from town to town, even the poor insane or besotted wreck of man or woman, feel the noble exception of your presence and your house, from the general bleakness and stoniness; to make such feel that they were greeted with a voice which made them both remember and hope?

What is vulgar, but to refuse the claim on acute and conclusive reasons? What is gentle, but to allow it, and give their heart and yours one holiday from the national caution? Without the rich heart, wealth is an ugly beggar

HE law of benefits is a difficult channel, which requires careful sailing, or rude boats. It is not the office of a man to receive gifts. How dare you give them? We wish to be self-sustained. We do not quite forgive a giver. The hand that feeds us is in some danger of being bitten. We can receive anything from love, for that is a way of receiving it from our-selves; but not from any one who assumes to bestow. We sometimes hate the meat which we eat, because there seems something of degrading dependence in living by it.

"Brother, if Jove to thee a present make,
Take heed that from his hands thou nothing take."
We ask the whole. Nothing less will content us. We arraign society, if it do not give us, besides earth, and fire, and water, opportunity, love, reverence and objects of veneration.

He is a good man who can receive a gift well.

HEN that love which is all-suffering, all-abstain-
ing, all-aspiring, which has vowed to itself that
it will be a wretch and also a fool in this world, sooner
than soil its white hands by any compliances, comes
into our streets and houses—only the pure and aspir-
ing can know its face, and the only compliment they
can pay it is to own it

Gifts of one who loved me—
'T was high time they came;
When he ceased to love me,
Time they stopped for shame.

E are such lovers of self-reliance that we excuse
in a man many sins, if he will show us a complete
satisfaction in his position, which asks no leave to be,
of mine, or any man's good opinion. But any deference
to some eminent man or woman of the world forfeits
all privilege of nobility. He is an underling: I have
nothing to do with him; I will speak with his master.

Necessity does everything well

UR tokens of compliment and love are for the
most part barbarous. Rings and other jewels
are not gifts, but apologies of gifts. The only gift is
a portion of thyself. Thou must bleed for me. Therefore, the poet brings his poem; the shepherd, his
lamb; the farmer, corn; the miner, a gem; the sailor,
coral and shells; the painter, his picture; the girl, a
handkerchief of her own sewing

It is an instance of our faith in ourselves that men
never speak of crime as lightly as they think: or
every man thinks a latitude safe for himself, which
is nowise to be indulged to another. The act looks very
differently on the inside, and on the outside: in its
quality, and in its consequences

We receive glances from the heavenly bodies, which call us to solitude, and foretell the remotest future. The blue zenith is the point in which romance and reality meet

GOOD sense and character make their own forms every moment, and speak or abstain, take wine or refuse it, stay or go, sit in a chair or sprawl with children on the floor, or stand on their head, or what else soever, in a new and aboriginal way: and that strong will is always in fashion, let who will be unfashionable

No services are of any value, but only likeness. When I have attempted to join myself to others by services, it proved an intellectual trick—no more. *They eat your service like apples, and leave you out.* But love them, and they feel you, and delight in you all the time

There is nothing so wonderful in any particular landscape as the necessity of being beautiful under which every landscape lies. Nature can not be surprised in undress. Beauty runs everywhere

No man is quite sane; each has a vein of folly in his composition, a slight determination of blood to the head, to make sure of holding him hard to some one point which Nature had taken to heart

Let the victory fall where it will, we are on that side.

Nature is loved by what is best in us

No man can write anything, who does not think that what he writes is for the time the history of the world; or do anything well, who does not esteem his work to be of importance

The world is mind precipitated, and the volatile essence is forever excaping again into the state of free thought

We are escorted on every hand through life by spiritual agents, and a beneficent purpose lies in wait for us

Let the stoics say what they please, we do not eat for the good of living, but because the meat is savory and the appetite is keen

Exaggeration is in the course of things. Nature sends no creature, no man into the world, without adding a small excess of his proper quality

We talk of deviations from natural life, as if artificial life were not also natural

Let us be men instead of woodchucks, and the oak and the elm shall gladly serve us, though we sit in chairs of ivory on carpets of silk

HE wise man is the State. He needs no army, fort or navy—he loves men too well; no bribe, or feast or palace, to draw friends to him; no vantage-ground, no favorable circumstance. He needs no library, for he has not done thinking; no church, for he is a prophet; no statute-book, for he has the lawgiver; no money, for he has value; no road, for he is at home where he is; no experience, for the life of the Creator shoots through him, and looks from his eyes

If the king is in the palace, nobody looks at the walls.

Things have their laws, as well as men; and things refuse to be trifled with

By fault of our dulness and selfishness, we are looking up to Nature; but when we are convalescent, Nature will look up to us

The boundaries of personal influence it is impossible to fix, as persons are organs of moral or supernatural force

We are encamped in Nature, not domesticated

Our exaggeration of all fine characters arises from the fact that we identify each in turn with the soul. But there are no such men as we fable; no Jesus, nor Pericles, nor Cæsar, nor Angelo, nor Washington, such as we have made

Each man is a hint of the truth, but far enough from being that truth, which yet he quite newly and inevitable suggests to us

What is strange, too—there never was in any man sufficient faith in the power of rectitude to inspire him with the broad design of renovating the State on the principle of right and love

The power of love, as the basis of a State, has never been tried

Every act hath some falsehood of exaggeration in it.

I verily believe if an angel should come to chant the chorus of the moral law, he would eat too much gingerbread, or take liberties with private letters, or do some precious atrocity

We consecrate a great deal of nonsense, because it was allowed by great men. There is none without his foible

HIS is the history of government—one man does something which is to bind another. A man who can not be acquainted with me taxes me; looking from afar at me, ordains that a part of my labor shall go to this or that whimsical end, not as I, but as he happens to fancy. Behold the consequence. Of all debts, men are least willing to pay the taxes. What a satire is this on government! Everywhere they think they get their money's worth, except for these. This undertaking for another is the blunder which stands in colossal ugliness in the governments of the world.

There is no end to the consequences of the act

We know nothing rightly, for want of perspective.

Every actual State is corrupt. Good men must not obey the laws too well

What satire on government can equal the severity of censure conveyed in the word *politic*, which now for ages has signified *cunning*, intimating that the State is a trick?

Nature seems to exist for the excellent

We see the foaming brook with compunction: if our own life flowed with the right energy, we should shame the brook

Any laws but those which men make for themselves are laughable

The less government we have, the better—the fewer laws, and the less confided power

Surely nobody would be a charlatan who could afford to be sincere

RE there not women who fill our vase with wine and roses to the brim, so that the wine runs over and fills the house with perfume; who inspire us with courtesy; who unloose our tongues, and we speak; who anoint our eyes, and we see? We say things we never thought to have said; for once, our walls of habitual reserve vanished, and left us at large; we were children playing with children in a wide field of flowers. Steep us, we cried, in these influences, for days, for weeks, and we shall be sunny poets, and will write out in many-colored words the romance that you are

It is a greater joy to see the author's author than himself

I wish to speak with all respect of persons, but sometimes I must pinch myself to keep awake, and preserve the due decorum

The sanity of society is a balance of a thousand insanities

F the aristocrat is only valid in fashionable circles, and not with truckmen, he will never be a leader in fashion; and if the man of the people can not speak on equal terms with the gentleman, so that the gentleman shall perceive that he is already really of his own order, he is not to be feared

Wild liberty develops iron conscience. Want of liberty, by strengthening law and decorum, stupefies conscience

HERE will always be a government of force, where men are selfish; and when they are pure enough to abjure the code of force, they will be wise enough to see how these public ends of the post-office, of the highway, of commerce, and the exchange of property, of museums and libraries, of institutions of art and science, can be answered

He is a rich man who can avail himself of all men's faculties. He is the richest man who knows how to draw a benefit from the labors of the greatest number of men, of men in distant countries and in past time.

ATURE is not democratic, nor limited-monar-chical, but despotic, and will not be fooled or abated of any jot of her authority, by the pertest of her sons: and as fast as the public mind is opened to more intelligence, the code is seen to be brute and stammering. It speaks not articulately, and must be made to

COUNT him a great man who inhabits a higher sphere of thought, into which other men rise with labor and difficulty; he has but to open his eyes to see things in a true light, and in large relations; whilst they must make painful corrections, and keep a vigilant eye on many sources of error. He is great who is what he is from nature, and who never reminds us of others

Better be a nettle in the side of your friend than his echo

HARACTER is higher than intellect. Thinking is the function. Living is the functionary. The stream retreats to its source. A great soul will be strong to live as well as strong to think. Does he lack organ or medium to impart his truths? He can still fall back on this elemental force of living them. This is a total act. Thinking is a partial act. Let the grandeur of justice shine in his affairs. Let the beauty of affection cheer his lowly roof. Those " far from fame," who dwell and act with him, will feel the force of his constitution in the doings and passages of the day, better than it can be measured by any public and designed display. And time shall teach him that the scholar loses no hour which the man lives. Herein he unfolds the sacred germ of his instinct, screened from influence. Thus, what is lost in seemliness is gained in strength

ET man learn that everything in Nature, even motes and feathers, goes by law and not by luck, and that what he sows he reaps. By diligence and self-command, let him put the bread he eats at his own disposal, that he may not stand in bitter and false relations to other men; for the best good of wealth is freedom. Let him practise the minor virtues. How much of human life is lost in waiting! Let him not make his fellow-creatures wait. How many words and promises are promises of conversation! Let his be words of fate

HE motive of science was the extension of man, on all sides, into Nature, till his hands should touch the stars, his eyes see through the earth, his ears understand the language of beast and bird and the sense of the wind; and through his sympathy heaven and earth should talk with him

O truth so sublime but it may be trivial tomorrow in the light of new thoughts. People wish to be settled; only as far as they are unsettled is there any hope for them. Life is a series of surprises. We do not guess today the mood, the pleasure, the power of tomorrow, when we are building up our being. Of lower states—of acts of routine and sense—we can tell somewhat; but the masterpieces of God, the total growths and universal movements of the soul, He hideth; they are incalculable

ND what is genius but finer love, a love impersonal, a love of the flower and perfection of things, and a desire to draw a new picture or copy of the same? It looks to the cause and life : it proceeds from within outward, while talent goes from without inward. Talent finds its models and methods and ends in society, exists for exhibition, and goes to the soul only for power to work. Genius is its own end, and draws its means and the style of its architecture from within, going abroad only for audience and spectator, as we adapt our voice and phrase to the distance and character of the ear we speak to. All your learning of all literatures would never enable you to anticipate one of its thoughts or expressions, and yet each is natural and familiar as household words. Here about us coils forever the ancient enigma, so old and so unutterable. Behold! there is the sun, and the rain, and the rocks : the old sun, the old stones. How easy were it to describe all this fitly : yet no word can pass. Nature is a mute, and man, her articulate speaking brother, lo! he also is a mute. Yet when genius arrives, its speech is like a river, it has no straining to describe, more than there is straining in Nature to exist. When thought is best, there is most of it. Genius sheds wisdom like perfume, and advertises us that it flows out of a deeper source than the foregoing silence, that it knows so deeply and speaks so musically because it is itself a mutation of the thing it describes. It is sun and moon and wave and fire in music, as astronomy is thought and harmony in masses of matter

THE GOSPEL ACCORDING TO
ELBERT HUBBARD

Ideas are born; they have their infancy, their youth—their time of stress and struggle—they succeed, they grow senile, they nod, they sleep, they die; they are buried and remain in their graves for ages. And then they come again in the garb of youth, to slaughter and slay—and inspire and liberate. And this death and resurrection goes on forever. In Time, there is nothing either new or old: there is only the rising and the falling of the Infinite Tide

AN! I wonder what a man really is! Starting from a single cell, this seized upon by another, and out of the Eternal comes a particle of the Divine Energy that makes these cells its home 〜 〜 Growth follows, cell is added to cell, and there develops a man—a man whose body, two-thirds water, can be emptied by a single dagger-thrust and the spirit given back to its Maker in a moment.

IXTY generations have come and gone since Cæsar trod the Roman Forum.

The pillars against which he often leaned still stand. The thresholds over which he passed are there. The pavements ring beneath your tread as they once rang beneath his 〜 〜 Three generations and more have come and gone since Napoleon trod the streets of Toulon contemplating suicide 〜 〜 Babes in arms were carried by fond mothers to see Lincoln, the candidate for President.

These babes have grown into men, are grandfathers, possibly, with whitened hair, furrowed faces, looking calmly forward to the end, having tasted all that life holds in store for them 〜 〜 And yet Lincoln lived but yesterday!

You can reach back into the past and grasp his hand, and look into his sad and weary eyes 〜 〜 A man!

Weighted with the sins of his parents, grandparents, great-grandparents, who fade off into dim spectral shapes in the dark and dreamlike past 〜 〜 No word of choice has he in the selection of his father and mother; no voice in the choosing of environment. Brought into life without his consent, and pushed out of it against his will—battling, striving, hoping, cursing, waiting, loving, praying; burned by fever,

torn by passion, checked by fear, reaching for friendship, longing for sympathy, hungering for love, clutch-
ing—nothing

MY heart goes out to you, O man, because
I can not conceive of any being greater,
nobler, more heroic, more tenderly loving,
loyal, unselfish and enduring than you are.

All the love I know is man's love
All the forgiveness I know is man's forgiveness.

All the sympathy I know is man's sympathy
And hence I address myself to man—to you—and
you I would serve
The fact that you are a human being brings you near
to me. It is the bond that unites us. I understand
you because you are a part of myself.

You may like me, or not—it makes no difference.
If ever you need my help I am with you.

Often we can help each other most by leaving
each other alone; at other times we need the hand-
grasp and the word of cheer
I am only a man—a mere man—but in times of lone-
liness think of me as one who loves his kind
What your condition is in life will not prejudice me
either for or against you
What you have done or not done will not weigh in
the scale
If you have been wise and prudent I congratulate
you, unless you are unable to forget how wise and
good you are—then I pity you.

If you have stumbled and fallen and been mired
in the mud, and have failed to be a friend to yourself,
then you of all people need friendship, and I am your
friend
I am the friend of convicts, insane people and fools—
successful and unsuccessful, college-bred and illiterate.

You all belong to my church
I could not exclude you if I would.

But if I should shut you out I would then close

the door upon myself and be a prisoner indeed. The spirit of friendship that flows through me, and of which I am a part, is your portion, too.

The race is one, and we trace to a common Divine ancestry.

I OFFER you no reward for being loyal to me, and surely I do not threaten you with pain, penalty and dire disaster if you are indifferent to me.

You can not win me by praise, promises or adulation

You can not shut my heart toward you, even though you deny and revile me.

Only the good can reach me, and no thought of love you send me can be lost or missent.

All the kindness you feel for me should be given those nearest you, and it shall all be passed to your credit, for you yourself are the record of your thoughts, and no error can occur in the count.

You belong to my church, and always and forever my friendship shall follow you, yet never intrude. I do not ask you to incur obligations nor make promises.

There are no dues. I do not demand that you shall do this or not do that. I issue no commands. I can not lighten your burden, and perhaps I should not even if I could, for men grow strong through bearing burdens.

If I can I will show you how to acquire strength to meet all your difficulties and face the duties of the day.

It is not for me to take charge of your life, for surely I do well if I look after one person.

If you err it is not for me to punish you. We are punished by our sins, not for them.

SOON or late I know you will see that to do right brings good, and to do wrong brings misery, but you will abide by the law and all good things be yours. I can not change these laws—I can not make you exempt from your own blunders and mistakes.

And you can not change the eternal laws for me, even
though you die for me

But perhaps I can point you the pathway that leads
to love, truth and usefulness, and this I want to do
because I am your friend

And then by pointing you the way I find it myself.
¶ You belong to me—you are a member of my church.
All are members of my church. None is excluded nor
can be excluded

So over the plains and prairies, over the mountains
and seas, over the cities and towns, in palaces, tenements, moving-wagons, dugouts, cottages, hovels,
sleeping-cars, autos, day-coach, caboose, cab, in solitary cells behind prison-bars, or wandering out under
the stars, my heart goes out to you, whoever you are,
wherever you are, and I wish you well.

¶ Only love do I send and a desire to bless and benefit.

Men are under the domain of Natural Law as much
as bees. Men succeed only by working with other men
and for other men

Man's business is to work—to surmount difficulties,
to endure hardship, to solve problems, to overcome
the inertia of his own nature: to turn chaos into cosmos by the aid of system—this is to live!

Keep in your heart a shrine to the ideal, and upon
this altar let the fire never die

A child does not need a religion until he is old enough
to evolve one, and then he must not be robbed of the
right of independent thinking by having a fully prepared plan of salvation handed out to him

Until men grant to women all the rights which they
demand for themselves, they will dwell in a Spiritual
Siberia

One who walks after another never goes in front of him; and one who is not able to do well by his own wit will not be able to profit by the works of other men

⌒

AKE an inventory of your spiritual assets. How do you stand on these? Mark yourself ten where you are perfect; then the rest mark down to about where you are, and see how it looks. Faith, system, energy, service, loyalty, purpose, kindness, economy, industry, courtesy, initiative, intention, frankness, evolution, education, fellowship, patience, courage, responsiveness, tenacity, ambition, harmony, prudence, integrity, obedience, thoroughness, mutuality, mastership, fraternity, endurance, enthusiasm, equanimity, good-cheer, reciprocity, cleanliness, helpfulness, personality, self-respect, orderliness, punctuality, self-control, co-operation, self-reliance, truthfulness, self-sacrifice, perseverance, individuality, concentration

⌒

Be a creator, not merely a creature and a consumer.

⌒

Nature is the best guide of which we know, and the love of simple pleasures is next, if not superior, to religion

⌒

Nature forever strives for a right adjustment, and sends satiety after license

⌒

A person may be very secretive and yet have no secrets

⌒

A wise man does not need advice, and a fool will not take it

⌒

The doctors help to evolve the ills they propose to cure—innocently, of course, but the fact remains

We flatter only those we fear—the highest applause is silence

We are brothers to all who have trod the earth

We want to do what is best for ourselves, and we have discovered that what is best for ourselves is best for others

No man is damned eternally as long as he tries

Inaction is only a gathering together of forces for the coming leap: the fallow years are just as natural, just as necessary, as the years of plenty

To know the worst is peace—it is uncertainty that kills

THIS secret, which I am about to impart, is the most valuable and far-reaching of any known to man

It is the key to health, happiness, wealth, power, success. It is the open sesame to Paradise, here and now

A secret is something known only to a few. Often the best way to retain a secret is to let others help you to keep it

The only way to retain love is to give it away—art and religion the same

This secret, which I am about to impart, will cause no thrill, save in the hearts of those who already know it

And all I can do for you, anyway, is to tell you the things you know, but which possibly you do not know you know until I tell you

SO here, then, is the secret: Let Motion equal Emotion

Must I elucidate? Very well, I will: There is only

one thing in the world, and that is Energy. This
Energy takes a myriad million forms; and its one
peculiarity is that it is always in motion. It has three
general manifestations: atmosphere, hydrosphere,
lithosphere—or, if you prefer, air, water and rock.
From air, water and rock we get fungi and mosses;
and then from these spring vegetation. Disintegrating
vegetation gives us animal life; and from the animal
to the vegetable kingdom, and the vegetable to the
animal—with the constant interchange of gas, water
and solid—gives us Nature's eternal program
In Nature there is nothing inanimate. Everything is
alive; everything is going somewhere, or else coming
back; nothing is static. Fixity is the one impossible
thing.
And the fallacy of fixity has been the one fatal
error of theology and all philosophies in the past
Progress consists in getting away from the idea of
the static
Nature's one business is to absorb and to dissipate
—to attract and repel—to take in and give out. And
everything which Nature makes is engaged in the
same business
Man takes in carbon and gives off nitrogen
The plant takes in nitrogen and gives off carbon.
All things are in motion, ebb and flow, action
and reaction, cause and effect, swirl and whirl
Centripetal and centrifugal forces make our life on
the planet Earth possible
The heart rests between beats. That which we call
static is merely equilibrium.
The tiger crouches for one of two reasons: to spring
or to die
And death is a form of life. Death is a combination
where the balance is lost, and gas, water and solids
are in wrong proportions. The only thing then is
to dissolve the body and use in new masses the sub-
stances that composed it

AN is the instrument of Energy. And if you wish to call this energy God, or the First Principle, or The Unknowable, there will be no quarrel. We will only divide when you insist on calling it a Super-Something, or a Superior Being

If there is any Being superior to man, we have thus far not the slightest evidence of His existence. Man is a part of the Divine Energy.

Also, there are no unique men, although men differ in quality, but not so much as we often think. What one man has attained, other men may attain

To talk about a Superior Being is a dip to superstition, and is just as bad as to let in an Inferior Being or a Devil

When you once attribute effects to the will of a personal God, you have let in a lot of little gods and devils—then sprites, fairies, dryads, naiads, witches, ghosts and goblins, for your imagination is reeling, riotous, drunk, afloat on the flotsam of superstition. What you know then does n't count. You just believe, and the more you believe the more do you plume yourself that fear and faith are superior to science and seeing

What I am now telling you is Science, and Science is the classified knowledge of the common people.

AN is a transformer of energy. This energy plays through him. In degree he can control it; or at least he can control his condition as a transmitter.

And the secret of being a good transmitter is to allow motion to equal emotion

To be healthy and sane and well and happy, you must work with your hands as well as with your head.

The cure for grief is motion

The recipe for strength is action.

To have a body that is free from disease and toxins, you must let motion equal emotion

Love for love's sake creates a current so hot that it blows out the fuse. But love that finds form in music, sculpture, painting, poetry and work is divine and beneficent beyond words.

❡ That is, love is an inward emotion, and if stifled, thwarted and turned back upon itself, tends to gloom, melancholy, brooding, jealousy, rage and death. But love that is liberated in human effort attracts love; so a current is created and excess emotion is utilized, for the good not only of the beloved, but also of the race. The love that lasts is a trinity—I love you because you love the things that I love. Static love soon turns to hate, or, to be more exact, try to make love a fixity and it dies

A lover out of a job is a good man for a girl to avoid.

❡ Safety lies in service. Going the same way, we will go hand in hand

Religion that takes the form of ecstacy, with no outlet in the way of work, is dangerous. This way horror lies. Emotion without motion tends to madness and despair

XPRESSION must equal impression. If you study you must also create, write, teach, give out. Otherwise, you will become a plaster-of-Paris cat or a brass monkey. If great joy has come to you, pass it along, and thus do you double it. You are the steward of any gift the gods have given you, and you answer for their use with your life. Do not obstruct the divine current. Use your knowledge and use it quickly, or it will disintegrate and putrefy

The school where the child learns, and then goes home and tells what he has learned, approaches the ideal

On the other hand, the college that imparts knowledge but supplies no opportunity for work is faulty in the extreme. A school for adults that does not supply work as well as facts is false in theory and vicious in practise. Its pupils do not possess health, happiness or power, except on a fluke

Emotion balanced by motion eliminates dead tissue

and preserves sanity. For lack of motion congestion
follows

Most sickness comes from a failure to make motion
balance emotion. Impress and express; inhale and
exhale; work and play; study and laugh; love and
labor; exercise and rest. Study your own case and
decide to get the most out of life. The education of
invalids is a terrific waste

Sickness, unhappiness, ignorance, all tend to inefficiency. And inefficiency is the only sin

Realize that you are a Divine Transformer.

Make motion equal emotion, and you will eliminate
fear, round out the century run, and be efficient to the
last. And to live long and well is to accept life in every
phase—even death itself—and find it good

To think is natural, and if not intimidated or coerced
a man will evolve a philosophy of life that is useful
and beneficent

What is the difference between domestic science and
keeping house? I 'll tell you: it is about the same as
the difference between securing a pass and accepting
the courtesies of the road

Remember this, you can always find excuses for not
doing the things which you do not want to do

Truth is an imaginary line dividing error into two
parts

The ideas that benefit a man are seldom welcomed
by him on first presentation

A little ignorance is not a dangerous thing

A gentleman is one whose virtues are not founded on
self-interest

Ozone and friendship will be our stimulants—let the drugs, tobacco and strong drink go forever. Natural joy brings no headaches and no heartaches. Get busy !

The man who blesses—who makes the world better— is the true priest

Do not dump your woes upon other people—keep the sad story of your life to yourself

Be on the lookout for the great joys and never let mosquitoes worry you into a passion

What a superb thing it would be if we were all big enough in mind to see no slights, accept no insults, cherish no jealousies, and admit into our heart no hatred !

We must breathe more, laugh more and love more.

That which perfects humanity can not destroy any religion except a bad one

Nature is lavish in the production of everything except great men

The wide domain of Happiness has never been mapped, but Sorrow has been surveyed and known in every part

To talk well is a talent, but to be a good listener is a fine art

Music vibrates through a man's being and rouses him to a higher life

Courage comes only to those who have done the thing before

HE supreme prayer of my heart is not to be learned, rich, famous, powerful or even "good," but simply to be radiant. I desire to radiate health, cheerfulness, calm courage and good-will

I wish to live without hate, whim, jealousy, envy, fear. I wish to be simple, honest, frank, natural, clean in mind and clean in body, unaffected—to say, " I do not know," if it be so, and to meet all men on an absolute equality—to face any obstacle and meet every difficulty unabashed and unafraid.

I wish others to live their lives, too—up to their highest, fullest and best. To that end I pray that I may never meddle, interfere, dictate, give advice that is not wanted, or assist when my services are not needed. If I can help people, I 'll do it by giving them a chance to help themselves; and if I can uplift or inspire, let it be by example, inference and suggestion, rather than by injunction and dictation. That is to say, I Desire to be Radiant—to Radiate Life!

A splendid woman is usually the daughter of her father, just as strong men have noble mothers

No person utterly miserable ever did a great work.

Let this be a world of friends

N history there are three men who conquered the world. These men are Alexander, Cæsar and Napoleon. Their method of conquering was through violence. These men had no desire to give themselves to the world; to make the world a better place because they were here; to merge themselves into the world and be lost in the mass. They were intent on honors, ease, luxury and lust for power

Alexander began the task when he was twenty years

of age, and he completed it when he was thirty. He died sighing for more worlds to conquer.

His teacher, Aristotle, twenty years his senior, foretold for him the end. To complete one task and not have another in sight was to die. Aristotle outlived Alexander and saw his prophecy come true.

Aristotle refused to have anything to do with the business of destruction, but he told Alexander that when his soldiers died, let them die at the point of the spear. What he meant was this: Let them die fighting, not in the hospital!

Alexander lost more men in battle than he lost by disease, so he surely had a pretty good hold on sanitary science; but his specialty was destruction and dissipation. From one standpoint it was a great feat he performed. With an army of thirty-five thousand men he flung himself against a Persian horde of over a million. He scattered them and destroyed them piecemeal

ALEXANDER marched Eastward through Persia, through Asia Minor, the Northern part of Africa and a small part of India. This was his world

We have mapped and platted the world within our own time. Today we know the geographical world. Yet we will never die from Alexander's disability. We see a milky way of worlds to conquer.

The worlds for us to conquer are economic, political, pedagogic, philosophic, artistic and scientific

Aristotle told Alexander that the dangers that confronted an army were not in the ranks of the enemy, but were in their own camp—which means all that you can read into it

In order that no one may feel there is danger of getting out of a job, I am going to give here a list of worlds that we have yet to conquer.

We have sighted these worlds, we know their orbit, and there is no excuse now to let them go unconquered

The University Militant is now engaged in fighting:
1. For the rights of women.
2. For the rights of children.
3. For the rights of criminals.
4. For the rights of dumb animals.
5. To make all work and business beautiful.
6. For the elimination of theological fetish—a thing that has caused more misery and bloodshed than all other causes combined.
7. For the elimination of medical superstition, to the end that mankind shall be freed from racial fear, one of the most prolific causes of insanity and disease.
8. For the eradication of parasitism, through the reformation of our social ideals and our systems of education, so that every man and woman shall know the joys of earning an honest living—this for the good of the individual and the preservation of the race
9. Against the tyranny of fashion as applied to clothes, housekeeping and social customs.
10. For the disarmament of the nations, and international arbitration, in order that this world shall cease to be a place of the skull

ALEXANDER, Cæsar and Napoleon each lived in a very limited world. They conquered all the world they could reach, and then they erected a shrine to the god Terminus.

Every individual lives in a limited world. And all the world we should attempt to conquer is our own world. Also, it is well to realize the dictum of Aristotle, that the foes of an army are those within its own camp. That is to say, our enemies are those which lurk in our won hearts—hate, fear, jealousy, sloth, greed, inertia, adpetite. To conquer the foes within is a task indeed. But the recipe for peace at home is a foreign war, and so the person who would be strong and efficient should enlist in the University Militant and help conquer the foreign foe, this as a part of the plan for conquering himself

Choose your division and enlist in the army that is
fighting for Human Rights. Don't be a neutral or a
camp-follower. Get in the fight and stand back to the
wall. Be one of a glorious minority. Be a Greek, and
never let yourself be swallowed up by a Persian mob.
Dare to stand alone, to fight alone, to live alone,
to die alone! Otherwise, you will not live at all—
you will only exist

I do not fear Nature, but I fear for the man who sets
himself in opposition to Nature

Conformists die, but heretics live on forever

RELIGION of just being kind would be a pretty
good religion—don't you think so? But a religion
of kindness and useful effort is nearly a perfect religion.
We used to think it was a man's belief concerning a
dogma that would fix his place in eternity. This was
because we believed that God was a grumpy, grouchy
old gentleman, stupid, touchy and dictatorial. A
really good man would not damn you, even if you
did n't like him; but a bad man would. As our ideas
of God changed, we ourselves changed for the better.
Or, as we thought better of ourselves we thought
better of God. It will be character that locates our
place in another world, if there is one, just as it is
our character that fixes our place here. We are weaving
character every day, and the way to weave the best
character is to be kind and to be useful. Think right,
act right; it is what we think and do that makes us
what we are

To know the great men dead is compensation for
having to live with the mediocre

It is easy to get everything you want, provided you
first learn to do without the things you can not get.

MAY it please the Court, I arise to present certain reasons why judgment should not be passed upon humanity. The time has not yet arrived when it is fair, reasonable, proper or right to judge my kind. Man is not yet created—he is only in process. I have a few excuses to make for him

Emerson says, " I have not yet seen a man." That is to say, he had never seen a man as excellent as the man he could imagine. And he thought the man that one man could create in imagination would some day become an actual, living reality. Before the act comes the thought ; before the building is complete, we draw the plans. This is true in all our activities—we have the feeling, the desire, the idea, the thought, and after this comes the deed. So Deity has the desire for a perfect man, and the universe is working toward that achievement

All the men we now see are fractional men—parts of men. To get a really great man we have to take the virtues of a score of men and omit the faults

The great man now is only supremely great after he is well dead, or to people who see him from a distance. To those who have to live with him he is at times more or less of a trial—a tax upon the patience and good nature of his friends.

For the individual, Nature has little thought— her care is for the race. What her intentions are we think we, in part, know. She desires to incarnate herself in the form of perfect men and women. The reason we know this is because it is the chief instinct in the minds of the best and strongest men and women to grow, to evolve, to become. After every achievement comes discontent. After every mountain scaled there are heights beyond. Always and forever we are lured and urged on. Hope, prayer, desire, aspiration are yearnings for perfection. For many this hope of perfection is centered in their children ; and with all,

in moments of calm, the needle points toward the
North. Deity creates through man—we are the Divine
Will

The old idea, now happily discarded by all thoughtful
people, that man loves darkness rather than light
is a libel on the race and a denial of the wisdom and
goodness of the Supreme Intelligence. Men have
sought to enslave other men, and these slaves struggling with their gyves and fetters have done many
things so strange, erratic and violent that it looked
like self-destruction, but so far as we know the life of
the present race, there has ever been progress and a
movement forward. The normal man hungers and
yearns after righteousness. It is, of course, admitted
that progress has often taken a zigzag course, as ships
tack and beat up against the wind at sea, and at times
humanity's craft has been becalmed, and we seemingly had lost our reckoning; but such periods of drift-
ing have been followed by a lifting of the fog, when
the forward movement was true and rapid

WHEN certain unmarried men, who had lost their
capacity to sin, sat indoors, breathing bad air,
and passed resolutions about what was right and what
wrong, making rules for the guidance of the people,
instead of trusting to the natural, happy instincts of
the individual, they ushered in the Dark Ages. These
are the gentlemen who blocked human evolution
absolutely for a thousand years. They dethroned the
Universal Intelligence and set up a theogony founded
on bad air, indigestion and fear. And yet, in absolute
fairness, the fact that there were prehistoric races
that have vanished, like the mound-builders, the cliff-
dwellers and the Aztecs, and left no successors, gives
ground for reasoning that these people were self-
destroyed, through failure to adjust themselves to
the Divine Economy. Then there are the civilizations
that once existed in Egypt, Assyria, Greece and Rome,
which were destroyed by a failure to obey the divine

law, but which in dying, like a rotting log that nourishes a bank of violets, have supplied to us rich legacies
of truth and beauty. After all her seeming failure,
Nature, or the Universal Energy—or God, if you please
—persistently kept on filling the hearts of men with a
desire for perfection, so that today millions of people are
studying the history of the nations gone, in order
that they may avoid the pitfalls of the past

A man is a transient, conscious, reasoning manifestation of Universal Energy; and the reason that
Nature does not care for the individual is because
in dying the man is not destroyed or lost. The particle
of energy which made the man has simply changed
its form

The very fact that we now, in this time and place,
are trying to understand the present by studying the
past, so that we may make a forecast of the future,
and help ourselves by helping others, is proof in itself
that the heart of the race is right.

The thought of the race for the first time in history
is monistic—we are all one. We are part and particle
of each other. To injure another is to injure yourself,
is becoming fixed in the race instinct. This is the
dominant idea of our time—reciprocity. In business,
the transaction where only one side prospers is
immoral. Mutuality is the watchword in all of man's
relations with man. Government exists only for the
increased happiness of the governed—he that is
greatest among you shall be your servant

These are ideas that have in the past been held by
a few, and these precious few have usually been killed
for giving expression to their thoughts. Now they are
everywhere expressed, and are gradually becoming
fixed in the race consciousness. Righteousness will
yet become a habit

Man could behold the Infinite, if only he would not
stand in his own shadow

THE laws of health are very simple, and for the most part are understood by all people of average intelligence

One reason why we do not all have good health is not because we are ignorant, but because inertia has us by the foot. The trouble is in our heads —we lack will

If a high degree of health were the rule, instead of the exception, we would cease to talk about it. We discuss health, because pallor, languor, and breaths that almost derail trolley-cars ride, Godiva-like, adown the times, and put us on the binkereens.

In one respect at least we have made head. It is no longer necessary to order people to keep personally clean—humanity's hide is now daily soaped, soaked and scrubbed. Whereas, in the days of Good Queen Bess, who they say was not so very good, the courtier who took a bath in his altogether between November and May was unknown

Even fifty years ago, the man who ordered a bath at a tavern was regarded as reckless of both health and money. It was an event! The water had to be heated in the kitchen and carried in buckets to his room, and a porter stood by to see that the carpets and plaster did not suffer. The danger of catching cold through bathing, except in hot weather, was considered very great. Scientific plumbing is less than forty years old. The famous Fifth Avenue Hotel did not have a single room with bath attached when it was built. Now everybody bathes, and we have ceased to talk about it. Will the time come when we will cease to advocate outdoor exercise, deep breathing and kind thoughts? I hope so

Tolerance is an agreement to tolerate intolerance

Don't pry the day open with a liquid jimmy, or Nemesis will surely pinch you

HE other day I wrote to a banker-friend inquiring as to the responsibility of a certain person. The answer came back, thus: " He is a Hundred-Point man in everything and anything he undertakes." I read the telegram and then pinned it up over my desk where I could see it. That night it sort of stuck in my memory. I dreamed of it. The next day I showed the message to a fellow I know pretty well, and said, " I 'd rather have that said of me than to be called a great this or that."
Oliver Wendell Holmes has left on record the statement that you could not throw a stone on Boston Common without caroming on three poets, two essayists, and a playwright
Hundred-Point men are not so plentiful.

A Hundred-Point man is one who is true to every trust; who keeps his word; who is loyal to the firm that employs him; who does not listen for insults nor look for slights; who carries a civil tongue in his head; who is polite to strangers, without being "fresh"; who is considerate toward servants; who is moderate in his eating and drinking; who is willing to learn; is cautious and yet courageous
Hundred-Point men may vary much in ability, but this is always true—they are safe men to deal with, whether drivers of drays, motormen, clerks, cashiers, engineers or presidents of railroads.

Paranoiacs are people who are suffering from fatty enlargement of the ego. They want the best seats in the synagogue, they demand bouquets, compliments, obeisance, and in order to see what the papers will say next morning, they sometimes obligingly commit suicide

HE paranoiac is the antithesis of the Hundred-Point man. The paranoiac imagines he is being wronged, and that some one has it in for him, and that the world is down on him. He is given to that which is strange, peculiar, uncertain, eccentric and erratic.

❦ The Hundred-Point man may not look just like all other men, or dress like them, or talk like them, but what he does is true to his own nature. He is himself ❦ ❦

He is more interested in doing his work than in what people will say about it. He does not consider the gallery. He acts his thought, and thinks little of the act ❦ ❦

I never knew a Hundred-Point man who was not brought up from early youth to make himself useful and to economize in the matter of time and money.

❦ Necessity is ballast ❦ ❦

The paranoiac, almost without exception, is one who has been made exempt from work. He has been petted, waited upon, coddled, cared for, laughed at and chuckled to ❦ ❦

The excellence of the old-fashioned big family was that no child got an undue amount of attention. The antique idea that the child must work for his parents until the day he was twenty-one was a deal better for the youth than to let him get it into his head that his parents must work for him.

❦ Nature intended that we should all be poor—that we should earn our bread every day before we eat it ❦ ❦

WHEN you find the Hundred-Point man you will find one who lives like a person in moderate circumstances, no matter what his finances are. Every man who thinks he has the world by the tail and is about to snap its demnition head off for the delectation of mankind, is unsafe, no matter how great his genius in the line of specialties ❦ ❦

The Hundred-Point man looks after just one individual, and that is the man under his own hat; he is one who does not spend money until he earns it; who pays his way; who knows that nothing is ever given for nothing; who keeps his digits off other people's property. When he does not know what to say, why, he says nothing, and when he does not know what to do, does not do it.We should mark on moral qualities, not merely mental attainment or proficiency, because in the race of life only moral qualities count. We should rate on judgment, application and intent. Men who, by habit and nature, are untrue to a trust are dangerous just in proportion as they are clever. I would like to see a university devoted to turning out safe men instead of merely clever ones.

How would it do for a college to give one degree, and one only, to those who are worthy—the degree of H. P.?

Would it not be worth striving for, to have a college president say to you, over his own signature: " He is a Hundred-Point man in everything and anything he undertakes "?

God, too, is only in process. He is getting an education out of His work, at His work

GENIUS is only the power of making continuous efforts. The line between failure and success is so fine that we scarcely know when we pass it: so fine that we are often on the line and do not know it. How many a man has thrown up his hands at a time when a little more effort, a little more patience, would have achieved success. As the tide goes clear out, so it comes clear in. In business, sometimes, prospects may seem darkest when really they are on the turn. A little more persistence, a little more effort, and what seemed hopeless failure may turn to glorious success. There is no failure except in no longer trying. There is no defeat except from within, no really insurmountable barrier save our own inherent weakness of purpose

Throw physic to the dogs—it will not hurt them, for they know better than to swallow it

HE Busy Man's Creed: I believe in the stuff I am handing out, in the firm I am working for, and in my ability to get results. I believe that honest stuff can be passed out to honest men by honest methods. I believe in working, not weeping; in boosting, not knocking; and in the pleasure of my job. I believe that a man gets what he goes after, that one deed done today is worth two deeds tomorrow, and that no man is down and out until he has lost faith in himself. I believe in today and the work I am doing; in tomorrow and the work I hope to do, and in the sure reward which the future holds. I believe in courtesy, in kindness, in generosity, in good-cheer, in friendship and in honest competition. I believe there is something doing, somewhere, for every man ready to do it. I believe I'm ready—RIGHT NOW!

Life is a gradual death. There are animals and insects that die on the instant of the culmination of the act for which they were created. Success is death, and death, if you have bargained wisely with Fate, is victory

Experience is the germ of power

Be sincere, but don't be too serious—at the last, nothing matters much

Avoid the pleasures that leave a burnt-sienna taste in your mouth

The only way to abolish a serving-class is for all to join it

Any man who can quietly override the wishes and ambitions of other men is first well feared, and then thoroughly hated

HERE is a common tendency to cling to old ways and methods. Every innovation has to fight for its life, and every good thing has been condemned in its day and generation.

Error once set in motion continues indefinitely, unless blocked by a stronger force, and old ways will always remain unless some one invents a new way and then lives and dies for it.

And the reason men oppose progress is not that they hate progress, but that they love inertia

Even as great a man as John Ruskin foresaw that the railroads would ruin England by driving the stages out of business and killing the demand for horses, thus ruining the farmer

Thomas Jefferson tells us, in his autobiography, of a neighbor of his who was "agin" the public schools, because, "when every one could read and write, no one would work."

Bishop Berkeley thanked God there was not a printing-press in Virginia, because printing-presses printed mostly lies, and their business was to deceive the people

In the time of Mozart, musicians were classed with stablemen, scullions and cooks. They ate below stairs and their business was simply to amuse the great man who hired them, and his assembled guests

HE word business was first used in the time of Chaucer to express contempt for people who were useful. The word was then spelled "busyness."

In those days the big rewards were given to men who devoted their lives to conspicuous waste and conspicuous leisure. He who destroyed most was king by divine right. And everybody took his word for it.

Even yet we find that if you would go in "good society" you had better not shoulder a trunk, sift ashes, sweep the sidewalk or carry a hoe upon your shoulder

To light cities by gas would set them afire.

Electricity was dangerous, and to put up wires was to invite the lightning to come into our houses and kill us all dead

But a few years ago any man who advertised in the newspapers was looked upon with suspicion, and even yet we have associations of professional men who stamp with their disapproval any individual among them who advertises

Such a one is called an " irregular."

But within five years' time great changes have occurred in this matter of advertising

In all the prominent cities there are clubs devoted to the study of advertising as a science.

The subject is taught in schools and colleges, and publicity is regarded now as eminently right, beautiful and necessary

Advertising is stating who you are, where you are, and what you have to offer the world in the way of commodity or service.

And the only man who should not advertise is the one who has nothing to offer, and he is a dead one —whether he knows it or not.

Yes, it is a fact that, if we look back through history, we will find that every good and beautiful thing has at one time or another been under the ban, and assailed as an evil

And the argument seems to be this: If you think a thing is right, never mind what the many say, stick to it

Work for it, live for it, die for it—this way immortality lies !

———

An ounce of performance is worth a pound of preachment

———

The New Thought is plain, simple, commonsense, God-given thought which all would think if they were unbought, unbribed and uncoerced

HE old and once popular view of life that regarded man as a sinful, lost, fallen, despised, despicable and damned thing has very naturally tended to kill in him enthusiasm, health and self-reliance. Probably it has shortened the average length of life more than a score of years.

When man comes to realize that he is part and particle of the Divine Energy that lives in all he sees and feels and hears, he will, indeed, be in a position to claim and receive his birthright. And this birthright is to be healthy and happy

The Religion of Humanity does not seek to placate the wrath of a Non-Resident Deity, nor does it worship an Absentee God

It knows nothing of gods, ghosts, goblins, sprites, fairies, devils or witches. I would not know a god if I saw one coming down the street in an automobile.

If ever a man existed who had but one parent, this fact of his agamogenesis would not be any recommendation to us, nor would it make special claim on our reverence and regard. Rather, it would place him outside of our realm, so that what he might do or say would not be vital to us. He would be a different being from us, therefore his experiences would not be an example for us to follow

The Religion of Humanity knows nothing of a vicarious atonement, justification by faith, miraculous conception, transubstantiation, original sin, Hell, Heaven, or the efficacy of baptism as a saving ordinance

It does not know whether man lives again as an individual after he dies or not

It is not so much interested in knowing whether a book is " inspired " as whether it is true.

It does not limit the number of saviors of the race, but believes that any man or woman who makes this world a better place is in degree a "savior" of mankind. It knows that the world is not yet saved from ignorance, superstition and incompetence, nor redeemed

from a belief in miracles. And hence it believes that
there must be saviors yet to come.

It believes that the supernatural is the natural
not yet understood

HE Religion of Humanity is essentially monistic
—it believes that there is but one thing in the
world. This one thing has been called by many names:
the Divine Energy, the Universal Intelligence, the
First Principle and " God." This One Thing has a
million myriad manifestations. It incarnates itself as
primordial gas, as matter, as vegetation, as animal
life

Its highest manifestation is man.

If you were asked what a man is, the definition
would be: Man is a transient, thinking, conscious,
reasoning, and sometimes unreasonable manifestation
of Divine Energy

But man is not yet created—he is only in process.
When you read history and find from what distance
the race has come, and see what tremendous progress
has been made, say within twenty-five years, one
thinks of the future possibilities of Man with reverence
and awe

And the part we now play, as forerunners and Mes-
siahs of the Coming Man, is enough to call out all our
sense of sublimity, all our love, all our heroism, all
our devotion

We have ceased to look upon the race with scorn and
suspicion; ceased to calumniate and libel our kind
by calling man a worm of the dust, born in sin and
conceived in iniquity; ceased to drone that pitiable
untruth, " and there is no health in us "; ceased to
disparage human reason; ceased to talk about " bodily
pleasures " and " worldliness," as if to enjoy life and
do the world's work were base, sinful and wrong

To devote ourselves to the service of Mankind, and
to realize that we can help ourselves, only by helping
others, this is the Religion of Humanity. By this

religion and through it we attain Health, Happiness and Prosperity, here and now. We eliminate fear, sickness and poverty, only as we cease to break Nature's laws, and by recognizing and having faith in the Supreme Intelligence of which we are a part.

This Intelligence is a form of motion—it is Energy —and we as parts of it are successful just in the degree that we move with it

Sanity consists in service. When we work for others, we benefit ourselves. To clutch for an exclusive good is to lose

Wisdom is the distilled essence of intuition, corroborated and proved by experience. And Wisdom tells us that life and life in abundance lies only in work, love, laughter—and work. And when I use the word work, I mean work with head, heart and hand

---

Righteousness is wise expediency

To remain on earth you must be useful, otherwise Nature regards you as old metal, and is only watching for a chance to melt you over

---

The law sent us our relatives, but, thank God, we can choose our friends ourselves

---

The sculptor produces the beautiful statue by chipping away such parts of the marble block as are not needed—it is a process of elimination

---

The test is this: Which do you love most, Victory or Truth?

Don't make promises—make good!

A man may belong to the Superior Class, but if his bones are full of pain and his mind perplexed, his social station availeth little

ORK to please yourself and you develop and strengthen the artistic conscience. Cling to that and it shall be your mentor in times of doubt; you need no other. There are writers who would scorn to write a muddy line, and would hate themselves for a year and a day should they dilute their thought with the platitudes of the fear-ridden people. Be yourself and speak your mind today, though it contradict all you have said before. And above all, in art, work to please yourself—that other self which stands over and behind you, looking over your shoulder, watching your every act, word and deed—knowing your every thought

Michelangelo would not paint a picture to order. " I have a critic who is more exacting than you," said Meissonier, " it is my other self." Rosa Bonheur painted pictures just to please her other self, and never gave a thought to any one else; and having painted to please herself, she made her appeal to the great common heart of humanity—the tender, the noble, the receptive, the earnest, the sympathetic, the lovable. That is why Rosa Bonheur stands first among the women artists of all time; she worked to please her other self. That is the reason Rembrandt, who lived at the time Shakespeare lived, is today without a rival in portraiture. He had the courage to make an enemy. When at work he never thought of any one but his other self, and so he infused soul into every canvas. The limpid eyes look down into yours from the walls and tell of love, pity, earnestness and deep sincerity. Man, like Deity, creates in his own image, and when he portrays some one else, he pictures himself, too—this provided his work is art.

If it is but an imitation of something seen somewhere, or done by some one else, or done to please a patron with money, no breath of life has been breathed into its nostrils, and it is nothing, save possibly dead perfection—no more. It is easy to please your other self? Try it for a day. Begin tomorrow morning and say: " This day I will live as becomes a man. I will be filled with good-cheer and courage. I will do what is right; I will work for the highest; I will put soul into every hand-grasp, every smile, every expression —into all my work. I will live to satisfy my other self." You think it is easy? Try it for a day

At last we must admit that the man who towers above his fellows is the one who has the power to make others work for him; a great success is not possible any other way

Belief is an error if it excludes belief in its opposite.

Individuality is a departure from a complete type, and so is never perfect

The germ of greatness is in every man, but we fall victims of arrested development

Immortality is reserved alone for those who have been despised and rejected of men

The alternating current gives power; only an obstructed current gives either heat or light; all good things require difficulty

Mankind is moving toward the light, and such is our faith now in the Divine Intelligence, that we do not believe that in our hearts were planted aspirations and desires that are to work our undoing.

Society does not punish those who sin, but those who sin and conceal not cleverly

The heroic man does not pose; he leaves that for the man who wishes to be thought heroic

ID you know: That lawyers are men; and judges are men; and that all laws are and were made by men; and that all priests and preachers are men; and that all religions were made and formulated by men;

And that all books were written by men;

And that all of the justice we know is man's justice;

And that what we call God's justice is only man's idea of what he would do if he were God;

And that this idea changes as man changes;

And that all love is man's love;

And all compassion, man's compassion;

And all sympathy, man's sympathy;

And all forgiveness, man's forgiveness;

And that there is nothing finer, greater, nobler in the world than man;

And that all beings, spirits and persons greater than man have been, and are, the creation of man's mind;

And that man is not yet created, but only in process of creation;

And that in his present transitional state he has partially abandoned intuition without fully getting control of his intellect;

And that all laws, creeds and dogmas are of only transient value, if of value at all; and should be eliminated when they no longer minister to human happiness;

And that now, for the first time in the history of the world, a very large number of people know these things; and are exercising their brains;

And that the brain is an organ and grows strong by use;

And that through right thinking we are gradually learning to control our bodies, our tempers, our desires, our imaginations;

And that the imagination is a searchlight which reveals the future;

And that by the use of imagination we now see

Paradise ahead; A Paradise of increasing effort,
work, endeavor—and increasing power; A Paradise
of this world, that is to come through health, work,
simplicity, honesty, mutuality, reciprocity and love?

Society supplies a relish for solitude

The pathway to success is in serving humanity.
By no other means is it possible, and this truth is
so plain and patent that even very simple folk recognize it

A friend is Nature's masterpiece

Any system can be defeated by one single man who
places himself out of harmony with it.

HE desire for friendship is strong in every
human heart. We crave the companionship
of those who understand. The nostalgia of
life presses, we sigh for " home," and long
for the presence of one who sympathizes with our
aspirations, comprehends our hopes, and is able to
partake of our joys. A thought is not our own until
we impart it to another, and the confessional seems
to be a crying need of every human soul
One can bear grief, but it takes two to be glad.
We reach the Divine through some one, and by
dividing our joy with this one we double it, and come
in touch with the Universal. The sky is never so blue,
the birds never sing so blithely, our acquaintances
are never so gracious, as when we are filled with love
for some one else
Being in harmony with one we are in harmony with
all. The lover idealizes and clothes the beloved with
virtues that exist only in his imagination. The beloved
is consciously or unconsciously aware of this, and
endeavors to fulfil the high ideal; and in the con-

templation of the transcendent qualities that his
mind has created, the lover is raised to heights otherwise impossible

Should the beloved pass from this earth while such a
condition of exaltation exists, the conception is
indelibly impressed upon the soul, just as the last
earthly view is said to be photographed upon the
retina of the dead.

The highest earthly relationship is in its very
essence fleeting, for men are fallible, and living in a
world where the material wants jostle, and time and
change play their ceaseless parts, gradual obliteration
comes and disillusion enters. But the memory of a
sweet affinity once fully possessed, and snapped by
Fate at its supremest moment, can never die from
out the heart. All other troubles are swallowed up
in this; and if the individual is of too stern a fiber
to be completely crushed into the dust, time will
come bearing healing, and the memory of that once
ideal condition will chant in his heart a perpetual
eucharist

And I hope the world has passed forever from the
nightmare of pity for the dead; they have ceased
from their labors and are at rest.

But for the living, when death has entered and
removed the best friend, Fate has done her worst;
the plummet has sounded the depths of grief, and
thereafter nothing can inspire terror.

At one fell stroke all petty annoyances and cor-
roding cares are sunk into nothingness.

The memory of a great love lives enshrined in
undying amber. It affords a ballast 'gainst all the
storms that blow, and although it lends an unutterable sadness, it imparts an unspeakable peace. Where
there is this haunting memory of a great love lost,
there are also forgiveness, charity and sympathy that
make the man brother to all who suffer and endure.

The individual himself is nothing: he has nothing

to hope for, nothing to lose, nothing to win, and this constant memory of the high and exalted friendship that was once his is a nourishing source of strength; it constantly purifies the mind and inspires the heart to nobler living and diviner thinking. The man is in communication with Elemental Conditions.

To have known an ideal friendship, and have it fade from your grasp and flee as a shadow before it is touched with the sordid breath of selfishness, or sullied by misunderstanding, is the highest good. And the constant dwelling in sweet, sad recollection of the exalted virtues of the one that is gone, tends to crystallize these very virtues in the heart of him who meditates them

One great, strong, unselfish soul in every community would actually redeem the world

An ounce of loyalty is worth a pound of cleverness.

OMMERCE is no longer exploitation. It is human service, and no business concern can hope to prosper which does not meet a human need and add to human happiness The indiscriminate giving to the poor was a mistaken policy. It tended to make poverty perpetual. Now we aim to give just one thing, and that is opportunity. Business aims to render life safe and secure. To supervise wisely the great corporations is well; but to look backward to the days when business was polite pillage and regard our great business concerns as piratical institutions carrying letters of marque and reprisal is a grave error, born in the minds of little men. When these little men legislate they set the brakes going up hill Charity and piracy are things of the past. They were always closely akin, for pirates were very charitable, and ever in their train were troops of sturdy beggars.

¶ Business will yet do away with graft and begging.
Reciprocity, co-operation and mutuality are the
important words now ⚬⚬ ⚬⚬
Laws for the regulation of trade should be most
carefully scanned. That which hampers, limits, crip-
ples and retards must be done away with. That which
gives freedom, security, and peace must be encouraged. We are moving toward the rising sun; and no
man can guess the splendor, and the riches and the
beauty that will yet be ours. Let America lead the
way! ⚬⚬ ⚬⚬

It may be proved with much certainty that God
intends no man to live in this world without working.

Take off your hat to the man who minds his own
business ⚬⚬ ⚬⚬

HRISTIANITY supplies a Hell for the
people who disagree with you and a Heaven
for your friends ⚬⚬ ⚬⚬
The distinguishing feature of Christianity is
the hypothesis that man is born in sin and conceived
in iniquity: that through Adam's fall we sinned all,
and to save us from eternal death or eternal damnation, the Son of God died on the cross, and this
Son was God, Himself. These things are still in its
creeds and confessions of faith. Has the Roman Catholic Church or any of the orthodox Protestant churches
officially repudiated its creed, and made a new one
founded on industry, reciprocity, sweetness and light?
¶ Christianity is not a unique religion. It has traits
in common with many other religions. It is a con-
glomeration of Judaism and Egyptian mythology,
with the protests of Jesus and the ideas of Paul fused
in the pomps and pride of Rome. It is a combination
of morality and superstition, and they never form a
chemical mixture. Man is the only creature in the

animal kingdom that sits in judgment on the work of the Creator and finds it bad—including himself and Nature. God, personally, we are told, looked upon His work and called it good. There is where the clergy of Christendom take issue with Him.

No greater insult was ever offered to God than the claim that His chief product, man, is base at heart and merits damnation

Be moderate in the use of all things, save fresh air and sunshine

Better mend one fault in yourself than a hundred in your neighbor

He has achieved success who has lived well, laughed often and loved much.

FROM being regarded as The Book, the Bible is now looked upon as one of many books, and is only worthy of respect as it instructs and inspires. We read it with the same reverence that we read Emerson and Whitman.

The preacher was once a commanding figure in every community. Now he is regarded as a sort of poor relation. The term " spiritual adviser " is only a pleasantry. We go to the businessman for advice, not the priest. If a book is listed on the " Index," all good Catholics read it in order to know how bad it is

Those who institute heresy trials have no power to punish—they only advertise.

Christianity was evolved, as all religions have been—it was not inspired. It grew in a natural way and it declined by the same token.

Whether it has benefited the race is a question which we need not discuss now. That it ministered to poverty and disease is true, and that it often

created the ills which it professed to cure is equally
a fact

Poverty, ignorance, repression, superstition, coercion,
disease, with nights of horror and days of fear, are
slinking away into the past; and they have slunk
further and further away the more Christianity's
clutch upon the throat of the race has been loosened.
The night is past—the day is at hand! The East
is all aglow! Health, happiness, freedom and joy are
all calling to us to arise and sing our matin to labor.
Our prayer is, "Give us this day our daily work,
and we will earn our daily bread."
Our religion is one of humanity. Our desire is to
serve. We know that we can help ourselves only as
we help others, and that the love we give away is the
only love we keep

We have no fears of the future, for we have no reason
to believe that the Power which cares for us in this
life will ever desert us in another

Know what you want to do, hold the thought firmly,
and do every day what should be done, and every
sunset will see you that much nearer the goal

Nothing that can be poured out of a bottle and taken
with a spoon will take the place of a sawbuck

Bring me cheerful messages, or none!

Creeping into the lives of men everywhere is the
thought that co-operation is better than competition
—we need one another. And by giving much we will
receive much

The Greeks regarded a woman who had brains with
suspicion. So do we

Education is an achievement, not a bequest

We need an education which fits a boy to get a living, creates a desire for more education, implants ideals of service, and lastly, teaches him how to spend leisure in a rational manner. Then we can get along with less government

Humanity wants help, the help of strong, sensible, unselfish men

HAT is good which serves—man is the important item, this earth is the place, and the time is now. So all good men and women and all churches are endeavoring to make earth, heaven and all agree that to live now and here the best one can, is the fittest preparation for a life to come

We no longer accept the doctrine that our natures are rooted in infamy, and that the desires of the flesh are cunning traps set by Satan, with God's permission, to undo us. We believe that no one can harm us but ourselves, that sin is misdirected energy, and that there is no devil but fear, and that the universe is planned for good. On every side we find beauty and excellence held in the balance of things. We know that work is a blessing, that Winter is as necessary as Summer, that night is as useful as day, that death is a manifestation of life, and just as good. We believe in the Now and Here. We believe in You, and we believe in a Power that is in Ourselves that makes for Righteousness

These things have not been taught us by the rich— a Superior Class who governed us and to whom we paid taxes and tithes—we have simply thought things out for ourselves, and in spite of them.

We have listened to Coleridge, Emerson, Brisbane, Charles Ferguson and others, who said : " You should use your reason and separate the good from the bad, the false from the true, the useless from the useful.

Be yourself and think for yourself; and while your conclusions may not be infallible they will be nearer right than the conclusions forced upon you by those who have a personal interest in keeping you in ignorance. You grow through exercise of your faculties, and if you do not reason now you will never advance. We are all sons of God, and it doth not yet appear what we shall be. Claim your heritage!"

The world welcomes an idea, but an idea stuffed with sawdust—hardly!

Hate is a ptomaine, good-will is a panacea

Once we thought work was a curse; then it came to us that it was a necessary evil; and yesterday the truth dawned upon us that it is a blessed privilege.

Life is a search for power

In a world where death is, there is no time to hate.

IN this matter of bodily health, just a few plain rules suffice. And these rules fairly followed soon grow into a personal habit. And the habit is a pleasure

Fortunately, we do not have to superintend our digestion, our circulation, the work of the millions of pores that form the skin, or the action of the nerves.

Folks who get fussy about their digestion and assume a personal charge of nerves, have nerves," and are apt to have no digestions.

"I have a pain in my side," said the woman to the busy doctor

"Forget it!" was the curt advice.

Get the Health Habit, and forget it, is excellent advice. It is the same with your soul as it is with your body

The man who is always stewing about his soul has a very small and insignificant one.

You don't have to trouble about your soul's salvation

Everything in the universe worth saving will be saved.

Don't worry

That advice of the busy doctor should be used by the preacher, and when the black-ant breed come around fussing about their souls, the advice should be, " Forget it ! "

⟨⟩

He is best educated who is most useful

⟨⟩

Complete success alienates a man from his fellows, but suffering makes kinsmen of us all

⟨⟩

EACHING things out of season is a woful waste of time. It is also a great consumer of nerve-force, for both pupil and teacher.
For instance, the English plan of having little boys of eight study Latin and Greek killed a lot of boys, and probably never helped a single one to shoulder life's burden and be a better man

Knowledge not used, like anything else not used, is objectionable and often dangerous.

Nature intends knowledge for service, not as an ornament or for purposes of bric-a-brac.

" Delay adolescence—delay adolescence ! " cries Stanley Hall. The reason is plain. The rareripe rots. What boy well raised, of ten or twelve, can compare with your street gamin who has the knowledge and the shrewdness of a grown-up broker ! But the Arab never becomes a man

The awkward and bashful boy from the country— with mind slowly ripening in its rough husk, gathering gear as he goes, securing knowledge in order to use it, and by using it, making it absolutely his own, and gaining capacity for more—is the type that scores.

❡ The priestly plan of having one set of men do all
the thinking, and another set all the work, is tragedy
for both ❧ ❧

To quit the world of work in order to get an education
is as bad as quitting the world of work and struggle
in order to be " good." The tendency of the classical
education is to unfit the youth for work. He gains
knowledge, like the gamin, in advance of his needs.

❡ The boy of eighteen who enters college and graduates at twenty-two, when he comes home wants to
run his father's business. Certainly he will not wash
windows ❧ ❧

He has knowledge, but no dexterity—he has learning,
but no competence ❧ ❧

He owns a kit of tools, but does not know how to
use them. And now, if his father is rich, a place is
made for him where he can do no damage, a genteel
and honorable place, and he hypnotizes himself and
deceives his friends with the fallacy that he is really
doing something ❧ ❧

In the meantime the plain and alert young man
brought up in the business keeps the chimes on the
barrel, otherwise 't would busticate.

❡ Use and acquaintance should go hand in hand.
Skill must be applied. All great writers learned to
write in just one way—by writing. To acquire the
kit is absurd—get the tools one at a time as you need
them ❧ ❧

College has just one thing to recommend it, and that
is the change of environment that it affords the pupil.
This is what does him good—new faces, new scenes,
new ideas, new associations. The curriculum is nil—
if it keeps the fledgling out of mischief it accomplishes
its purpose. But four years in college tends to ossi-
fication instead of fluidity—and seven years means
the pupil gets caught and held by environment: he
stays too long ❧ ❧

Alexander von Humboldt was right—one year in any

college is enough for any man. One year gives him inspiration and all the spirit of good there is in it; a longer period fixes frats, fads and fancies in his noodle as necessities

Men are great only as they train on. College may place you in the two-thirty list, but you get into the free-for-all only by letting the Bunch take your dust.

❡ Happy is the man, like Ralph Waldo Emerson, who is discarded by his Alma Mater, or like Henry Thoreau, who discarded her

In any event—in God's name, get weaned!

The pathway to success is in serving humanity. By no other means is it possible, and this truth is so plain and patent that even very simple folk recognize it

Man is a creating animal, and the natural desire of the child to "make things" should never be discouraged

Civilization is the expeditious way of doing things

IF you have health, you probably will be happy; and if you have health and happiness, you will have all the wealth you need, even if not all you want.

❡ Health is the most natural thing in the world. It is natural to be healthy, because we are a part of Nature—we are Nature. Nature is trying hard to keep us well, because she needs us in her business
Nature needs man so he will be useful to other men.

❡ The rewards of life are for service
And the penalties of life are for selfishness.

❡ Human service is the highest form of self-interest for the person who serves

We preserve our sanity, only as we forget self in service

To center on one's self, and forget our relationship

to society, is to summon misery, and misery means
disease

Unhappiness is an irritant. It affects the heart-beats
or circulation first; then the digestion; and the person
is ripe for two hundred nineteen diseases, and six
hundred forty-two complications

The recipe for good health is this: Forget it
What we call diseases are merely symptoms of mental
conditions

Our bodies are automatic, and thinking about your
digestion does not aid you. Rather it hinders, since
the process of thinking, especially anxious thinking,
robs the stomach of its blood, and transfers it to the
head

If you are worried enough, digestion will stop absolutely

The moral is obvious: Don't Worry

HERE are three habits which, with but one
condition added, will give you everything in the
world worth having, and beyond which the imagination of man can not conjure forth a single addition
or improvement. These habits are the Work Habit,
the Health Habit and the Study Habit.

If you are a man and have these habits, and also
have the love of a woman who has these same habits,
you are in Paradise now and here, and so is she
Health, Books and Work, with Love added, are a
solace for all the stings and arrows of outrageous
fortune—a defense 'gainst all the storms that blow;
for through their use you transmute sadness into
mirth, trouble into ballast, pain into joy

Do you say that religion is still needed?

Then I answer that Work, Study, Health and
Love constitute religion. Moreover, any religion that
leaves any of these out is not religion, but fetish

Yet most formal religions have pronounced the love
of man for woman and woman for man an evil thing.

They have proclaimed labor a curse

They have said that sickness was sent from God;
and they have whipped and scorned the human body
as something despicable, and thus have placed a
handicap on health, and made the doctor a necessity.

And they have said that mental attainment was a
vain and frivolous thing, and that our reason was a
lure to lead us on to the eternal loss of our soul's
salvation

Now, we deny it all, and again proclaim that these
will bring you all the good there is: Health, Work,
Study—Love!

Work means safety for yourself and service to mankind. Health means much happiness and potential
power. Study means knowledge, equanimity and the
evolving mind. Love means all the rest!

But Love must be a matter of reciprocity, not a
one-sided affair. " I love you because you love the
things that I love."

A man who marries a woman in order to educate her
falls a victim to the same fallacy that a woman does
who marries a man expecting to reform him

If you marry a woman who is not on your mental
wire, you 'll either go down to her level or you will
live in a water-tight compartment and go to purgatory through mental asphyxiation.

Choose this day the habits you would have rule
over you

———

The divine in Man is the only hint we get in life that
there is anything divine in the universe

———

Men who fight with folks of little worth win nothing.

———

Any man who has a job has a chance!

———

The truth is that in human service there is no low or
high degree: the woman who scrubs is as worthy of
respect as the man who preaches

Friendships, for the most part, are real, substantial and lasting. They are built on positive qualities, while enmities are a vapor that only awaits the sunshine, to be dissipated into nothingness

The folks who do big things are not in bondage to their bodies

Every duty well done makes the next duty easier to do

I THINK I know what love is for, although I 'm not quite sure. I think love is given us so we can see a soul. And this soul we see is the highest conception of excellence and truth we can bring forth. This soul is our reflected self. And from seeing what one soul is, we imagine what all souls may be—and thus we reach God, who is the Universal Soul

If you don't know what to do, suppose you don't.

Falling in love is the beginning of all wisdom, all sympathy, all compassion, all art, all religion; and in its larger sense is the one thing in life worth doing

The thought of getting safely out of the world has no part in the life of the Enlightened Man—to live fully while he is here is his problem—one world at a time is enough for him

If college education were made compulsory by the State, and one-half of the curriculum consisted of actual, useful, manual labor, most of our social ills would be solved and we would be well on the highway toward the Ideal City

We can do without being loved, but we can not afford to live without love

In the sky of truth the fixed stars are few, and the shepherds who tend their flocks by night are quite as apt to know them as are professed and professional Wise Men of the East

A man's theories are apt to smile sadly at his practise, over the gaping gulf that separates the ideal from the real

A seer is the scout of civilization

Y father has practised medicine for seventy years, and is still practising

I, also, have studied the so-called science of medicine

I am fifty-five years old; my father is ninety

We live neighbors, and daily ride horseback together or tramp through the fields and woods. Today we did our little jaunt of five miles and back across country.

I have never been ill a day—never consulted a physician in a professional way; and, in fact, never missed a meal except through inability of access.

The old gentleman and I are not fully agreed on all of life's themes, so existence for us never resolves itself into a dull neutral gray.

He is a Baptist and I am a Vegetarian

Occasionally he refers to me as "callow," and we have daily resorts to logic to prove prejudice, and history is searched to bolster the preconceived, but on the following important points we stand together, solid as one man:

First—Ninety-nine people out of a hundred who go to a physician have no organic disease, but are merely suffering from some functional disorder, caused by their own indiscretion

Second—Individuals who have organic diseases nine times out of ten are suffering from the accumulated evil effects of medication

Third—That is to say, most diseases are the result of medication which has been prescribed to relieve and take away a beneficent and warning symptom on the part of Nature

Most of the work of doctors in the past has been to prescribe for symptoms, the difference between actual disease and a symptom being something that the average man does not even yet know.

And the curious point is that on these points all physicians, among themselves, are fully agreed, what I say here being merely truism, triteness and commonplace

AST week, in talking with an eminent surgeon, he said: "I have performed over a thousand operations of laparotomy, and my records show that in every instance, except the cases of habit, the individual was given to what you call the 'Beecham habit.'"

The people you see waiting in the lobbies of doctors' offices are, in a vast majority of cases, suffering through poisoning caused by an excess of food

Coupled with this goes the bad results of imperfect breathing, irregular sleep, lack of exercise and improper use of stimulants, or the thought of fear, jealousy and hate

All these things, or any one of them, will, in very many persons, cause fever, chills, cold feet, congestion and faulty elimination

To administer drugs to a man suffering from malnutrition caused by a desire to " get even," and a lack of fresh air, is simply to compound his troubles, shuffle his maladies, and get him ripe for the ether-cone and the scalpel

Nature is forever trying to keep people well, and most so-called " disease " (which word means merely lack of ease) is self-limiting, and tends to cure itself.

If you have appetite, do not eat too much

If you have no appetite, do not eat at all.

❡ Be moderate in the use of all things, save fresh air and sunshine ❧ ❧

The one theme of Ecclesiastes is moderation ❧ ❧

Buddha wrote it down that the greatest word in any language is " equanimity."

❡ William Morris said that the finest blessing of life was systematic, useful work.

❡ Saint Paul declared that the greatest thing in life was love ❧ ❧

Moderation, equanimity, work and love—you need no other physician ❧ ❧

In so stating I lay down a proposition agreed to by all physicians; which was expressed by Hippocrates, the father of all medicine, and then repeated in better phrase by Epictetus, the slave, to his pupil, the great Roman Emperor, Marcus Aurelius, and which has been known to every thinking man and woman since: Moderation, Equanimity, Work and Love ! ❧ ❧

Recipe for success : Subdue yourself—devote yourself.

Wholesale condemnation is usually a subtle form of flattery ❧ ❧

You had better be a round peg in a square hole than a square peg in a square hole. The latter is in for life, while the first is only an indeterminate sentence ❧ ❧

A thought is mental dynamite ❧ ❧

To benefit others, you must be reasonably happy : there must be animation through useful activity, good-cheer, kindness and health—health of mind and health of body ❧ ❧

To succeed you must get out of your groove and change safety for experience. And anyway, does n't stability lie in motion? ❧ ❧

I‾T is qualities that fit a man for a life of usefulness, not the mental possession of facts.
The school that best helps to form character, not the one that imparts the most information, is the college the future will demand
I do not know of a single college or university in the
world that focuses on qualities, excepting Tuskegee.
At Harvard, Yale, Dartmouth, Columbia and
Princeton, cigarettes are optional, but a stranger,
seeing the devotion to them, would surely suppose
the practise of cigarette-smoking was compulsory
The boy who does not acquire the tobacco habit at
college is regarded as eccentric.
Many college professors teach the cigarette habit
by example
At all our great colleges gymnasium work is optional.
Instead of physical culture there is athletics, and those
who need the gymnasium most are ashamed to be
seen there
How would the scientific cultivation of these do?
Bodily Qualities—Health of digestion, circulation,
breathing, manual skill, vocal speech, and ease in
handling all muscles
Mental Qualities—Painstaking, patience, decision,
perseverance, courage, following directions, tact, concentration, insight, observation, mental activity,
accuracy and memory
Moral Qualities—Putting one's self in another's place,
or thoughtfulness for others, which includes kindness,
courtesy, good-cheer, honesty, fidelity to a promise,
self-control, self-reliance and self-respect

Was n't that a queer story they used to tell us about
God working for six days and then getting tired and
never doing anything afterward!

To eliminate the needless and keep the good is the
problem of progress

I BELIEVE in the Motherhood of God

I believe in the blessed Trinity of Father, Mother and Child

I believe that God is here, and that we are as near Him now as ever we shall be. I do not believe He started this world a-going and went away and left it to run itself

I believe in the sacredness of the human body, this transient dwelling-place of a living soul, and so I deem it the duty of every man and every woman to keep his or her body beautiful through right thinking and right living

I believe that the love of man for woman, and the love of woman for man is holy; and that this love in all its promptings is as much an emanation of the Divine Spirit as man's love for God, or the most daring hazards of the human mind.

❡ I believe in salvation through economic, social and spiritual freedom

I believe John Ruskin, William Morris, Henry Thoreau, Walt Whitman and Leo Tolstoy to be Prophets of God, who should rank in mental reach and spiritual insight with Elijah, Hosea, Ezekiel and Isaiah

I believe that men are inspired today as much as ever men were.

❡ I believe we are now living in Eternity as much as ever we shall

I believe that the best way to prepare for a Future Life is to be kind, live one day at a time, and do the work you can do the best, doing it as well as you can.

I believe we should remember the week-day to keep it holy

I believe there is no devil but fear

I believe that no one can harm you but yourself

I believe in my own divinity—and yours

I believe that we are all sons of God, and it doth not yet appear what we shall be

I believe the only way we can reach the Kingdom

of Heaven is to have the Kingdom of Heaven in our
hearts

I believe in every man minding his own business

I believe in freedom—social, economic, domestic,
political, mental, spiritual

I believe in sunshine, fresh air, friendship, calm sleep,
beautiful thoughts

I believe in the paradox of success through failure

I believe in the purifying process of sorrow, and I
believe that death is a manifestation of life

I believe the Universe is planned for good

I believe it is possible that I shall make other creeds,
and change this one, or add to it, from time to time
as new light may come to me

When in doubt, mind your own business

People who give you something for nothing, usually
equalize the matter by expecting something for
nothing in return

To make mistakes is human, but to profit by them
is divine

I THINK it really better, if you have to choose,
to drink beer out of an earthen pot—as did the
father of John Sebastian Bach—and be kind and
gentle, than to have a sharp nose for other folks'
faults and be continually trying to pinch and prod
the old world into the straight and narrow path of
virtue

As we grow better we meet better people

To love one's friends, to bathe in life's sunshine,
to preserve a right mental attitude—the perceptive
attitude, the attitude of gratitude—and to do one's
work—these make up an ideal life

COURTESY in every line of life is now the growing rule

No strong man lowers himself by giving somebody a lift, no matter who that " somebody " is. It may be an ignorant foreigner, unversed in our ways and language, but there is a right way and a wrong way, even in pantomime.

And to the clerk who would succeed, I say, cultivate charm of manner. Courteous manners in little things are an asset worth acquiring. When a customer approaches, rise and offer a chair. Step aside and let the store's guest pass first into the elevator. These are little things, but they make you and your work finer

To gibe visitors, or to give fresh and flippant answers, even to stupid or impudent people, is a great mistake. Meet rudeness with unfailing politeness and see how much better you feel.

Your promise to a customer is your employer's promise. A broken promise always hurts ; and it shows weakness in the character of a business organization, just as unreliability does in an individual

If your business is to wait on customers, be careful of your dress and appearance. Do your manicuring before you reach the store. A toothbrush is a good investment. A salesman with a bad breath is dear at any price. Let your dress be quiet, neat and not too fashionable. To have a prosperous appearance helps you inwardly and helps the business

Give each customer your whole attention, and give just as considerate attention to a little buyer as to a big one

If asked for information, be sure you have it before you give it. Do not assume that the location or fact is so now because you once thought it so.

Don't misdirect. Make your directions so clear that they will be a real help

And the more people you direct, and the higher the

intelligence you can rightly lend, the more valuable
is your life

The most precious possession in life is good health.
Eat moderately, breathe deeply, exercise outdoors
and get eight hours' sleep. And cultivate courtesy
as a business asset

The conservative keeps the reformer from going too
fast and plucking the fruit before it is ripe

Our admiration is so given to dead martyrs that we
have little time for living heroes

Keep your ray of reason! It is your only guiding star.
He who says you would see better if you would blow
it out is a preacher

The Ideal Life is only the normal or natural life as
we shall some day know it

HE Reverend Sydney Smith once made up
a list of things that we could do without
It will be remembered that he finally ended
by declaring we could eliminate everything
but cooks

Yet Charles Lamb used to go without food in order
to save money to buy books. And Andrew Lang said
that if there were no good books in Heaven he would
not want to go there.

Also, we find several modern cults founded on the
idea of eliminating cooks by eating raw food
I know a man who consumes only nuts, raisins, prunes
and milk, and he seems to thrive on the diet
Our ancestors only a few hundred years ago ate their
meat raw and worshiped fire.

Nevertheless, in spite of these quillets and quibbles,
the fact remains that Sydney Smith is right—the
person who prepares food for the people is a necessity.

❧ Let us define a bit : The cook is the individual who prepares our food for us

But before food is prepared it must be secured, and so we must have the farmer who evolves the food out of the ground

In the preparation of hare-soup, the first move, we are told, is to " catch your hare," to which the would-be joker has written an advertisement for a certain firm that supplies hair-dye and explains, " The first requisite in dyeing your hair is to secure your hair."

I PASS up this persiflage and rise into the higher ether of pragmatic philosophy.

❧ We hear much about the elimination of the middle-man, but I have never yet seen a sharp, definite, crystalline definition of what a middleman is

Technically, a middleman is any one who stands between the producer and the consumer.

❧ But most of the people who use the expression " middleman " regard him as an animated example of lost motion, a specimen of economic slack

No doubt there are several professions and occupations that could be abolished from civilized society with decided advantage

Edward Bellamy declared advertising to be an economic waste ; and he explained that the cost of advertising was always counted in and added to the value of the article and ultimately was paid for by the consumer

He then made his calculation that by eliminating advertising the cost of the article to the consumer would be much reduced.

❧ To the argument we make no exception, but to the assumption that all advertising is economic waste a demurrer must here be entered.

❧ Advertising is telling who you are, where you are, and what you have to offer the world in the way of service or commodity. If nobody knows who you are, or what you have to offer, you do no business, and the world is the loser through giving you absent treatment

Life is too short for the consumer to employ detectives to ferret out merchants who have the necessities of life to sell

People who want to buy things do not catch the seller, chloroform him and cram the orders into his pockets.

Parties who want milk should not seat themselves on a stool in the middle of a field, in hope that the cow will back up to them

This would be as vain as for a man to step out of his office on Broadway and shoot into the air in the hope of firing into a flock of ducks that might be flying over

ADVERTISING is the proper education of the public as to where the thing can be found, and therefore it is a necessity.

We are parts and particles of one another, but a little of the kindly glue of human brotherhood is needed in order to fasten us together.

The policeman who keeps the crossing clear, and at the same time informs us as to the location of the post-office and the First National Bank, is no doubt, in one sense, an economic waste. On the other hand, he is an economic necessity. He is a necessary middle-man

He relieves the congestion of traffic, and granting the hypothesis that he does not misdirect us as to the location of the post-office, he speeds us on our way

The musician who so delightfully entertains us, the lecturer who informs us, and the preacher who relieves all tendency to insomnia, or serves as a social promoter, all are middlemen

We say that food is a primal need

Next to this comes affection—for we can not love on half-rations. People who are not properly nourished bicker without ceasing; so Love flees and stands aloof, naked and cold, with fingers to his lips.

¶ Granting that food is a primal need, food then must be cooked and served. The very simple service of the cafeteria, where you flunky for yourself and pocket your own fee, is a necessity.

¶ Somebody must cook and somebody must serve. Otherwise, all of us would have to do the thing for ourselves, and then all our efforts would be taken up in the search for eats and we would be reduced to the occupation of the Caveman.

¶ Civilization is a great system of transfers. Each one does the thing he can do best and works for the good of all

It is all for each, and each for all

So any man who does a needed service for humanity should not be classed with the parasites, although he be a middleman

WISE businessmen keep out of court. They arbitrate their differences—compromise—they can not afford to quit their work for the sake of getting even. As for making money, they know a better way.

¶ In theology we are waiving distinctions and devoting ourselves to the divine spirit as it manifests itself in humanity. We are talking less about another world and taking more notice of the one we inhabit. Of course we occasionally have heresy trials, and pictures of the offender and the accusing bishop adorn the first page, but heresy trials not accompanied by the scaffold or the fagots are innocuous and exceedingly tame. In medicine we have more faith in ourselves and less in prescriptions

In pedagogy we are teaching more and more by the natural method—learning by doing—and less and less by means of injunction and precept.

¶ In penology we seek to educate and reform, not to suppress, repress and punish

That is to say, the gods are on high Olympus, but the Greeks are at our door.

¶ Humanity needs us

Society is in process of evolution. Man is yet primitive. All that has gone before is a preparation for better things to come, but we are moving rapidly, and, I believe, securely toward nobler things

Some degree of personal independence is absolutely necessary to good work

No man ever did or can do a great work alone

Complete success alienates a man from his fellows, but suffering makes kinsmen of us all

Wealth is an engine that can be used for power if you are an engineer; but to be tied to the flywheel of an engine is rather a misfortune

No man is to be pitied except the one whose Future lies behind

Every misery and every crime is evidence that Nature's law has been transgressed

Paths of kindness are paved with happiness

Some people are so great that outwardly they may conform to the petty customs of the court, but inwardly the soul towers over the trifling annoyances, and all the vain power of the fearing, quibbling, little princes can not touch them

Worked by the owner a farm yields well. Renters can not be expected to do as good. Nor can man's mind be cultivated best by proxy

He who influences the thought of his times influences all the times that follow. He has made his impress on eternity

IT requires two to make a home. The first home was made when a woman, cradling in her loving arms a baby, crooned a lullaby. All the tender sentimentality we throw around a place is the result of the sacred thought that we live there with some one else. It is our home. The home is a tryst—the place where we retire and shut the world out. Lovers make a home, just as birds make a nest, and unless a man knows the spell of the divine passion I can hardly see how he can have a home at all; for of all blessings no gift equals the gentle, trusting, loving companionship of a good woman

The judge is a worse sinner than the woman he condemns, for he sins in his strength and against the light, while she stumbles in the dark and in her weakness

Science is love with seeing eyes

That man only is really worthy to be called educated who is able to do at least one useful thing well; who has a sympathy which is universal, and who is in the line of evolution

EDUCATION means growth, evolution—efficiency
That man is best educated who is most useful
There is no such thing as a science of education, any more than there is a science in medicine
Some of the very strongest and most influential men who have ever lived were men who never had any " advantages."
Of course it is equally true that great numbers of college graduates have gone to the front; but, on the other hand, a college degree is no proof of competence.
And so long as some men who are not college-bred

take first place on the roster of fame, and other men who are college-bred sink out of sight, most thinking men are quite willing to admit there is no such thing as a science of education ◦◦ ◦◦

Of the college men who succeed, who shall say they succeeded by and through the aid the college gave, or in spite of it?

❧ Yet many men who win will wail, " If I only had the advantage of college training! "

❧ If so it might have ironed all the individuality out of them ◦◦ ◦◦

Yet I would have every man have a college education, in order that he might see how little the thing is really worth. I would have every man rich, that he might know the worthlessness of riches ◦◦ ◦◦

O take a young man away from work, say at eighteen years of age, and keep him from useful labor, in the name of education, for four years, will some day be regarded as a most absurd proposition. It is the most gigantic illusion of the age. Set in motion by theologians, the idea was that the young person should be drilled and versed in " sacred " themes.

❧ Hence, the dead languages and the fixed thought that education should be esoteric.

❧ This separation from the practical world for a number of years, where no useful work was done and the whole attention fixed on abstract themes and theories, often tended to cripple the man so that he could never go back to the world of work and usefulness. He was no longer a producer, and had to be supported by tithes and taxes ◦◦ ◦◦

And, of course, as he did not intend to go back to the world of work and usefulness, it really did n't make any difference if he did sink into a pupa-like condition of nullity ◦◦ ◦◦

In the smaller colleges many instances are found of students working their way through school. My experience leads me to believe that such students stand a very much better chance in the world's race than those who are made exempt from practical affairs by having everything provided. The responsibility of caring for himself is a necessary factor in man's evolution

And the point of this preachment lies right here— that to make a young man exempt from the practical world, from eighteen to twenty-two, is to run the risk of ruining him for life. Possibly you have taken opportunity from him and turned him into a memory machine

THERE are persons who are always talking about preparing for life. The best way to prepare for life is to begin to live.

A school should not be a preparation; a school should be life

Isolation from the world in order to prepare for the world's work is folly. You might as well take a boy out of the blacksmith-shop in order to teach him blacksmithing

College is a make-believe, and every college student knows it. From the age of fourteen and upward the pupil should feel that he is doing something useful, not merely killing time; and so his work and his instruction should go right along hand in hand

The educated man is the useful man.

And no matter how many college degrees a man has, if he can not earn an honest living he is an educated ignoramus, and is one with the yesterdays, doing pedagogic goose-step adown the days to dusty death.

Only through liberty can men progress and grow

God never made a gymnasium—He did, however, make a garden

He who passes out to the world a counterfeit life gets paid for it in Confederate money

The advantage of college lies in stimulus, and not in information. The stimulus we need, but the information we can get through a clerk

If I supply you a thought you may remember it and you may not. But if I can make you think a thought for yourself, I have indeed added to your stature

The more practical a man is, the larger his stock of Connecticut commonsense, the greater is his disillusionment as his children grow to manhood

Aim for the bull's-eye, not for acreage

We desire at least a modicum of intellectual honesty, and the man who shuffles his opinions in order to match ours is seen through quickly. We want none of him

Nothing unmasks a man like his use of power

Who are my brethren? All those who think as I do, who breathe the same mental atmosphere—these know all that I know

Woman's inaptitude for reasoning has not prevented her from arriving at truth; nor has man's ability to reason prevented him from floundering in absurdity.

Logic is one thing, and commonsense another

Our own are those who are in our key; and when this is struck we answer back out of the silence

It is better to be victimized occasionally than to go through life filled with suspicion

Wise initiative is the finest gift of God to man

*Y*ESTERDAY woman was a chattel. Now she is, in law, a minor. Tomorrow she will be free, or partially so—that is to say, as free as man

These changes have gradually come about through isolated discoveries that a woman might be a man's comrade and friend—that a man and a woman may be mental mates

Then for the first time there existed honesty in the relation, for surely I do not have to prove that honesty between master and slave is either an accident or a barren ideality. There must be a community of interest

Love for its own sake can only exist between a man and a woman mentally mated, for only then is complete, unqualified, honest expression possible

Men who marry for gratification, propagation, or the matter of buttons and socks, must expect to cope with and deal in a certain amount of quibble, subterfuge, concealment and double, deep-dyed prevarication

And these things will stain the fabric of the souls of those who juggle them and leave their mark upon futurity

The fusion of two minds in an idea has given a new joy to the race, a zest to life and a reason for living.

*L*OVE is for the lover. And in this new condition, where the mental equality of the woman is being acknowledged, there will be no tyranny, and therefore no concealment and untruth.

There will be simplicity and frankness, and these are the essence of comradeship.

And where there is comradeship, there can love and reason walk hand in hand.

Love and reason!

Love for its own sake, with honesty and truth for counsel and guide, is the highest good. It is the supreme endowment of God. And under these conditions he who loves most is most blessed

Love and ownership.

Love and " rights."

Love and finesse.

Love and management

These things are very old, but love and reason are a new combination. And it can exist only where there is the unconditional admission of equality.

Such a partnership means a doubling of every intellectual joy, and an increased sympathy with every living thing—a oneness that knows no limit.

It means universality

We reach God through the love of one.

We can gain the Kingdom of Heaven by having the Kingdom of Heaven in our hearts.

Love for love's sake—there is nothing better

It sweetens every act of life

Love grows by giving

The love we give away is the only love we keep

Insight, sympathy, faith, knowledge and love are the results of love—they are the children of parents mentally mated.

Love for love's sake

The man with a healthy mouth is never sick; the sick man never has a healthy mouth

---

It does not take much strength to do things, but it requires great strength to decide on what to do

---

Be a man and a friend to everybody

Live one day at a time, do your work as well as you can, and be kind

---

A good laugh is sunshine in the house

Believe in the divinity of the child, not in its depravity.

The industrious man is light-hearted—the man who works is the happy man

System is crystallized commonsense

Morality is simply the attitude we adopt towards people we personally dislike

HE very first item in the creed of common-sense is obedience

Perform your work with a whole heart

Revolt may be sometimes necessary, but the man who tries to mix revolt and obedience is doomed to disappoint himself and everybody with whom he has dealings

To flavor work with protest is to fail in the protest and fail in the work.

When you revolt, why, revolt—climb, hike, get out, defy—tell everybody and everything to go to hades! That disposes of the case. You thus separate yourself entirely from those you have served—no one misunderstands you—you have declared yourself

The man who quits in disgust when ordered to perform a task which he considers menial or unjust may be a pretty good fellow; but the malcontent who takes your order with a smile and then secretly disobeys is a dangerous proposition

To pretend to obey and yet carry in your heart the spirit of revolt is to do half-hearted, slipshod work.

If revolt and obedience are equal in power, your engine will then stop on the center, and you benefit no one, not even yourself

HE spirit of obedience is the controlling impulse that dominates the receptive mind and the hospitable heart. There are boats that mind the helm and there are boats that do not. Those that do not get holes knocked in them sooner or later.

To keep off the rocks, obey the rudder

Obedience is not slavishly to obey this man or that, but it is that cheerful mental state which responds to the necessity of the case, and does the thing without any back talk—uttered or expressed.

Obedience to the institution—loyalty!

The man who has not learned to obey has trouble ahead of him every step of the way. The world has it in for him continually, because he has it in for the world

The man who does not know how to receive orders is not fit to issue them to others. But the individual who knows how to execute the orders given him is preparing the way to issue orders, and better still, to have them obeyed

There is known to me a prominent business house that by the very force of its directness and worth has incurred the enmity of many rivals. In fact, there is a very general conspiracy on hand to put the institution down and out

In talking with a young man employed by this house he yawned and said, " Oh, in this quarrel I am neutral."

" But you get your bread and butter from this firm, and in a matter where the very life of the institution is concerned I do not see how you can be a neutral."

And he changed the subject

I think that if I enlisted in the Japanese army I would not be a neutral

BUSINESS is a fight—a continual struggle—just as life is. Man has reached his present degree of development through struggle

Struggle there must be and always will be.

The struggle began as purely physical. As man evolved it shifted ground to the mental, the psychic and the spiritual, with a few dashes of Caveman proclivities still left

But, depend upon it, the struggle will always be— life is activity. And when it gets to be a struggle in well-doing, it will still be a struggle. When inertia gets the better of you it is time to telephone the undertaker

The only real neutral in this game of life is a dead one.

Eternal vigilance is not only the price of liberty, but of every other good thing.

A business that is not safeguarded on every side by active, alert, attentive, vigilant men is gone. As oxygen is the disintegrating principle of life, working night and day to dissolve, separate, pull apart and dissipate, so there is something in business that continually tends to scatter, destroy and shift possession from this man to that. A million mice nibble eternally at every business venture.

The mice are not neutrals, and if enough employees in a business house are neutrals, the whole concern will eventually come tumbling about their ears

I like that order of Field Marshal Oyama, " Give every honorable neutral that you find in our lines the honorable jiu-jitsu hikerino."

Righteousness is only a form of commonsense

Do not stop to think about who are with you, and what men are against you. It matters little at the last—both the ability to harm and the ability to help are overestimated

When you recognize a thing in the outside world, it is because it was yours already

Life is a movement outward, an unfolding

A pessimist is a man who has been compelled to live with an optimist

When a church becomes fashionable it ceases to be the House of God

HE world bestows its big prizes, both in money and in honors, for but one thing.

¶ And that is Initiative

What is Initiative?

¶ I 'll tell you: It is doing the right thing without being told

But next to doing the right thing without being told is to do it when you are told once. That is to say, carry the Message to Garcia!

¶ Next, there are those who never do a thing until they are told twice: such get no honors and small pay.

¶ Next, there are those who do the right thing only when Necessity kicks them from behind, and these get indifference instead of honors, and a pittance for pay. This kind spends most of its time polishing a bench with a hard-luck story

Then, still lower down in the scale than this, we find the fellow who will not do the right thing even when some one goes along to show him how, and stays to see that he does it: he is always out of a job, and receives the contempt he deserves, unless he has a rich Pa, in which case Destiny patiently awaits around the corner with a stuffed club.

¶ To which class do you belong?

○—

The mud-slinger never comes into court with clean hands

○—

You get what you prepare for

○—

That which has been done is dead; that which is now being done is dying; that only is alive which remains to do

○—

Power left to itself attains a terrific impulse

○—

The recipe for perpetual ignorance is: Be satisfied with your opinions and content with your knowledge.

WHENEVER you go out of doors, draw the chin in, carry the crown of the head high, and fill the lungs to the utmost; drink in the sunshine; greet your friends with a smile, and put soul into every hand-clasp

Do not fear being misunderstood; and never waste a minute thinking about your enemies. Try to fix firmly in your mind what you would like to do, and then without violence of direction you will move straight to the goal

Keep your mind on the great and splendid things you would like to do; and then, as the days go gliding by, you will find yourself unconsciously seizing upon the opportunities that are required for the fulfilment of your desire, just as the coral insect takes from the running tide the elements it needs. Picture in your mind the able, earnest, useful person you desire to be, and the thought you hold is hourly transforming you into that particular individual

Thought is supreme. Preserve a right mental attitude —the attitude of courage, frankness and good-cheer. To think rightly is to create

All things come through desire, and every sincere prayer is answered. We become like that on which our hearts are fixed. Carry your chin in and the crown of your head high. We are gods in the chrysalis

Science stands for the head, religion for the heart.

Debt is the devil in disguise

If your neighbor's team is stuck in the mud, it is not quite enough to advise him to " hitch his wagon to a star."

For the first time in the history of the world, it is the general feeling that free speech is a good thing, and that the masses can safely be trusted with it

No god was ever jealous, but the man who invents him always is

Society is a relish for solitude

Worry is futile and senseless, being born often of a blindness that will not wait

Life is the continuous adjustment of internal to external relations

The basis of commonsense is to know that good men may differ, yet in their differences agree

Think less about your rights, more about your duties.

Knowledge consists in a sense of values—a fine discernment for trouble lies in the mass

It is a fine thing to have ability, but the ability to discover ability in others is the true test

The millennium will come, only through scientific acceptance of piety

True life lies in laughter, love and work

What you want to do is to walk more and eat less; also love more and hate less, and this " germ theory " will take care of itself

To act as we should is the moral part : to know how to act is the intellectual part

The question still remains whether discipline is not a matter of gratification to the person in power, rather than a sincere desire and honest attempt to benefit the person disciplined

ARTIN LUTHER the German, John Calvin the Frenchman, and John Knox the Scotchman, lived at the same time. They constitute a trinity of strong men who profoundly influenced their times; and the epoch they made was so important that we refer to it as " The Reformation." They form the undertow of that great tidal wave of reason, the Italian Renaissance. And as the chief business of the Hahnemanian School of Medicine was to dilute the dose of the Allopaths, and the Christian Scientists confirmed the Homeopaths in a belief in the beauties of the blank tablet, so did Luther, Calvin and Knox neutralize the arrogance of Rome, and dilute the dose of despotism. Ernest Renan thought that Martin Luther put progress back five hundred years, " by effecting a compromise with the Catholic Church, supplying the people something just as good, at less cost."

Yet the great Renan must have known that fanaticism is a disease of the mind, just as alcoholism is a disease of the body, and the rational cure for both is the diminishing dose. That is, you are weaned from one thing by the substitution of something less harmful

The cure by violence and revulsion works sometimes, but it is unreliable and often unsafe

Mankind can be released from the power of weakness by slow degrees only

Christian Science has eliminated the doctor, reducing the rank of priest to that of reader, and thrown away the bell, candle and curse, but it still finds it expedient, if not absolutely necessary, to have its " Book " and " Church."

And behold one great Life-Insurance Company has instructed its agents by circular thus: " Christian Scientists as a class are extra good risks and should be solicited."

Then comes Doctor Hughson Harding, the cele-

brated neurologist of London, and says, " Christian
Science, by lessening nerve-tension, and increasing
the self-reliance of the patient, brings about a normal
flow of the secretions, and thus doubtless increases
the average length of human life in a very perceptible
degree."

Renan's idea that humanity could have been jumped
from the hypnotic dazzle of Rome into the clean,
calm sunlight of reason at a bound, if Luther had
not interposed " with something just as good," is
not reasonable. Mankind must get used to the light
by degrees

And if Protestantism is " a compromise with truth,"
as Diderot and so many others have averred, let us
just remember that life itself is a compromise, and
that progress is only possible through courteously
giving the rights of the road and making way for
vehicles, even though you do not exactly love the
occupants nor admire their millinery

NATURE intended that each animal should live
to an age approximating five times the number
of years which it takes to reach its bodily maturity.
Man reaches his height and maximum strength at
twenty, and should therefore live to be a hundred.

The brain, being the last organ developed, and
growing until man is past seventy, should sit secure
and watch every organ decline. As it is, the brain, with
over one-half of the individuals who live to be seventy,
loses its power before the hands and feet, and death
reaps something less than a man—all through too
much exercise of the brain, or not enough

Glancing once more at Doctor Harding's remark,
it is very evident that if the sum of human happiness
can be increased, life will be much extended, and the
danger of dying at the top obviated.

Of all the mental and physical polluters of life,
nothing exercises such a poisonous effect as fear

Fear paralyzes the will, and either stagnates the

secretions or turns them loose in a torrent
Jealousy, cruelty, hate, revenge, all are forms of fear.

Abolish fear, and every man and woman is an orator and an artist. The criminal and the untruthful person are obsessed by fear until the genial current of their life is turned awry. A man, like a horse, is safe until he gets in the fell clutch of fear.

When the Shah of Persia was asked the average length of human life in his country, he replied, " Some die old, some die young—only God can tell how long anybody will live."
Luther died at sixty-three, Calvin at fifty-three, and John Knox at fifty-seven. Luther and Knox were in prison, and Calvin escaped only by flight. All were under sentence of death; all lived under the ban of fear. All were literally scared to death, and all have literally scared to death thousands upon thousands of other people
Now if you were asked what factor in human life had contributed most to fear, would you not be compelled in truth to say, Theology?

Theology, by diverting the attention of men from this life to another, and by endeavoring to coerce all men into one religion, constantly preaching that this world is full of misery, but the next world would be beautiful—or not, as the case may be—has forced on men the thought of fear where otherwise there might have been the happy abandon of Nature
Next to theology, in point of harm, is medicine, which is the study of the abnormal, and the constantly iterated thought that the " family physician " was a necessary adjunct to life itself; which thought has bred in mankind the fallacy of looking to the doctor for relief from pain, instead of to ourselves. Should we not understand the Laws of Life sufficiently, so as to be as well and as happy as birds and squirrels?

The third great engine of human misery has been the law. Seventy per cent of the members of all our law-making bodies are lawyers. Very naturally, lawyers in making laws favor laws that make lawyers a necessity. If this were not so, lawyers would not be human.

Until very recent times, and in degree I am told it is so yet, laws are for the subjection of the many and the upholding of the privileges of the few. The few employ a vast lobby, while all the many can do is to obey, or be ground into the mire. All the justice the plain people have, they have had to fight for, and what we get is a sop to keep us quiet. The law, for most people, is a great, mysterious, malevolent engine of wrath. A legal summons will yet blanch the cheek of most honest men, and an officer at the door sends consternation into the family. The District Attorney prosecutes us—we must defend ourselves. " And if you have no money to hire a lawyer, you are adjudged guilty and for you justice is a by-word," says Edward Lauterbach, the eminent lawyer

And here is the argument : The fear of death, as taught by the clergy ; the fear of disease, as fostered by the doctors ; and the fear of the law, as disseminated by lawyers, has created a fog of fear that has permeated us like a miasma, and cut human life short one-third, causing the brain to reel and rock at a time when it should be the serene and steadfast pilot of our lives. " What, then," you ask; " shall we go back to savagery? "

And my answer is, No, we must, and will, and are, going on, on to Enlightenment

⟃⟄

You can live forty days without food, but you can not possibly live four minutes without air. These things being true, is it wise to stuff ourselves with food and starve ourselves for want of air?

⟃⟄

When sympathy finds vent in vengeance, and " love " takes the form of strife, the doctor is getting ready his ether-cone

Life consists in molting our illusions. We form creeds today only to throw them away tomorrow. The eagle molts a feather because he is growing a better one.

A sect is merely a point of view

The best preparation for good work tomorrow is to do good work today; the best preparation for life in the hereafter is to live now

Live so as to get the approbation of your Other Self, and success is yours. But pray that success will not come any faster than you are able to endure it

Do not take life too seriously—you will never get out of it alive

The soul grows by leaps and bounds, by throes and throbs. A flash, and a glory stands revealed for which you have been groping blindly through the years

The education that aims at mere scholarly acquire-ment, rather than useful intelligence, will have to step down and out. The world needs competent men; then, if their hearts are right, culture will come as a matter of course. To go in search of culture is to accumulate that which is rotten at the core

We grow through expression—if you know things there is a strong desire to express them. It is Nature's way of deepening our impressions—this thing of recounting them. And happy, indeed, if you know a soul with whom you can converse at your best

Man is the instrument of Deity

Through sin do men reach the light, and that which teaches can not be wholly bad

HE secret of success is this : There is no secret of success

Carry your chin in and the crown of your head high. We are gods in the chrysalis

Success is a result of mental attitude, and the right mental attitude will bring success in everything you undertake

In fact, there is no such thing as failure, except to those who accept and believe in failure. Failure! There is no such word in all the bright lexicon of speech, unless you yourself have written it there

A great success is made up of an aggregation of little ones. These finally form a whole.

The man who fills a position of honor and trust has first filled many smaller positions of trust

The man who has the superintendence of ten thousand men has had the charge of many small squads.

And before he had charge of a small squad he had charge of himself

The man who does his work so well that he needs no supervision has already succeeded

And the acknowledgment of his success is sure to follow in the form of a promotion.

The world wants its work done, and civilization is simply a search for men who can do things

UCCESS is the most natural thing in the world.

The man who does not succeed has placed himself in opposition to the laws of the universe

The world needs you—it wants what you produce— you can serve it, and if you will, it will reward you richly

By doing your work you are moving in the line of least resistance—it is a form of self-protection

You need what others have to give—they need you. To reciprocate is wisdom. To rebel is folly.

To consume and not produce is a grave mistake, and upon such a one Nature will visit her displeasure.

The common idea is that success means great

sacrifice, and that you must buy it with a price. In one sense this is true

To succeed you must choose. If you want this you can not have that. Success demands concentration—oneness of aim and desire.

Choose this day whom you will serve

Paradoxically, it is true that you must " sacrifice " some things to gain others

If you are a young man and wish to succeed in business, you will have to sacrifice the cigarettes, the late hours, the dice, the cards, and all the round of genteel folly which saps your strength and tends to unfit you for your work tomorrow

HAT awkward and uncouth country boy who went to work yesterday is concentrating on his tasks—he is doing the thing, high or low, mental or what not—yes! He is not so very clever, his trousers bag at the knee, and his sleeves are too short, but his heart has but one desire—to do his work. Soon you will be taking your orders from him.

And let me say right here that the habit of continually looking out for Number One is absolutely fatal to success. Nature is on her guard against such, and if by accident they get into a position of power their lease on the place is short. A great success demands a certain abnegation—a certain disinterestedness

The man who can lose himself in his work is the man who will succeed best

Courtesy, kindness and concentration—this trinity forms the sesame that will unlock all doors.

Good-cheer is twin sister to good health

Isn't it the part of wisdom not to put an enemy into your mouth to steal away your brains? Isn't it wise to so fill your working hours that the night comes as a blessing and a benediction—a time for sweet rest and sleep?

These things mean a preparation for good work. And

good work means a preparation for higher work ≈
Success is easy. We do not ascend the mountain by
standing in the valley and jumping over it ≈
Success is only difficult to the man who is trying to
lift himself by tugging at his boot-straps ≈

Our quarrel with the world is only our quarrel with
ourselves. When we are at peace with self, we are at
peace with God ≈

Weep not peeling other people's onions ≈

If you want to find the spring of perpetual youth,
go and dig in the sand with the children, or hoe in
the garden—then you will tap that spring all right.

Your neighbor is the man who needs you ≈

It does not make much difference what a person
studies—all knowledge is related, and the man who
studies anything, if he keeps at it, will be learned.

Theology is Classified Superstition ≈

Appreciation of the worthy can come only from those
who are not unworthy ≈

To have friends is a great gain, but to achieve an
enemy is distinction ≈

The major habit or the minor sin trips its victim
over the bank at an unguarded point, and to get back
to safety, strong and friendly hands must reach out.

Only one get mad at a time ≈

If your friend reveals his humanity and the world
forsakes him, it is your opportunity—stand by him!

ES, yes, I am a Zionist. I long to be a citizen of the Eternal City of Fine Minds. I would belong to that brotherhood which cultivates the receptive heart and the generous mind. My neighbors are often hundreds of miles apart. They are the men and women of earth who think and feel and dream, and ask themselves each morning, " What is Truth? " We think better of Pilate for his question. To meet a god face to face and not ask would have betokened complete imbecility. But Jesus did not answer. He could not. All truth is relative, and that message which comes out of the great Silence to you can only be interpreted to another who, too, has listened and heard. Yes, let us all be Zionists and dwell in the New Jerusalem of Celestial Truth

If calamity, disgrace or poverty come to your friends —then is the time they need you

Reformers are those who educate people to appreciate the things they need

N the beginning of his career man is repressed and suppressed by Nature. Fear haunts his footsteps. The shadows of the forests are filled with the unknown. To get out into the open—out into the clearing—where he can see, is his desire

And in the great order of things this is well, for the impulse to see and know leads to all that is good. But here we find that great primal fear of the forest —the place of hiding! It was the monkey that took to the plains, that stood upright and observed, and learned to run, that evolved into a man.

Out on the plains the man recovers from his fright and looks around. He finds a few trees, and near them is a bubbling spring of water

He is refreshed by the water, and the shade is grateful.

Then it dawns upon him by slow degrees that trees and water always go together, and that society is only possible where these things exist.

Surely that Texas man was right: Water, trees and society are all that Hell lacks of being Paradise.

MAN contrives to divert the water of streams and plants trees

These trees grow, just in proportion as they are wisely watered and cultivated. And here is a thing that man does not know until way along in the game, that is, that in cultivating the trees he cultivates himself.

But man notes this, that where trees grow, showers come, too, from the skies, for water and foliage mutually attract

So, from a state of fear of the forest, man learns to love the tree. From being depressed by Nature, he co-operates with her

He perceives that man himself is a part of Nature and under the domain of the same great natural laws that control the tree

The last lesson is that in a great degree we not only can co-operate with Nature, but we can also control her. So, from being a victim, man becomes a master.

This discovery of unity and oneness, and next the mastership, is the work of those rare souls, men of great faith, great originality, individuality and power of initiative whom, for lack of a better term, we call geniuses

It is easy to say, " We are part of all we see and hear and feel," when many others are saying the same. But how was it when men sang, " This world is but a desert drear, Heaven is my home "?

The genius is the man who stands at the pivotal point and flings into the teeth of entrenched prejudice his own thought, pitting himself against the ignorance of the past

With no uncertain tone and without apology he lifts

up his voice and cries aloud, " They have said unto you in olden times, * * * but I say unto you!" And again, " A new commandment I give unto you, that ye love one another."

This is a busy world, but the age is calling for men who can help bear its burdens, who can do things, whose faces are turned toward the sunrise. There is no place for the man who lives in the squabbles of the past

Good habits are the mentors that regulate our lives.

Our happiest moments are when we forget self in useful effort

It is safe to say that governments have committed far more crimes than they have prevented

Words of wisdom will ever be interpreted by fools according to their folly, and words of foolishness will sometimes have truth read into them by guileless minds

You had better be standard by performance than by pedigree

The man who thinks out what he wants to do, and then works and works hard, will win, and no others do, or ever have, or can—God will not have it so

Send the flowers when the man gets well, instead of when he does n't

The serene point of view is obtainable only by holding the spirit in equipoise; by letting slip the shackles of hurry; by anchoring fast to the one greatest thing, " Peace."

The church increases morality at the expense of intellect, and thus tends to keep man forever a mental minor

---

Success depends on loyalty and co-operation

E need some one to believe in us—if we do well, we want our work commended, our faith corroborated. The individual who thinks well of you, who keeps his mind on your good qualities, and does not look for flaws, is your friend. Who is my brother? I 'll tell you: he is the one who recognizes the good in me

---

Industrialism, as it changes and betters human environment, is the true civilizing agent

---

Undying faith is possible only for those who are not afraid of being unpopular

---

To undertake to supply people a thing you think they need, but which they do not want, is to have your head elevated on a pike, and your bones buried in the potter's field

---

HE history of all dogmatic and " revealed " religions is, in truth, but a history of man's endeavors to discover or invent some plan or scheme or method whereby he may shirk his personal responsibility, or shift it to other shoulders than his own, or in some manner escape the natural consequences of its conscious and intentional evasion or violation

---

Success is ten per cent opportunity, and ninety per cent intelligent hustle

---

Recipe for having food taste like that which mother used to make: Walk five miles before dinner

BIG business is a steamship bound for a port called Success. It takes a large force of men to operate this boat. Eternal vigilance is not only the price of liberty, but it is the price of every other good thing, including steamboating

To keep this steamship moving, the captain requires the assistance of hundreds of people who have a singleness of aim—one purpose—a desire to do the right thing and the best thing in order that the ship shall move steadily, surely and safely on her course.

Curiously enough, there are men constantly falling overboard. These folks who fall overboard are always cautioned to keep away from dangerous places ; still, there are those who delight in taking risks. These individuals who fall off, and cling to floating spars, or are picked up by passing craft, usually declare that they were " discharged." They say the Captain or the Mate or their comrades had it in for them.

I am inclined to think that no man was ever " discharged " from a successful concern—he discharges himself

When a man quits his work—say, oiling the engine or scrubbing the deck—and leans over the side calling to outsiders, explaining what a bum boat he is aboard of, how bad the food is and what a fool there is for a Captain, he gradually loosens his hold until he falls into the yeasty deep. There is no one to blame but himself, yet probably you will have hard work to make him understand this little point.

When a man is told to do a certain thing, and there leaps to his lips, or even to his heart, the formula, " I was n't hired to do that," he is standing upon a greased plank that inclines toward the sea. When the plank is tilted to a proper angle, he goes to Davy Jones' locker, and nobody tilts the fatal plank but the man himself

And the way the plank is tilted is this : the man takes

more interest in passing craft and what is going on
on land, than in doing his work on board ship
So I repeat : no man employed by a successful concern
was ever discharged. Those who fall overboard get
on the greased plank and then give it a tilt to the
starboard
If you are on a greased plank, you had better get off
from it, and quickly, too.

Loyalty is the thing!

To subjugate another is to subjugate yourself

A man who formally accepts a creed is bonded to the
past. All creeds and most laws tend to cripple progress.

People who say, " There's no use talking," usually
keep right on doing it

He who will not accept orders has no right to give
them ; he who will not serve has no right to command ;
he who can not keep silence has no right to speak.

I HOLD these truths to be self-evident :
That man was made to be happy ;
That happiness is only attainable through
useful effort ;
That the best way to help ourselves is to help others ;
That useful effort means the proper exercise of all
our faculties ;
That we grow, only through this exercise ;
That education should continue through life, and
the joys of mental endeavor should be, especially,
the solace of the old ;
That where men alternate work, study and play in
right proportion, the brain is the last organ of the
body to fail. Death for such has no terrors ;
That the possession of wealth can never make a man
exempt from useful, manual labor ;

That if all would work a little, none would be over-worked;

That if no one wasted, all would have enough;

That if none were overfed, none would be underfed;

That the rich and " educated " need education quite as much as the poor and illiterate;

That the presence of a serving class is an indictment and a disgrace to our civilization;

That the disadvantage of having a serving class falls most upon those who are served, and not upon those who serve—just as the real curse of slavery falls upon the slaveowner;

That the presence of a serving class tends toward dissolution instead of co-operation;

That the people who are waited on by a serving class can not have a just consideration for the rights of others, and that they waste both time and substance, both of which are lost forever, and can only partially be made good by additional human effort;

That the person who lives on the labor of others, not giving himself in return to the best of his ability, is really a consumer of human life;

That the best way to abolish a serving class is for all to join it;

That in useful service there is no high nor low;

That all duties, offices and things useful and necessary are sacred, and that nothing else is or can be

The Via Media is the route you take when a frank expression might hurt your business

Brain-work is just as necessary as physical exercise, and the man who studies his own case, and then plays one kind of work off against another, finds a continual joy and zest in life, and his days shall be long upon the land

No man is ever any better than he wants to be

ATURE makes the crab-apple, but without man's help she could never evolve the pippin. Nature makes the man, but unless the man takes charge of himself, he will never evolve into a Master. He will remain a crab-apple man. So Nature requires men to co-operate with her. And of course in this statement I fully admit that man is but a higher manifestation of Nature ⁓ ⁓ Nature knows nothing of time—time is for men. And the fleeting quality of time is what makes it so valuable to us. If life were without limit, we would do nothing. Life without death would be appalling. It would be a day without end—a day with no night of rest. Death is a change—and death is a manifestation of life ⁓ ⁓

We are allowed to live during good behavior, and this is what leads men toward truth, justice and beauty, for these things mean an extension of time, and happiness instead of misery.

We work because life is short, and through this work we evolve. The Master is a man who has worked wisely and intelligently, and through habit has come to believe in himself ⁓ ⁓

Men are strong just in proportion as they have the ability to say NO, and stand by it. Look back on your own life—what was it that caused you the most worry, wear, vexation, loss and pain? Wasn't it because you failed to say NO at certain times and stick to it? ⁓ ⁓

This vice of the inability to say NO comes from lack of confidence in yourself.

You think too much of the opinions of other people and not enough of your own. "Put your name right here—it is only a matter of form, you know—just between friends." ⁓ ⁓

And you sign your name. The years go by, and there comes a time when you pay for your weakness in blood and tears ⁓ ⁓

And the real fact is that the good opinion of the best
people comes from your saying NO, and not weakly
yielding and putting your name to a subscription,
or a contract which was none of yours ·

Cultivate self-confidence and learn to say NO. It
is a great thing to be a man, but it is a finer thing
to be a Master—Master of yourself ·

I AM going to write a little here on the subject of
jealousy. There is only one kind of jealousy, and
that is Sex Jealousy. People often use the word when
the thing they refer to is covetousness. We may covet
a man's talent, or his possessions, or we may dislike
a person, conceiving against him a prejudice and
thus belittle him; but jealousy is another matter.
Jealousy is not the exclusive possession of the highly
organized, nor the extremely sensitive, nor the irritable, nor the weak. The fact is, the strongest natures
are more given to jealousy than the weaker ones,
and the most patient man may manifest the disease
in its most virulent form. Shakespeare, who knew the
human heart as no other writer ever has, gives us a
picture of jealousy. The play of Othello is simply a
portrayal of this passion. And the man Othello is
surely not a man afflicted with " nerves "—he is a
great, serene and self-sufficient personality. He is
healthy, honest, trustful, truthful, and filled with a
childlike confidence ·

But Othello is a man—a strong, well-sexed man.
Beware how you arouse such a one!

Othello's intellect was no match for the cold,
calculating brain of Iago, and he was played upon
by this plotting, soulless knave until his love for
Desdemona was curdled into hate, and he killed that
which, in all the world, he loved best.

Only the strongly sexed are ever jealous. Weak
natures are indifferent—they transfer affection easily
—there is n't much to bestow—the change is easily

effected, and the past forgotten. But the strong give themselves, and the bonds they make are fastened to their souls with hoops of steel. Love, to such, is no light matter

Jealousy seems the absolute reversal of love. It is the swinging from the sunny warmth of the Equator to the frigid cold of the North Pole

ONCE heard Doctor James Bryce Howard, lecturer on Pathology at Bellevue, make a statement to the effect that cancer was caused by jealousy. His argument was something like this: Jealousy at once affects the circulation, and the emotion strikes at the organs of reproduction. In moments of goodwill, when the mind is calm, the circulation is complete, strong, natural; the secretions are active, the pores open, the glands do their perfect work. Let a spasm of hate and fear sweep over the person, and the heart thumps in wild alarm, and then dies down until you can scarcely detect its throb. The skin grows cold, the pores close, the secretions cease as though a sirocco of death had swept over the body. There is congestion in the parts, then fever, and Nature is working hard to restore an equilibrium. That is just the way cancer grows—there is a stoppage in the circulation, and Nature tries to clear it away by sending more blood to the part. This increased nutrition causes a growth to form, and Nature, who works always according to general laws, not caring for the individual, kills the patient in an effort to cure him. More women suffer from cancer than men, and three-fourths of all cases of cancer with women are in the mammary glands, or are connected directly with the sex organs. And in summing up the case the Doctor says: " Cancer is caused by misdirected or abnormal sex emotion. If we could bring about perfect love relations we would do away with cancer as well as most other diseases."

There is no form of woe that will cause a suffering

so terrible as jealousy. It grows by what it feeds upon
—a suspicion! Ah! it clutches for it, even though it
knows it is poison. It lies in wait, it watches, it listens;
and finding the proof it wants, suffers more than ever.
It suffers if it finds proof, and suffers if it does n't.
For bodily pain, Nature is pitiful, and quickly sends
insensibility. But for the woes of the heart, there is
only lingering torture—nights of tossing unrest, and
days of lagging, leaden misery.

In bereavement by death there soon comes calm
and sweet peace, in thought of the virtues of the loved
one gone. We consider and dwell upon the good that
was in the dead; but in jealousy we think only of the
worst in the living. It is a blasting, withering hate
towards that which we love best. It corrodes the heart
and makes the man hate himself. It forms a trinity
of hate—hate for the woman he loves, hate for the
suspected person, hate for himself.

That is why it stings so—the jealous person can
not justify himself. And so those who are most jealous
always affirm they are not so at all, and scout the
idea in hysterical emphasis. So far, the passion of
jealousy has never been analyzed. Many men have
written upon it, and all they attempt to do is to
describe its manifestations. The cause of jealousy
is never equal to the tragedy that tears and rends
the soul, and so no cause is ever sufficient. To analyze
it perfectly, we must perfectly comprehend the human
heart, and this we can never do. Human nature, at
last, remains the great riddle of God—contradiction
and paradox confront us at every turn. And should
we possibly come to know one soul, this gives no
index to others, for in Nature there are no duplicates.

WHO can explain why a woman with a great and
tender love for a man will at times tantalize
him into a frenzy? Who can tell why the simple-
hearted Moor, Othello, who loved the gentle Desdemona, should conceive such a hatred for her,

prompted by a flimsy and groundless suspicion,
that he takes her life? Where these insurrections
of the heart are born that wreck and rend the souls
of men is to us unguessed—we simply do not know.
Jealousy seems a sort of rudimentary savage instinct
that has come down to us from a time when its manifestation was a violence that knew no restraint, but
with tooth and claw struck its object dead, so only
the strongest survived. But now we partially hold the
savage hate in check, and jealousy, instead of hurting
the other person, hurts worst the one who is jealous.
We hug the hate and let it gnaw at our vitals, and
poison all the well-springs of our life with its venom.

The cure is not easy, and only a person of heroic
moral fiber can face the truth and bring philosophy
to bear, to heal and cure. At first thought, indifference
is the panacea—cease to love at all—be a stoic—
but this is to sink below jealousy, and not to rise
above it

To say that jealous people ought to separate is trite;
and it is true that people having totally different
temperaments should not force their personal presence
on each other to tantalize and taunt and make this
earth a hell

Separation is better than lingering death. But jealousy
may possibly come to those couples who really need
each other. In it always is the element of dissatis-
faction with self, and no pain and disappointment
equals this—when we are disappointed with ourselves.
Yet very seldom are we quite honest and frank with
ourselves; instead of laying the blame at home, we
bestow it on another. But let us be honest—the man
who is jealous is himself to blame for the most part.

CONCERNING these tragedies of the heart, the
wise man does not dogmatize. His heart throbs
for all those who suffer. And in his own life he would
not escape the pangs of disprized love by loving less;
rather does he love more. He seeks to send his love

to all, and make it universal. That he concentrates his affection on certain ones more than others may be true, but he fixes his thought upon the good that is in them, and waives all else.

❡. Folly, dissipation, absurdity, extravagance, are all about us; but these things do not rend our souls, cause us sleepless nights, and turn the genial current of our lives awry. Let us remember that we can not afford to admit hate into our hearts—we are the ones who suffer—the wrong is not ours, and so we will not take it in

Each soul is a center in itself, and the mistakes of others—the follies of wife or child, husband or parent—are none of ours. We are individuals—we came into the world alone, we live alone, and we die alone; and we must be so girded round by right that no fault of another can touch us. God is on our side—nothing can harm us but ourselves. Let us make sure that we are right, and then the follies of others will pass by us unscathed. And above all, remember it is not for us to punish. " Vengeance is mine: I will repay, saith the Lord."

⊂⊃

Two necessities in doing a great and important work: a definite plan and limited time

⊂⊃

To try many things means power: to finish a few is immortality

⊂⊃

To act in absolute freedom and at the same time realize that responsibility is the price of freedom is salvation

⊂⊃

The best service a book can render you is, not to impart truth, but to make you think it out for yourself

⊂⊃

Health and happiness can be found only out of doors.

For disobedience the man and woman were put out of the Garden—they have wandered far—and they can only return hand in hand

If you have not known poverty, heart-hunger and misunderstanding, God has overlooked you, and you are to be pitied

Theology is not what we know about God, but what we know we do not know about Nature

Men congratulate themselves on their position, no matter what it is; the world is wrong, not they

A few conquer by fighting, but more battles are won by submitting

Martyr and persecutor are usually cut from the same piece

The businessman is the man who gets the business.

What is the good of eternally discussing the future? If God is or is not, we are bound to keep doing the best we can, one day at a time, just the same

So long as millions of men gain a living by evolving the machinery of war and training for war we will have war

The object of education is that a man may benefit himself by serving others

We grow strong through assuming responsibilities— by bearing burdens and doing things we acquire power

Health is a gift, but you have to work to keep it

NO woman is worthy to be a wife who on the day of her marriage is not absolutely and entirely in an atmosphere of love and perfect trust; the supreme sacredness of the relation is the only thing which, at the time, should possess her soul. Is she a bawd that she should bargain? Women should not " obey " men any more than men should obey women. There are six requisites in every happy marriage; the first is Faith, and the remaining five are Confidence. Nothing so compliments a man as for a woman to believe in him— nothing so pleases a woman as for a man to place confidence in her

Obey? God help me! Yes, if I loved a woman, my whole heart's desire would be to obey her slightest wish. And how could I love her unless I had perfect confidence that she would only aspire to what was beautiful, true and right? And to enable her to realize this ideal, her wish would be to me a sacred command; and her attitude of mind toward me I know would be the same. And the only rivalry between us would be as to who could love the most; and the desire to obey would be the one controlling impulse of our lives

We gain freedom by giving it, and he who bestows faith gets it back with interest. To bargain and to stipulate in love is to lose

THE woman who stops the marriage ceremony and requests the minister to omit the word " obey " is sowing the first seed of doubt and distrust that later may come to fruition in the divorce-court.

The haggling and bickerings of settlements and dowries that usually precede the marriage of " blood " and " dollars " are the unheeded warnings that misery, heartache, suffering and disgrace await the principals.

Perfect faith implies perfect love; and perfect love casteth out fear. It is always the fear of imposition, and a lurking intent to rule, that causes the woman to haggle over a word—it is absence of love, a limitation, an incapacity. The price of perfect love is an absolute and complete surrender

Keep back part of the price, and yours will be the fate of Ananias and Sapphira. Your doom is swift and sure. To win all we must give all

Only the exiled can sympathize with the exile—only the downtrodden and sore-oppressed understand the outcast

Until you come to realize that many things you were sure of are not so, and many you scouted are true, you have not begun to live

The value of the thinker who writes, or the writer who thinks, or a businessman who acts, is that he supplies arguments for the people, and confirms all who are on his wire in their opinions, often before unuttered

Keep in your heart a shrine to the ideal, and upon this altar let the fire never die

Since language can never explain to one who does not already know, and as words are never a vindication, silence when ballasted by soul is effective beyond speech

Upon every face is written the record of the life the man has led: the prayers, the aspirations, the disappointments, all he hoped to be and was not—all are written there ; nothing is hidden, nor indeed can be.

Men are changed only as you change their surroundings. Transportation changes environment. And the railroads are the most important in the world today —barring nothing

IT is a great thing to teach. I am never more complimented than when some one addresses me as " teacher." To give yourself in a way that will inspire others to think, to do, to become—what nobler ambition ! To be a good teacher demands a high degree of altruism, for one must be willing to sink self—to die, as it were—that others may live. There is something in it very much akin to motherhood—a brooding quality. Every true mother realizes at times that her children are only loaned to her—sent from God—and the attributes of her body and mind are being used by some Power for a purpose. The thought tends to refine the heart of its dross, obliterate pride, and make her feel the sacredness of her office. All good men everywhere recognize the holiness of motherhood—this miracle by which the race survives

There is a touch of pathos in the thought that while lovers live to make themselves necessary to each other, the mother is working to make herself unnecessary to her children. And the entire object of teaching is to enable the scholar to do without his teacher. Graduation should take place at the vanishing-point of the teacher

Yes, the efficient teacher has in him much of this mother quality. Thoreau, you remember, said that genius is essentially feminine; if he had teachers in mind his remark was certainly true. The men of much motive power are not the best teachers—the arbitrary and imperative type, that would bend all minds to match its own, may build bridges, tunnel mountains, discover continents and capture cities, but it can not teach. In the presence of such a towering personality freedom dies, spontaneity droops, and thought slinks away into a corner. The brooding quality, the patience that endures, and the yearning of motherhood, are all absent. The man is a commander, not a teacher; and there yet remains a grave doubt whether the

warrior and ruler have not used their influence more
to make this world a place of the skull than the abode
of happiness and prosperity. The orders to kill all
the firstborn, and those over ten years of age, were
not given by teachers

THE teacher is one who makes two ideas grow
where there was only one before
Just here seems a good place to say that we live in
a very stupid, old world, round like an orange and
slightly flattened at the poles. The proof of this seemingly pessimistic remark, made by a hopeful and
cheerful man, lies in the fact that we place small
premium, either in honor or in money, on the business of teaching. As in olden times, barbers and scullions ranked with musicians, and the Master of the
Hounds wore a bigger medal than the Poet Laureate,
so do we pay our teachers the same as coachmen and
coal-heavers, giving them a plentiful lack of everything but overwork.

I will never be quite willing to admit that this
country is enlightened, until we cease the inane and
parsimonious policy of trying to drive all the really
strong men and women out of the teaching profession
by putting them on the payroll at one-half the rate,
or less than that which the same brains and energy
can command elsewhere. In the year of our Lord,
Nineteen Hundred Six, in a time of peace, we appro-
priated four hundred million dollars for war and war
appliances, and this sum is just double the cost of
the entire public-school system in America. It is not
the necessity of economy that dictates our actions
in this matter of education—we simply are not enlightened

But this thing can not always last—I look for the
time when we shall set apart the best and noblest
men and women of earth for teachers, and their
compensation will be so adequate that they will be
free to give themselves for the benefit of the race,

without apprehension of a yawning almshouse. A liberal policy will be for our own good, just as a matter of cold expediency ; it will be enlightened self-interest.

Why not be a Top-Notcher? A Top-Notcher is simply an individual who works only for the interest of the institution of which he is a part, not against it

Men are great only as they are kind

Civilization is not a thing apart, any more than Art is. Civilization is an evolution, and evolution is motion, Each day we have a new civilization

The man who does not relax and hoot a few hoots voluntarily, now and then, is in great danger of hooting hoots and standing on his head for the edification of the pathologist and trained nurse, a little later on.

The great books are those the authors had to write to get rid of; only immortal songs are those sung because the singer could not help it

He who stands still is lost

A man's measure is his ability to select men and materials and organize them

It takes at least five men to make one bad woman ; and it takes at least five women to make a preacher.

Our finest flowers are often weeds transplanted

The art of winning in business lies in working hard, and not taking the game too seriously

The big winners are invariably men who have snatched success from the jaws of failure

T was not so very long ago that the profession of teaching was entirely in the hands of theologians. All things secular and sacred, that were taught to young or old, were taught by priests. Priests decided what books should be printed and what not. The priest decided as to what should be taught, and how it should be taught, and beyond him there was no appeal

Instead of refuting natural science by natural science, theology sought to silence science by citing Scripture.

Galileo, writing in Sixteen Hundred Ten, complains because the theologians would not so much as look through his telescope, but sat back and declared him an " infidel " and an " atheist."

Two popes, Pope Alexander the Seventh and Pope Urban the Eighth, placed interdicts upon Galileo and forbade his teaching that the earth revolved, under serious penalty. The works of Galileo and Copernicus were forbidden to all good Catholics, and were upon the Index for more than two hundred fifty years, or until the year Eighteen Hundred Thirty-six. For teaching the truths of natural science Bruno was burned alive, and his ashes scattered to the four winds.

HE policy of every formal religion has always been to allow the fullest possible play to individuality, and yet not risk the life of the institution, the institution being the important thing—the individual, secondary. This is the idea of society in general as well. Individuals, however, threaten at times the life of the institution or system, by an excess of strength, and these powerful individuals it has been thought necessary to subdue and suppress. So, when one reads history he notes the fact that in days gone by nations have killed, banished or disgraced their men of genius

This has always been done with the avowed purpose of protecting the State or the prevailing religious system. Socrates, Pericles, Jesus, Anaxagoras, Aris-

totle, Savonarola, Copernicus, Galileo, Bruno, Huss,
Wycliff, are the types that society has suppressed.
That those who have done the destroying did not
know what they were doing is probably very true.
In one way they were surely self-deceived—they
thought they were working for the good of the State
or their religious system, when what they really feared
was the curtailment of their own individual power.
Men do the things they wish, and absolve their consciences at their convenience. And forever do they
deceive themselves as to their motives.

❡ Said Archbishop Ireland: " The enemies of the
Church have been inside the Church, not outside
of it. The supreme blunders of churchmen have been
in suppressing strong men—in thwarting individuality.
All the good law and all the good order which the
State or the Church enjoys today may be traced back
over some route to the words and deeds of men who
rebelled against the kind of law and the kind of order
that they found administered by its ' constituted
guardians '; by men who dared to appeal from the
' keepers of divine truth ' to divine truth itself—from
the ' trustees of God ' to God Himself."

The time to mind somebody else's business is when
he does n't

We do not fight for truth—we fight for electrotypes,
old books, old clothes, old sermons, old creeds, old
barrels. Persecution and martyrdom are usually struggles for inertia and junk

---

Strength comes from solitude, a waiting, a communion
with the best in us, which is at one with the divine
spark

If pleasures are greatest in anticipation, just remember
that this is also true of troubles

I make mistakes, of course; but I do not respond to encores

The sense of universality is heaven

Let 's keep the windows open to the East, be worthy, and some time we shall know

Sanity lies in your ability to think individually and act collectively

THOSE who manage religious systems have small faith in a Supreme Being or Universal Order. Luther, left alone, would have soon settled down into a country parson, and his protestantism would have diffused itself in the form of a healthful attenuation. All extremes tend to cure themselves. Well has it been said that Luther retarded civilization a thousand years. It was the absurd and foolish rancor of priests and popes that by opposition lifted Luther into a world-power, and made possible a thousand warring, jarring, quibbling sects and systems, consuming one another and the time and substance of mankind, in their vacuous and inept theological antics

Luther prolonged the life of theology by presenting it in a palatable capsule, just at a time when the intelligence of the world was making wry faces getting ready to spew it.

Pope Leo the Thirteenth, the wisest man who ever sat in the papal chair, once wrote: " The real enemies of the Church have been those o'er-zealous churchmen who have sought to stamp out error by violence, forgetful that man is little and our God is great, and that in His wisdom the Father of all has provided that evil left alone shall soon exhaust itself, and right, of itself, will surely prevail. Impatient defense of our holy religion springs from limitation and lack of faith. Against its avowed enemies the Church stands secure, but against those who are quick to draw the sword and strike off the ear of Malchus, we are often powerless. If the servants of the Church had ever taught by example, through love and patience, even now the reign of our God would be universal, as the flowers of Spring carpet the gentle hillside slopes." These gentle words of Pope Leo lose none of their quality, even when the obvious fact is pointed out that the man who struck off the ear of the high-priest's servant was the very man who founded the Church

The reason there are now so few professors to teach theology is on account of the scarcity of scholars who will pay for being taught. The demand always keeps pace with the supply where salaries and honors are involved. If there were a vast number of people who wanted to be taught alchemy, astrology and palmistry, there would not be wanting teachers to teach these things.

When augury was in vogue and men foretold the future by the flight of birds, in all first-class colleges there were endowed chairs held down by High-Test, Non-Explosive great men learned in the noble science of augury

If there were now emoluments and honors for teaching alchemy, astrology, palmistry and augury, there would be pedagogic preparatory schools for all these things, richly endowed by good men who did not understand them, but assumed that other people did

The science of theology is the science of episcopopagy. It starts with an assumption and ends in a fog Nobody ever understood it, but vast numbers have pretended to, because they thought others did. Very slowly we have grown honest, and now the wise man and the good man accept the doctrine of the unknowable

Gradually the consensus of intelligence has pushed theology off into the dustbin of oblivion, with alchemy and astrology

Theology is not meant to be understood—it is to be believed. A theologian is an ink-fish you can never catch. And in stating this fact I fully appreciate that I am laying myself open to the charge of being a theologian myself

HEN a prominent member of Congress, of slightly convivial turn, went to sleep on the floor of the House of Representatives, and suddenly awakening, convulsed the assemblage by loudly demanding, " Where am I at? " he propounded an inquiry that is classic. With the very first glimmering of intelligence and as far back as history goes, man has always asked this question and three others:

Where am I?
Who am I?
What am I here for?
Where am I going?

A question implies an answer, and so, coeval with the questioner, the man who answered has exacted a living from the man who asked, also titles, gauds, jewels and obsequies. Further than this, the volunteer who answered has declared himself exempt from all useful labor. This volunteer is our theologian. Walt Whitman has said:

" I think I could turn and live with animals, they are
          so placid and self-contained,
I stand and look at them long and long.
They do not sweat and whine about their con-
          dition,
They do not lie awake in the dark and weep for their
          sins,
They do not make me sick discussing their duty to
          God,
Not one is dissatisfied, not one is demented with the
          mania of owning things,

Not one kneels to another, nor to his kind that lived
      thousands of years ago,
Not one is respectable or unhappy over the whole
      earth."

But we should note this: Whitman merely wanted
to live with animals, he did not desire to become one.
He was not willing to forfeit knowledge; and a part
of that knowledge was, that man has some things
yet to learn from the brute

MUCH of man's misery has come from his persistent questioning
The book of Genesis is certainly right, when it tells
us that man's troubles come from his desire to know.
The fruit of the tree of knowledge is bitter, and man's
digestive apparatus has been ill-conditioned to assimilate it. But still we are grateful, and good men never
forget that it was woman who gave the fruit to man—
men learn nothing alone. In the Garden of Eden, with
everything supplied, man was an animal; but when
he was turned out and had to work, strive, struggle
and suffer, he began to grow into something better.

The theologians of the Far East have told us that
man's deliverance from the evils of life must come
through the killing of desire; we reach Nirvana—
rest—through nothingness. But within a decade it
has been borne in upon a vast number of thinking
men of the world that deliverance from discontent
and sorrow was to be had, not through ceasing to
ask questions, but by asking one more. The question
is this: " What can I do? "

And having asked the question, we must set to
work answering it ourselves
When man went to work, action removed the doubt
that theory could not solve.

The rushing winds purify the air; only running
water is pure; and the holy man, if there be such,
is the one who loses himself in persistent, useful effort.
The saint is the man who keeps his word and is on

time. By working for all, we secure the best results
for self, and when we truly work for self, we work
for all. The priestly class evolves naturally into being
everywhere as man awakens and asks questions. Only
the unknown is terrible, says Victor Hugo. We can
cope with the known, and at the worst we can overcome the unknown by accepting it. Verestchagin,
the great painter, who knew the psychology of war
as few men have, and went down to his death gloriously, as he should, on a sinking battleship, once said,
" In modern warfare, when man does not see his
enemy, the poetry of battle is gone, and man is rendered by the unknown into a quaking coward."
Enveloped in the fog of ignorance every phenomenon
of Nature causes man to quake and tremble—he
wants to know. Fear prompts him to ask, and greed
for power, place and pelf replies

O succeed beyond the average is to realize a
weakness in humanity and then bank on it. The
priest who pacifies is as natural as the fear he seeks
to assuage—as natural as man himself.

So the first man is in bondage to his fear, and
exchanges this for bondage to a priest. First, he fears
the unknown; second, he fears the priest who has
power over the unknown

Soon the priest becomes a slave to the answers he
has conjured forth. He grows to believe what he at
first pretended to know. The punishment of every
liar is that he eventually believes his lies. The mind
of man becomes tinted and subdued to what he works
in, like the dyer's hand.

So we have the formula:

Man in bondage to fear

Man in bondage to a priest.

The priest in bondage to a creed

Then the priest and his institution become an integral
part and parcel of the State, mixed in all its affairs.
The success of the State seems to lie in holding belief

intact and stilling all further questions of the people, transferring all doubts to this volunteer class that answers—for a consideration.

❡ Naturally the man who does not accept the answers is regarded by the priest as the enemy of the State— that is, the enemy of mankind ✒ ✒

To keep this questioner down has been the chief concern of every religion. And the problem of progress has been to smuggle the newly discovered truth past Cerberus, the priest, by preparing a sop that was to him palatable. From every branch of science, the priest has been routed, save sociology alone. Here he has stubbornly made his last stand, and is saving himself alive by slowly accepting the situation and transforming himself into the promoter of a social club ✒ ✒

The priest is society's walking delegate. He is the self-appointed business agent of Divinity—and no contract between God and man, man and man, or man and woman, is valid unless ratified by him.

❡ All who do not belong to his union are scabs ✒ ✒

THE evolution of the race is mirrored in the evolution of the individual. Look back on your own career—your first dawn of thought began in an inquiry, " Who made all this—how did it all happen? " ✒ ✒

And theology comes in with a glib explanation : the fairies, dryads, gnomes and gods made everything, and they can do with it all as they please. Later, we concentrate all of these personalities in one god, with a devil in competition, and this for a time satisfies.

❡ Later, the thought of an arbitrary being dealing out rewards and punishments grows dim, for we see the regular workings of cause and effect. We begin to talk of energy, the divine essence and the reign of law. We speak as Matthew Arnold did of a " Power, not ourselves, that makes for righteousness." But Emerson believed in a Power that was in himself, that made for righteousness ✒ ✒

Metaphysics reaches its highest stage when it affirms,
" All is one," " All is Mine," just as theology reaches
its highest conception when it becomes monotheistic
—having one God and curtailing the personality of
the Devil to a mere abstraction.

⁋ But this does not long satisfy, for we begin to ask,
" What is this One? " or " What is Mind? "
Then positivity comes in and says that the highest
wisdom lies in knowing that we do not know anything,
and never can, concerning a First Cause. All we find
is phenomena, and behind phenomena, phenomena.
⁋HE laws of Nature do not account for the origin
of the laws of Nature. Spencer's famous chapter
on the origin of the unknowable defines the limits of
human knowledge. And it is worth noting that the
one thing which gave most offense in Spencer's work
was this doctrine of the unknowable. This, indeed,
forms but a small part of the work of this great man,
and if it were all demolished there would still remain
his doctrine of the known. The bitterness of theology
toward science arises from the fact that as we find
things out we dispense with the arbitrary, handmade
god, and his business agent, the priest.

⁋ Men begin by explaining everything, and the explanations given are always for other people, Parents
answer the child, not telling him the actual truth,
but giving him that which will satisfy—that which
he can mentally digest. To say,"the fairies brought it,"
may be all right until the child begins to ask who the
fairies are, and wants to be shown one, and then we
have to make the somewhat humiliating confession
that there are no fairies.

⁋ But now we preceive that this mild fabrication in
reference to Santa Claus and the fairies is right and
proper mental food for the child. His mind can not
grasp the truth that some things are unknowable;
and he is not sufficiently skilled in the things of the
world to become interested in them—he must have

a resting-place for his thoughts, and so the fairy-tale comes in as an aid to the growing imagination ✿ ✿ Only this—we place no penalty in disbelief in fairies nor do we make offers of reward to all who believe that fairies actually exist. Neither do we tell the child that people who believe in fairies are good, and that those who do not are wicked and perverse ✿ ✿

The theological and metaphysical stages are necessary, but the sooner man can be graduated out of them the better. Hate, fear, revenge and doubt are all theological attributes, detrimental to man's best efforts.

❡ Moral ideas were an afterthought, and really form no part of theology. All beautiful, altruistic impulses thrive better when separated from theology ✿ ✿

AND the sum of the argument is, that all progress in mind, body and material things has come to man through the study of cause and effect. And just in degree as he abandoned the study of theology as futile and absurd, and centered on helping himself here and now, has he prospered.

❡ Man's only enemy is himself, and this is on account of his ignorance of this world, and his superstitious belief in another. Our troubles, like diseases, all come from ignorance and weakness, and through our ignorance are we weak and unable to adjust ourselves to better conditions. The more we know of this world the better we think of it, and the better we are able to use it for our advancement.

❡ So far as we can judge, the unknown cause that rules the world by unchanging laws is a movement forward to happiness, growth, justice, peace and right. Therefore, the scientist, who perceives that all is good when rightly received and rightly understood, is really the priest and holy man—the mediator and explainer of the mysterious. As fast as we understand things they cease to be supernatural. The supernatural is the natural not yet understood. The theological priest who believes in a God and a Devil is the real modern infidel ✿ ✿

The man of faith is the one who discards all thought of " how it first happened," and fixes his mind on the fact that he is here. The more he studies the conditions that surround him, the greater his faith in the truth that all is well

If men had turned their attention to humanity, discarding theology, using as much talent, time, money and effort in solving social problems, as they have in trying to wring from the skies the secrets of the unknowable, this world would now be a veritable paradise. It is theology that has barred the entrance to Eden, by diverting the attention of men from this world to another

ALL religious denominations now dimly perceive the trend of the times, and are gradually omitting theology from their teachings and taking on ethics and sociology instead. We are evolving theology out and sociology in. Theology has ever been the foe of progress and the enemy of knowledge. It has professed to know all, having a revelation direct from the Creator Himself, and has placed a penalty on all investigation and advancement.

The age of enlightenment will not be here until every church has evolved into a schoolhouse, and every preacher is both a teacher and a pupil

---

The best way to get even is to forget

If men could only know each other, they would never either idolize or hate

---

Every spirit makes its house, but as afterwards the house confines its spirit you had better build well.

The mouth indicates the flesh ; the eye the soul

Too often the reformer has been one who caused the rich to band themselves against the poor

Parties who fuss about saving their souls, probably
have no souls worth saving

The valuable man in any business is the man who can
and will co-operate with other men. Men succeed
only as they utilize the service and ideas of other
men. Co-operate!

The wise hold all earthly things lightly—they are
stripping for eternity

There is a sweet recompense in mutual deprivations,
where trials and difficulties only serve to cement
affection

Strong drink makes no man more useful; but it renders
many a useful man useless

Men who make themselves useful are needed

Literature should be the product of the ripened mind
—the mind that knows the world of men and which
has grappled with earth's problems. Letters should
not be a profession in itself—to make a business of
an art is to degrade it. Literature should be the
spontaneous output of the mind that has known
and felt. To work the mine of spirit as a business
and sift its product for hire is to overwork the vein
and palm off slag for useful metal

It is better to be only sometimes right than to be
at all times wrong

He who imparts cheerfulness is adding to the wealth
of the world

You can not reform a man who has a great many
little faults, but no big ones

NY one taking a trip up the Rhine can not but be seriously impressed with the fact that the chief business of man, until yesterday, was war

At every bend of the storied river is a castle. Each point of vantage is crowned with a redoubt, or the ruins of one, where men, armed with every known weapon of their time, once bade defiance to other men, and challenged their brothers. No man could travel without an armed guard—every man went laden with the instruments of death.

The history of the race is a history of war and blood. The men who could kill most and quickest were the men who owned the earth, and those who destroyed most were those to whom all honors were paid. Very gradually things have changed, until over the fairest portion of the earth, life and property are now secure. Men who mind their own business have nothing to fear, and those are safest who carry no weapons. The honors are going to men who build up, who can create. Within proper limits we may express ourselves upon any subject of vital interest—we give men the right to their own opinions, and everywhere it is understood that a man has a perfect right to be wrong in his conclusions as well as right

NO more striking proof of change is found than in the fact that recently we have found public opinion forcing arbitration upon men who "had nothing to arbitrate." The men who owned those rock-ribbed fortresses and castles on the Rhine once had nothing to arbitrate. They took their position and held it—but not forever.

It is the people who rule, for strong men are only strong as they are backed up by the people. When the people think deeply and think sanely, and vibrate together, "the rulers" quickly fall into line

And now it has come to pass that people object to being used as stones and sticks to fight the battle of

the seeming strong. Their quibbles, quarrels, feuds and selfish struggles for power are none of ours. Helen and Paris may elope for all of us—that is their affair —and all Priam's loud calls of " To arms ! " fall upon the ears of men who have work to do at home.
❧ And here is a prophecy : In America conscription will never again be attempted. It has gone and gone forever. Arbitrate your differences—you both are right, and both are wrong. Fighting may test which side is the stronger, but not which side is more nearly right ☙ ☙

Calm deliberation will bring us near to Truth, but heat, anger, strife and war only drive her far afield. HAT the world is fast getting rid of the thought of physical strife is very sure, but let us not plume ourselves too much about it—we have a long way to travel yet. The idea of danger is strong upon us ; we have not gotten rid of the thought of struggle and strife ☙ ☙

" Society is in league against all of its members," wrote Emerson. And as once every clan was at enmity with every other clan, and every nation at war with every other nation, so yet does man in his heart distrust every other man. Suspicion, hate, jealousy, apprehension—all forms of fear—fill the hearts of men. The newspapers that have the largest circulation are those whose columns bulge with tales of disgrace, defeat and death. If joy comes to you the news will go unheralded, but should great grief, woe, disgrace, and hopes dashed upon the rocks be your portion, the wires will flash the news from continent to continent, and flaring headlines will tell the tale to people who never before heard of you ☙ ☙

ND all this goes to prove that it is a satisfaction to a vast number of people to hear of the downfall of others—it is a gratification to them to know that disaster has caught some one in the toils. The newspapers print what the people want, and thus

does the savage still swing his club and flourish his
spear

Ride in any American city, on the morning cars,
or upon any suburban train, and note the greedy grab
for the daily papers, and observe how the savory
morsels of scandal are rolled beneath the tongue. So
long as men glory in the defeat of other men, it is a
perversion of words to call this a Christian land.
But as clan once united with clan, and nation with
nation for a mutual protection, so do a goodly number
of people now recognize that men should unite with
men—not only in deeds, but in thought—for a mutual
benefit

To hold a thought of fear is to pollute the mind—
prejudice poisons, jealousy is a thing to zealously
avoid, and hate hurts worst the one who hates

AND the argument is this: So long as the thought
of rivalry is rife, and jealousy, fear, unrest and
hate are in the mind, we are still in the savage state.
❡ War robs men of their divine birthright, and turns
the tide of being back to chaos. You have so much
life—what will you do with it? If you lose it pulling
down other lives, you shall soon forfeit your own. And
even though you do not do an overt destructive act,
the thought of hate and fear reacts to your disadvantage, honeycombs the will and tends to destroy the
tissue of your body

Every school, factory, store and institution is to a
degree a hotbed of strife, jealousy and heart-burning.
Plot and counterplot fill the air. There is disappointment, discontent and apprehension everywhere. The
employees or helpers unite in friendships, and all
exclusive friendships breed factions, feuds, and tend
in the end to separate men. Beware of chums—they
only pool their weaknesses. He is strongest who stands
alone. Be a friend to all—stand by all—speak well
of all. If you lend a willing ear to any man's troubles,
you make them your own, and you do not lessen his.

By listening to tales of trouble you absorb trouble—
that is to say, you take discord into your being. And
the more discord you have in your cosmos, the weaker
are you—you are that much nearer death and dissolution. The more harmony you possess, the stronger
you are. The institution that succeeds in a masterly
way is the one that has at its head a man of strong,
stern and inflexible purpose. The more this man keeps
his eye on the central idea—the more he focuses on
his work—and keeps fear and hesitation and distrust
at bay, the more sure he is to win.

The soil is bounteous, the mountains full of precious
gifts, the opportunity to work is everywhere. Society
needs men who can serve it—humanity wants help,
the help of the strong, sensible, unselfish man. The
age is crying for men—civilization wants men who
can save it from dissolution ; and those who can benefit
it most are those who are freest from prejudice, hate,
revenge, whim and fear

TWO thousand years ago lived One who saw the
absurdity of a man loving only his friend—He
saw that this meant faction ; lines of social cleavage,
with ultimate discord ; and so He painted the truth
large, and declared we should love our enemies and
do good to those who might despitefully use us. He
was one with the erring, the weak, the insane, the
poor, and so free was He from prejudice and fear
that we have confounded Him with Deity, and con-
fused Him with the maker of the worlds. He was one
set apart, because He had no competition in the matter
of love. It is not necessary for us to leave our task
and pattern our lives after His ; but if we can imitate
His divine patience and keep thoughts of discord out
of our lives, we, too, can work such wonders that men
will indeed truthfully say that we are the Sons of God.

There is n't so much rivalry here—be patient,
generous, kind, even to foolish folk and absurd people.
Do not extricate yourself—be one with all—be uni-

versal. So little competition is there in this line that
any man, in any walk of life, who puts jealousy, hate
and fear behind him, can make himself distinguished.
And all good things shall be his—they will flow to
him. Power gravitates to the man who can use it—
and love is the highest form of power that exists. If
ever a man shall live who has infinite power, he will
be found to be one who has infinite love. And the
way to be patient and generous—to free yourself
from discord—is not to take a grip on yourself and
strive to be kind—not that. Just don't think much
about it, but lose yourself in your work 🙖 🙖

DO not go out of your way to do good, but do good
whenever it comes your way. Men who make a
business of doing good to others are apt to hate others
in the same occupation. Simply be filled with the
thought of good, and it will radiate—you do not have
to bother about it, any more than you need trouble
about your digestion. Do not be disturbed about
saving your soul—it will be saved if you make it
worth saving. Do your work. Think the good. And
evil, which is a negative condition, shall be swallowed
up by good. Think no evil; and if you think only good,
you will think no evil. Life is a search for power. To
have power you must have life, and life in abundance.
And life in abundance comes only through great love.

⊂⊃

Do not separate yourself from plain people; be one
with all—be universal 🙖 🙖

⊂⊃

The test at the last is this: What effect has a man's
life had on civilization? 🙖 🙖

⊂⊃

No man can make others think unless he himself is
a thinker 🙖 🙖

⊂⊃

The outcome of the battle is of no importance—
but how did you fight? 🙖 🙖

'HERE has recently been erected on the campus of The Roycroft Shop, a statue of Michelangelo. The figure is of heroic size, in bronze, and was cast by Gorham and Company, of Providence

The original of this statue was a commission from the United States Government. The result can now be seen in the Congressional Library at Washington. ⁋ The statue at Roycroft, however, is not a replica of the one in Washington—it is better than that— it is an evolution from it

Every great masterpiece is an evolution, be it a statue, a poem, a painting—or a man.

⁋ Whether Paul Bartlett will ever make a nobler and more subtle " Michelangelo " than this last, remains to be seen. As it is, a critic has said of it as Ruskin said of a painting by Turner, " One can not, by any flight of the imagination, suggest how it could be improved upon."

Here we get a portrait of a sculptor by a sculptor. Michelangelo was the greatest artist the world has ever seen, and there be those who aver, and not without reason, that Paul Bartlett is the greatest of living sculptors.

⁋ I hope that my love and admiration for Paul Bartlett, the man, does not blind me to any possible defects in his art, but it seems to me that in this Roycroft " Michelangelo," Bartlett has done a piece of work— inspired work—that will live as one of the world's masterpieces

⁋ Michelangelo was a primitive genius. He had no ancestors, and he left no successors. The art of the world is mostly imitative. Just as our religions are not spontaneous inspirations, but inheritances from the dead, so are our ideals of art and beauty a legacy from the outworn past

And as Michelangelo gave us the greatness and grandeur of Moses, the Liberator, in living marble, so has Paul Bartlett caught the nobility and power of Michelangelo, the Super-Artist, in bronze.

¶ No man or woman who has lived and loved, suffered and aspired, hoped and struggled, can look upon Bartlett's " Michelangelo," without being hushed into silence

The very young, the heedless, the vain, the self-centered, the smug, the calloused, will pass it by. But all those who through toil and pain have entered into citizenship in the Celestial City of Fine Minds, will pause and pay this noble and beauteous bronze the tribute of a sigh

CLOTHED in the garb of labor, his face furrowed and seamed ; the nose mutilated by the crashing blow from Torrigiano's hammer ; the luster of the eyes dimmed by toil and tears ; the pose one of patience, courage and heroic strength—there he stands, chisel in hand, absorbed, proud, erect and defiant.

¶ He seems to be looking at an imaginary statue—an uncompleted statue—perhaps the " Moses." The sunken cheeks tell of years of yearning and aspiration, but the swelling muscles in the legs and arms, the lean and corded neck, the deep chest, the splendid hands—the big, bony, manly, competent, helpful, honest hands—speak of one from whom time has taken slight toll. Thus has the artist combined for us the effects of age, wisdom, experience, a subtle sense of pensive melancholy, and a persistence that never tires ; so also does he give us the feeling of supreme strength and exultant health.

¶ As Moses lived one hundred twenty years, and his natural strength was unabated, so might this man be of a like age

With it all goes that great look of disinterestedness which only bronze or death can typify.

¶ On the face of the dead we often see this divine aloofness

Life carries with it anxiety, pain, desire and apprehension, but the last enemy having been met, ignoble men sometimes suddenly become possessed of great dignity ❧ ❧

The craft and greed are gone—their pettiness and peevishness are spent—they ask for nothing.

❡ You can neither bribe nor buy them; your flattery falls on ears no longer alert for praise; your approbation or blame alike are vain; the muscles, freed from pain and fear, relax into the suggestion of a smile, and the peace that passeth understanding—the possession of the dead alone—steals over all ❧ ❧

No wonder that the voices of the living are hushed into whispers in the presence of the majesty of death.

❡ So into the bronze that endureth forever, Paul Bartlett has graven the majesty of life in death, and hope and love in all, and with the self-sufficiency that comes from having given all, now has won all.

❡ Michelangelo faces the East!

The years will pass and be counted into the eternity that lies behind: the breezes of Spring will blow— birds will mate and flowers bloom—Summer will come with scorching sun; Autumn will follow with falling leaves; the snows of Winter will sift and fall; generations will be born, live and die—but there, riveted to the rock, tenoned and mortised in granite, this man will stand oblivious and indifferent to the centuries as they stalk by. He faces the East! ❧ ❧

◦━◦

Love is all. I say to you that man has not sufficient imagination to exaggerate the importance of love.

◦━◦

That man only is really worthy to be called Educated who is able to do at least one useful thing well; who has a sympathy which is universal, and who is in the line of evolution ❧ ❧

◦━◦

The selfish wish to govern is often mistaken for a holy zeal in the cause of humanity ❧ ❧

I N that wonderful impressionistic painting, " Waiting," we see a woman seated on the sands of the sea ; the woman's back is toward us and over her head is held tightly a tattered shawl. A bulge to the right of the shawl tells that within her arms the woman holds a child. You do not see the child, yet you know 't is there—hugged closely to the mother's heart. You do not see the woman's face, but you know that she is looking out upon the restless, tossing tide ; and you know that she is waiting for a ship that will never return. However, if you have never waited for a footstep that shall never come, and listened for a voice that shall never more be heard, the picture will mean little to you. But if you have lived and suffered and known and felt, you will see despair written large across the dull, threatening gray of that sky ; and wrecked hopes in every curve and line of the angry waves; and the long monotonous stretch of yellow sands will speak to you of a hope that never dies, and the bulge in the shawl will tell of a love that is stronger than death

To be gay your life must be one that suffers no surfeit

There is only one thing worth praying for, and that is to be in the line of evolution

J UST as long as trade was trickery, business barter, commerce finesse, government exploitation, slaughter honorable, and murder a fine art; when religion was superstition, piety the worship of a fetish and education a clutch for honors, there was small hope for the race. But with the supremacy of science, the introduction of the one-price system in business, and the gradually growing conviction that honesty is man's most valuable asset, we behold light at the end of the tunnel

God does n't need us so much as His children do;
so let us help them, and let God shift for Himself.

Abstinence is not enough : you must make life positive
—do something

ORK is for the worker! Work is for the
worker! Did I say that once before? Very
well, I think I will print it twelve times a
year. Work is for the worker!
¶ We become robust only through exercise, and
every faculty of the mind and every attribute of the
soul grows strong only as it is exercised. So you had
better exercise only your highest and best, else you
will give strength to habits or inclinations that may
master you, to your great disadvantage. Work is for
the worker, and work is a blessing. The Bible does
not teach that—it teaches that work is a form of
punishment, and only a very grim necessity at best.
Even the New Testament is full of sympathy and
condolences for the bearer of burdens and those who
are heavy laden. There is much about looking forward
to a sweet rest in Heaven, but not a word about getting
onto your job. Heaven, to many, is a long rest, and
no religion has ever pictured a paradise where happiness came through useful activity. No wonder that
the jolly, jolly mariners, sitting forevermore upon the
windless, glassy floor, grew aweary of the monotony.
¶ There are no glad congratulations in the Bible for
the man who has found his work—only pity. And
then, where in Holy Writ do you find any statement of
this patent truth : There is a certain amount of work
to do in the world, and the reason some folks have
to work from daylight to dark is because some other
folks never work at all? It was a Philistine who had
to discover and voice that. A certain amount of work
is very necessary to growth. Work is a blessing, not a
curse, because through it we acquire strength—

strength of mind and strength of body. To carry a responsibility gives a sense of power. Men who have borne responsibility know how to carry it, and with heads erect, and the burden well adjusted to their shoulders, they move steadily forward. Those who do not know better, drag their burdens behind them with a rope

There is no reformation in degradation

The more one knows, the more one simplifies

THE civilized world is just now experiencing a great mental and spiritual awakening. It is an awakening similar to that of Greece in the time of Pericles; of Rome in the time of Augustus; of Italy in the time of Michelangelo—say, in the year Fourteen Hundred Ninety-two, when Columbus set sail and the invention of printing gave learning to the people

We are living in the greatest time the world has ever seen—in a time that will live in history as The Great American Renaissance. Some will call it " The Age of Electricity." Others will call it " The Age of Concrete."

Beginning with a shower of inventions and discoveries about Eighteen Hundred Seventy-six, this awakening has extended to every domain of human thought and endeavor. The vast changes, for example, in the matter of transportation, only symbol the changes that have occurred in our ideals of right and wrong.

Within thirty years' time we have evolved: a new science of Education; a new science of Medicine; a new science of Theology; a new science of Penology, and a new science of Business

EMERSON defines commerce as the taking of things from where they are plentiful to where they are needed

Business is that field of endeavor which undertakes to supply the materials to humanity that life demands.
⟨ Until recently we spoke of Theology, Law and Medicine as " The Three Learned Professions." ⟩⟨ If we use the phrase now, it is only in a Pickwickian sense—for we realize that there are fifty-seven varieties of learned men ⟩⟨
Of all professions the greatest and most important is that of commerce or business. Medicine and law have their specialties—a dozen each—but business has ten thousand specialties or divisions.
⟨ The best lawyers are now businessmen, and their work is to keep the commercial craft in a safe channel, where it will not split on the rocks of litigation, nor founder in the shallows of misunderstanding ⟩⟨ Every good lawyer will tell you this: " To make money you must satisfy your customers." ⟩⟨
HE greatest change in business came with the One-Price System. This has all been brought about since the Civil War. The old idea was for the seller to get as much as he possibly could for everything he sold. Short weight, short count and inferiority in quality were considered quite right and proper. When you bought a dressed turkey from a farmer, if you did not discover the stone inside the turkey when you weighed it and paid for it, there was no redress. The laugh was on you. And moreover a legal maxim, *caveat emptor*—" Let the buyer beware! " —made larceny legally safe. Dealers in clothing guaranteed neither fit nor quality, and everything you accepted, once wrapped up and in your hands, was yours beyond recall—" Let the buyer beware! " ⟩⟨
FEW hundred years ago business was transacted mostly through fairs, ships, and by peddlers. Your merchant at that time was a peripatetic rogue, who reduced prevarication to a system.
⟨ The booth gradually evolved into a store, with the methods and customs of the irresponsible keeper

intact; the merchants cheated their neighbors and chuckled in glee until their neighbors cheated them, which of course they did. Then they cursed each other, began again and did it all over. John Quincy Adams tells of a certain deacon, who kept a store near Boston, who always added in the year 1775 at the top of the column, as seventeen dollars and seventy-five cents.

The amount of misery, grief, disappointment, shame, distress, woe, suspicion and hate caused by a system which wrapped up one thing when the buyer expected another, and took advantage of his innocence and ignorance as to quality and value, can not be computed in figures. Suffice it to say, that duplicity in trade has had to go. The self-preservation of the race demanded honesty, square dealing, one price to all. The change came only after a struggle ♠ ♠ But we have gotten thus far, that the man who cheats in trade is tabu. Honesty as a business asset is fully recognized. If you would succeed in business you can not afford to sell a man something he does not want; neither can you afford to disappoint him in quality any more than in count ♠ ♠

OTHER things being equal, the merchant who has the most friends will make the most money. We make money out of our friends, for our enemies will not deal with us. To make a sale and acquire an enemy is poor policy. To a peddler or a man who ran a booth at a bazaar or fair, it was "get your money now or never." Buyer and seller were at war. One transaction and they never met again. The air was full of hate and suspicion, and the customs of the road were refined to a point where hypocrisy and untruth took the place of violence.

The buyer was as bad as the seller—if he could buy below cost he boasted of it. To catch a merchant who had to have money was glorious—we smote him hip and thigh. Later, we discovered that being strangers he took us in ♠ ♠

HE One-Price System has come as a necessity, since it reduces the friction of life and protects the child or simple person in the selection of things needed, just the same as if the buyer were an expert in values and a person who could strike back if imposed upon. Safety, peace and decency demanded the One-Price System

When we reach the point where we see that all men are brothers, we will have absolute honesty and one price.

And so behold we find the Government making favoritism in trade a crime and enforcing the One-Price System by law. And just remember this: Law is the crystallization of public opinion, and no law that is not backed up by the will of the people can be enforced

As we grow better we have better laws.

In Kansas City the other week three men were fined forty thousand dollars each for cutting prices. They were railroadmen, and railroadmen have only one thing to sell, and that is transportation. To cut the price on it and sell to some at a less figure than to others is now considered not only immoral, but actually criminal

The world moves. And this change in the methods of business and in our mental attitude toward trade has all grown out of a dimly perceived but deeply felt belief in the Brotherhood of Man, or the Solidarity of the Race; also, in the further belief that life in all its manifestations is divine

HEREFORE, he who ministers to the happiness and well-being of the life of another is a priest and is doing God's work. Men must be fed, they must be clothed, they must be housed. It is quite as necessary that you should eat good food, as that you should read good books, hear good music, hear good sermons, or look upon beautiful pictures.

The necessary is the sacred. There are no menial

tasks. " He that is the greatest among you shall be your servant." The physical reacts upon the spiritual and the spiritual on the physical, and rightly understood are one and the same thing.

⁋ We change men by changing their environment, that is, the conditions under which they live ๑๑ ๑๑ Commerce changes the environment and gives us a better society. To supply good water, better sanitary appliances, better heating apparatus, better food, served in a more dainty way—these are all tasks worthy of the highest intelligence and devotion that can be brought to bear upon them, and every Christian preacher in the world today so recognizes, believes and preaches ๑๑ ๑๑

We are ceasing to separate the secular from the sacred.

⁋ That is sacred which serves ๑๑ ๑๑

Once, a businessman was a person who not only throve by taking advantage of the necessities of people, but who banked on their ignorance of values. But all wise men know now that the way to help yourself is to help humanity.

⁋ We benefit ourselves only as we benefit others. And the recognition of these truths is what has today placed the businessman at the forefront of the learned professions—he ministers to the necessities of humanity ๑๑ ๑๑

My opinion is, that the great business houses of the country are influencing civilization for good to an extent that only the children of the coming generation will realize—and realizing, will thank us ๑๑ ๑๑

Success is voltage under control—keeping one hand on the transformer of your cosmic kilowatts ๑๑ ๑๑

Let us get free from fetish, be it religious, medical or pedagogic ๑๑ ๑๑

A man possessing Initiative is a Creator ๑๑ ๑๑

T is perfectly safe to say that ninety-nine men out of a hundred, in civilized countries, are opposed to war *⊛ ⊛*

Savages like to go to war; we do not *⊛ ⊛* We are farmers, mechanics, merchants, manufacturers and teachers, and all we ask is the privilege of attending to our own business. We own our homes, love our friends, are devoted to our families, and do not interfere with our neighbors any more than is necessary.

⟨ We have work to do, and wish to work while it is called the day. We recognize that life is short, and the night cometh. Leave us alone! *⊛ ⊛*

⟨ But they will not—these demagogues, politicians and rogues intent on the strenuous life. We wish to be peaceable and want to be kind, but they say this life is warfare and we must fight.

⟨ Of course we would fight to protect our homes; but our homes are not threatened, nor our liberties, either, save by the men who chew the ubiquitous clove and insist on the strenuous life.

⟨ Leave us alone! *⊛ ⊛* We wish to pay off the mortgages on our houses, to educate our children, to work, to read, to meditate, to prepare for old age and quick-coming, cool, all-enfolding death *⊛ ⊛* But they will not leave us alone—these men who insist on governing us and living off our labor. They tax us, eat our substance, conscript us when they wish, draft our boys into their wars to fight farmers whose chief offenses are that they wear trousers that bag at the knee and cultivate an objectionable style of whisker.

⟨ They call themselves the superior class. They live off the labor of our hands. They essay the task of governing us for a consideration. They deceive us— this superior class—they hoodwink us; they betray us; they bulldoze us by the plea of patriotism *⊛ ⊛* They deceive us, and oh, the infamy and the shame of it! they deceive us in the name of the bleeding

Christ—the gentle Christ whose love embraced the
world, and whose pitying eyes look down upon us
from a cross—the Christ who distinctly taught that
war was wrong, and that the only rule of life should be
to do unto others as we would be done by

FEW people, comparatively, think for themselves,
and so this deception, being backed up by many
alleged educated people, acts as a hypnosis on the
many, and being peaceably disposed, they accept it.
❧ And now, this superior class, intent on taxing us,
may declare war and maintain standing armies. And
so we find Canada lusting for a navy. All the myriads
of men who live off the government depend upon the
government to tax the many, and in order to tax
successfully, standing armies are maintained
The plea that the army is needed for the protection
of the country is fraud and pretense.
❧ The French Government affrights the people by
telling them that the Germans are ready and anxious
to fall upon them; the Russians fear the British; the
British fear everybody; and now in America, we are
told we must increase our navy and add to our army
because Europe may at any moment combine with
Japan and wipe us off the Rand-McNally map.
❧ This is fraud and untruth. The plain people in
France, Germany, England and America are opposed
to war. We only wish to be let alone. Men with wives,
children, sweethearts, homes, aged parents, horses,
cattle, crops and flowers, do not want to go off and
fight some one. We are peaceable and wish to be kind.
We fear war: we hate it
We would like to obey the Golden Rule.
❧ But the superior class will not have it so—they
pass conscription laws over in Europe and use the
army thus conscripted to conscript other men

WAR is the sure result of the existence of armed
men. That country which maintains a large
standing army will sooner or later have a war on hand.

The man who prides himself on fisticuffs is going, some day, to meet a man who considers himself the better man, and they will test the issue.

❡ Germany and England have no issue save a desire to see who is the better man. They have fought once —more than that, several times—and they will fight again. Not that the people want to fight, but the superior class fan fright into fury and make men think they must fight to protect their homes.

❡ So the people who wish to follow the teachings of Christ are not allowed to do so, but are taxed, outraged, deceived by " kinks "—by the superior class who demand that we shall lead the strenuous life, when all we ask is the privilege of doing our work.

❡ Christ taught humility, meekness, the forgiveness of one's enemies, and that to kill was wrong. The Bible teaches men not to swear, but the superior class swear us on the Bible which they do not believe ⚬ ⚬

THE question is, How are we to relieve ourselves of these cormorants who toil not, but who are clothed in broadcloth and blue, with brass buttons and many costly accouterments; who feed upon our substance, and for whom we delve and dig?

❡ Shall we fight them? ⚬ ⚬
No, we do not believe in bloodshed; and besides that they have the guns and the money, and they would use these guns bought by money they never earned —taxed out of us—they would use these guns and use their army to kill us off speedily.

❡ They have the money and the guns and can hold out longer than we ⚬ ⚬
But who composes this army that they would order to fire upon us? ⚬ ⚬
Why, our neighbors and brothers—deceived into the idea that they are doing God's service by protecting their country from its enemies.

❡ Thus do they siphon our resources and turn our true brothers upon us to subdue and humiliate us.

You can not send a telegram to your wife, nor an express package to your friend, nor draw a check for your grocer, in time of war, until you first pay the tax to maintain armed men who can quickly be used to kill you; and who surely will imprison you if you do not pay.

❡ An army is a menace ◆◆

The only relief lies in education. Educate men not to fight, and that it is wrong to kill. Teach them the Golden Rule, and yet again teach them the Golden Rule. Silently defy this fuss, feathers and fury idea, by refusing to bow down to the fetish of bullets. Cease supporting the Hobsons who cry for war, and spout patriotism for a consideration. Let them go to work as we do ◆◆

AMERICA can never become the Ideal Republic —the home and refuge of all that is best in art and science, the fulfilment of the dreams of seers and prophets—until we cease modeling our political policy after the rotting monarchies of Europe ◆◆ Force expends itself and dies. Every army is marching to its death; nothing but a skull and a skeleton fill helmet and cuirass; the aggressor is overcome by the poison of his pride; victory is only another name for defeat—but the spirit of gentleness and of love is eternal. Only by building on that can we hope as a nation to live ◆◆

Leave us alone !

❡ We wish to do our work. We wish to beautify our homes, to educate our children, to love our neighbors.

❡ Leave us alone ! ◆◆

Your false cry of danger and " Wolf! Wolf! " shall not alarm us. We pay your war taxes of a million dollars a day, only because we have to, and we will pay no more and no longer than we have to ◆◆ We will educate men ◆◆

And all the time our silent influence will be going out. We will educate men into the thought that the life of peace and good-will is better than the strenuous life of strife, bloodshed and red war. "Peace on Earth!"—it can only come when men do away with armies, and are willing to do unto other men as they would be done by.

❡ Leave us alone!

It is a great blessing to be born into a family where strict economy of time and money is necessary. The idea that nothing shall be wasted and that each child must carve out for himself a career is a thrice-blessed privilege. Rich parents are an awful handicap to youth: few, indeed, there be who have the strength to stand prosperity

Mother Nature is kind, and if she deprives us of one thing she gives us another—happiness seems to be meted out to each and all in equal portions

WE take an interest in the lives of others, because when we think of another we always imagine our relation to him. Then, too, other lives are to a degree repetitions of our own life. There are certain things that come to every one, and the rest we think might have happened to us, and may yet. So, as we read, we unconsciously slip into the life of the other man and confuse our identity with his. To put ourselves in his place is the only way to understand and appreciate him and so enrich our own lives. It is imagination that gives us this faculty of transmigration of souls; and to have imagination is to be universal; not to have it is to be provincial

We pay for everything we receive—nay, all things can be attained if we but pay the price. One of the very few Emancipated Men in America bought redemption from the bondage of selfish ambition at a terrible price

ALL men recognize in their hearts that they must have the good-will of some other men. To be separated from your kind means death, and to have their good-will is life—and this desire for sympathy and this alone shapes conduct. We are governed by public opinion, and until we regard all mankind as our friends, and all men as brothers, so long will men combine in sects and cliques, and keep the millennium of Peace and Good-Will a dim and distant thing

I WISH to be simple, honest, frank, natural, clean in body and mind, unaffected—ready to say, " I do not know," if it be so, to meet all men on an absolute equality—to face any obstacle and meet every difficulty unabashed and unafraid—to cultivate the hospitable mind and the receptive heart

THERE is only one thing in the world—and that is Divine Energy. Herbert Spencer defined dirt as useful matter in the wrong place, and so we may say that the bad man is a good man who has misdirected his energies. When we once acknowledge that this is God's world, and that we are His children, there is no high or low in human service. We will pity, but we will not blame

Business is eminently a divine calling. We do not differentiate it from any other calling, no matter how noble, how beautiful, how altruistic.

There is a romance of business, and a heroism of business, that literature will yet take note of. The antique phrase about the three learned professions will have to go. There are fifty-seven varieties of learned men. To do your work with a whole heart up to your highest and best is an eminently religious motive

And when in doubt, to mind your own business is eminently ethical and wise

Enlightened self-interest endorses the Golden Rule.

IT is well to realize that it is the patient man who wins. To do your work, and not be anxious about results, is the best way to go after and secure a big result. This does not mean that you are to sell yourself as a slave. If your present position does not give you an opportunity to grow, and you know of a better place—why, go to the better place, by all means. The point I make is simply this: If you care to remain in a place, you can never better your position by striking for higher wages or favors of any kind

The employee who drives a sharp bargain and is fearful that he will not get all he earns, never will. There are men who are set on a hair-trigger—always ready to make demands when there is a rush of work, and who threaten to walk out if their demands are not acceded to. The demands may be acceded to, but this kind of help is always marked on the time-book for dismissal, when work gets scarce and business dull. Such men are out of employment about half the time, and the curious part of it is, they never know why. As a matter of pure worldly wisdom—just cold-blooded expediency—if I were an employee I would never mention wages. I would focus right on my work and do it

The man that endures is the man that wins. I would never harass my employer with inopportune propositions. I would give him peace, and I would lighten his burdens. Personally I would never be in evidence, unless it were positively necessary—my work would tell its own story

The cheerful worker who goes ahead and makes himself a necessity to the business—never adding to the burden of his superiors—will sooner or later get all that is his due, and more. He will not only get pay for his work, but he will get a bonus for his patience and another for his good-cheer.

The man who makes a strike to have his wages

raised from fifteen to eighteen dollars a week may get the increase, and then his wages will stay there. Had he kept quiet and just been intent on making himself a five-thousand-dollar man, he might have gravitated straight to a five-thousand-dollar desk. I would not risk spoiling my chances for a large promotion by asking for a small one. And it is but a trite truism to say that no man ever received a large promotion because he demanded it—he got it because he could fill the position, and for no other reason. Ask the man who receives a ten-thousand-dollar-a-year salary how he managed to bring it about, and he will tell you that he just did his work as well as he could. Never did such a man go on a strike. The most successful strike is a defeat; and had this man been a striker by nature, sudden and quick to quarrel, jealous of his rights, things would have conspired to keep him down and under. I do not care how clever he may be or how well educated, his salary would have been eighteen a week at the furthest, with a very tenuous hold upon his job ⁕ ⁕

HE that endureth unto the end shall be saved. At hotels the man who complains is the man against whom the servants are ever in league; and the man who complains most is the man who has the least at home ⁕ ⁕

If you are defamed, let time vindicate you—silence is a thousand times better than explanation. Explanations do not explain. Let your life be its own excuse for being—cease all explanations and all apologies, and just live your life. By minding your own business, you give others an opportunity to mind theirs; and depend upon it, the great souls will appreciate you for this very thing.

I am not sure that absolute, perfect justice comes to everybody in this world; but I do know that the way to get justice is not to be too anxious about it. As love goes to those who do not lie in wait for it,

so does the great reward gravitate to the patient man.
It is but common to believe in him who believes in
himself, but if you would do aught uncommon, believe
yet in him who does not believe in himself

Man creates both his god and his devil in his own
image. His god is himself at his best, and his devil
himself at his worst

Every man measures others by himself—he has only
one standard. When a man ridicules certain traits
in other men, he ridicules himself. How would he
know other men were contemptible did he not look
into his own heart and there see the hateful thing?

THE family whose members work together succeeds. And the success of this family is in exact
ratio to the love that cements them into a whole.
Of course, the more intellect you can mix with this
mutual love the better; but intellect alone is too cold
to fuse the dumb indifference of inanimate things
and command success.

Love is the fulfilling of life's law

The big merchant nowadays is the one who can keep
the peace between his department heads.

The concern that succeeds is the one where feud,
fuss and folly are kiboshed, and all hands work
together for a mutual end

The man who can forget his own personal feelings
and fuse his own interests with those of the house
is a sure winner. Nothing can hold such a one back.
Sanity shows itself in co-operation. Power does not
mean what you alone can do—it means what you
can get others to do by welding them into a whole
so they will work together

To be famous is to be slandered by the people who do
not know you

YMPATHY, Knowledge and Poise seem to be the three ingredients that are most needed in forming the Gentleman. I place these elements according to their value. No man is great who does not have Sympathy plus, and the greatness of men can safely be gauged by their sympathies. Sympathy and imagination are twin sisters. Your heart must go out to all men : the high, the low, the rich, the poor, the learned, the unlearned, the good, the bad, the wise and the foolish—it is necessary to be one with them all, else you can never comprehend them. Sympathy !—it is the touchstone to every secret, the key to all knowledge, the open sesame of all hearts. Put yourself in the other man's place : then you will know why he thinks certain things and does certain deeds. Put yourself in his place, and your blame will dissolve itself into pity, and your tears will wipe out the record of his misdeeds. The saviors of the world have simply been men with wondrous Sympathy. But Knowledge must go with Sympathy, else the emotions will become maudlin and pity may be wasted on a poodle instead of on a child ; on a field-mouse instead of on a human soul. Knowledge in use is wisdom, and wisdom implies a sense of values—you know a big thing from a little one, a valuable fact from a trivial one. Tragedy and comedy are simply questions of value ; a little misfit in life makes us laugh, a great one is tragedy and cause for expression of grief ⚘ ⚘

POISE is the strength of body and strength of mind to control your Sympathy and your Knowledge. Unless you control your emotions, they run over and you stand in the slop. Sympathy must not run riot, or it is valueless and tokens weakness instead of strength. In every hospital for nervous disorders are to be found many instances of this loss of control. The individual has Sympathy but not Poise, and therefore his life is worthless to himself and to the world.

⁋ He symbols inefficiency, and not helpfulness. Poise reveals itself more in voice than in words; more in thought than in action; more in atmosphere than in conscious life. It is a spiritual quality, and is felt more than it is seen. It is not a matter of bodily size, nor of bodily attitude, nor attire, nor of personal comeliness; it is a state of inward being, and of knowing your cause is just. And so you see it is a great and profound subject after all, great in its ramifications, limitless in extent, implying the entire science of right living. I once met a man who was deformed in body and little more than a dwarf, but who had such Spiritual Gravity—such Poise—that to enter a room where he was, was to feel his presence and acknowledge his superiority. To allow Sympathy to waste itself on unworthy objects is to deplete one's life forces. To conserve is the part of wisdom, and reserve is a necessary element in all good literature, as well as in everything else ⚬ ⚬

POISE being the control of our Sympathy and Knowledge, it implies a possession of these attributes, for without Sympathy and Knowledge you have nothing to control but your physical body. To practise Poise as a mere gymnastic exercise, or study in etiquette, is to be self-conscious, stiff, preposterous and ridiculous. Those who cut such fantastic tricks before high heaven as make angels weep, are men void of Sympathy and Knowledge trying to cultivate Poise. Their science is a mere matter of what to do with arms and legs. Poise is a question of spirit controlling flesh, heart controlling attitude.

⁋ Get Knowledge by coming close to Nature. That man is the greatest who best serves his kind. Sympathy and Knowledge are for use—you acquire that you may give out; you accumulate that you may bestow. And as God has given unto you the sublime blessings of Sympathy and Knowledge, there will come to you a wish to reveal your gratitude by giving them out again; for the wise man is aware that we retain spiritual qualities only as we give them away. Let your light shine. To him that hath shall be given. The exercise of wisdom brings wisdom; and at the last the infinitesimal quantity of man's knowledge, compared with the Infinite, and the smallness of man's Sympathy when compared with the source from which ours is absorbed, will evolve an abnegation and a humility that will lend a perfect Poise. The Gentleman is a man with perfect Sympathy, Knowledge and Poise

The voice is the true index of the soul. The clear, low, musical modulation belongs only to the men and women who think and feel. To possess a beautiful voice you must be genuine

The man who thinks out what he wants to do, and then works and works hard, will win, and no others do, or ever have, or can—God will not have it so.

AURICE MAETERLINCK says that one bee can never make honey, for the reason that a bee alone has no intelligence. Bees succeed only by working for the good of other bees. A single bee, separated from the hive, is absolutely helpless, yet a hive of bees has a very great and well-defined purpose and intelligence And this intelligence, Maeterlinck calls " The Spirit of the Hive."
Occasionally a bee will go off to the fields and come back gorged with honey, bringing nothing for the common stock, and this bee is quickly killed—stung to death by a self-appointed committee who sit on the case, and seem to consider that any bee which loses sight of the Spirit of the Hive and works for private good is sick, criminally insane, and can not be allowed longer to cumber good space.

¶ Now it is quite probable that if we could communicate with a bee, and ask it why it makes honey,
it would say, " I make honey because I choose to,"
just as Schopenhauer's boulder that rolled down hill
explained that it did so because it found a peculiar
pleasure and satisfaction in so doing

Men think they do certain things because they choose,
but the actual fact is they simply succumb to the
strongest attraction and call it choice. Is n't a man
under the domain of Natural Law just as much as
a bee? I think so. The recognition of this great truth
concerning the Solidarity of the Race marks a mental
epoch in the onward and upward march.

¶ With the bee, there is seemingly no evolution. The
Spirit of the Hive is fixed within narrow limits

With man, the Spirit of the Hive, or, if you prefer,
the Spirit of the Times, or the " Zeitgeist," is a constantly changing spiritual entity

Ancient Athens was made and controlled by fourteen
men. But these masterly men did not represent the
" Zeitgeist," nor were they strong enough to form
the Spirit of the Hive. They kept the many in subjection by the seductive ecclesiasticon—by shows,
spectacles, pomps, processions—and when danger at
home became imminent, the mob was diverted by
a foreign war

As long as the actual " Zeitgeist " of Greece was
saturated with religious fanaticism, superstition and
a childish tantrum tendency, the fourteen great men
of Athens, who for just thirty-six years sat on the lid,
were in a very dangerous position.

¶ The miracle is that they kept the beast down and
under long enough to build the temples and embellish
them with undying works of art. But they were
allowed to do their work, only by pandering to the
hoi polloi idea that the statues represented the gods
in Elysium, and that the Pantheon was for the habitation of Zeus Himself. To find the Deity in yourself

by producing Art was a truth the many could not comprehend, and when Praxiteles hinted at it, his temerity cost him his life

When Phidias placed his own portrait with that of Pericles upon a sacred shield, the glory that was Greece got its death sentence

The mumble of discontent grew into a roar. Socrates was passed the hemlock, and all the fourteen actual gods who made the glory were either killed or ostracized—robbed, disgraced, undone.

¶ The "Zeitgeist" had its way. Socrates, Euclid, Pericles, Phidias, Herodotus, Empedocles and Sophocles no more represented the Spirit of the Hive that existed at Athens, than Jesus represented the "Zeitgeist" of Jerusalem in the age of Augustus Savonarola, Tyndale, Ridley, Huss, Wyclif, George Wishart, were martyrs all to the Spirit of the Times. Yet Socrates, Jesus, Savonarola, Old John Brown —none of Freedom's illustrious dead died in vain. They died that we might live; and as a single drop of aniline will tint an entire cask of water, so has the blood of martyrs tinted the Spirit of the Times and given us a peculiar and different "Zeitgeist" from that which we would otherwise have had.

¶ The death of Lincoln created a sentiment which the living man could not, and which in time brought the entire South to an acknowledgment of the righteousness of his cause

The "Zeitgeist," not being able to understand or assimilate the doctrines of the seers and prophets, killed them. The man who preaches doctrines or performs deeds contrary to the Spirit of the Times is ever regarded as the enemy of the State, a menace to society, and is snuffed out. Whether he be above the law or below it matters not: the saviors of the world have always been hanged between thieves. This full, frank, free expression which we now enjoy is the precious legacy of a blood-stained past. And it is for us, the living, to see that these dead shall not have died in vain. Familiarity breeds indifference, if not contempt, and whether there be men now living as great as those fourteen in the time of Pericles, it would be difficult to determine

But this we know—we have a Spirit of the Hive now that is making honey honestly, and that, too, of a satisfactory quality, while the honey of Hymettus was made by that immortal fourteen who worked by stealth, plot, plan and connivance

Our Spirit of the Times is of a kind unequaled in history. We have thousands upon thousands of men and women who are thinking great and noble thoughts and doing great and splendid work.

¶ Our " Zeitgeist " is sensitive, restless, alert, impressionable, progressive and is making for righteousness. The man who can imagine a better religion than now exists is allowed to throw his vision on the screen, and he who can imagine a better government than we now have, is not hanged for his pains, but is allowed to express his dream

Public opinion rules. No law that is contrary to the " Zeitgeist " can be enforced. Judges translate and interpret the laws to suit the Spirit of the Times. Every man who speaks out loud and clear is tinting the " Zeitgeist." Every man who expresses what he honestly thinks is true is changing the Spirit of the Times. Thinkers help other people to think, for they formulate what others are thinking. No person writes or thinks alone—thought is in the air, but its expression is necessary to create a tangible Spirit of the Times. The value of a thinker who writes, or of a writer who thinks, is that he supplies arguments for the people and confirms all who are on his wire in opinions often before uttered

If your religion does not change you, then you had better change your religion

To associate only with the sociable, the witty, the wise, the brilliant, is a blunder—go among the plain, the uneducated, the stupid, and exercise your own wit and wisdom. You grow by giving

Taste is the test of the mind

I T is well to cultivate a mild, gentle and sympathetic voice, and the one way to secure a mild, gentle and sympathetic voice is to be mild, gentle and sympathetic. The voice is the index of the soul. Children do not pay much attention to your words—they judge of your intent by your voice. Your voice reassures. " My sheep know my voice." We judge each other more by voice than by language, for voice colors speech, and if your voice does not corroborate your words, doubt will follow. We are won or repelled by a voice. Your dog does not obey your words—he does, however, read your intents in your voice

The best way to cultivate the voice is not to think about it. Actions become regal only when they are unconscious; and the voice that convinces, that holds us captive, that leads and lures us on, is used by its owner unconsciously. Fix your mind on the thought, and the voice will follow. If you fear you will not be understood, you are losing the thought—it is slipping away from you—and you are thinking of the voice. Then your voice rises to a screech, subsides into a purr, or bellows like the vagrant winds. Anxiety and intent are shown, and your case is lost. If you fear you will not be understood, you probably will not. If the voice is allowed to come naturally, easily and gently, it will take on every tint and emotion of the mind. So, to get back to the place of beginning, my advice is this: The way to cultivate the voice is not to cultivate it

The voice is the sounding-board of the soul. God made

it right. If your soul is filled with truth, your voice
will vibrate with love, echo with sympathy, and fill
your hearers with the desire to do, to be and to become.
Your desire will be theirs. By their voices ye shall
know them

Peace—be still! Feel that, and then say it, and your
voice shall be a word of command that even the elements will obey

———

All suffering is caused by an obstacle in the path of
a force. See that you are not your own obstacle

———

Knowledge is the distilled essence of our intuitions,
corroborated by experience

———

LIFE is a voyage, and we are all sailing under
sealed orders

We plan, plot, scheme and arrange, and some
fine day Fate steps in and our dreams are
tossed into the yeasty deep.

¶ We grin and bear it—anyway we bear it: it is the
only thing to do

We swallow our disappointment, and the years pass,
as the years do, for that is a way things have. " And,"
says Doctor Draper, " over the evening of our dreams
there steals the thought that we have been used by
an Unknown Power for an Unseen End."

¶ Gabriel is always out of the particular thing we
want most, but he gives us something else just as
good—and the strange part is, it is just as good. We
never ask for loss, disappointment and grief, but these
are the packages often handed us.

¶ " Merciful Christ! Is this for me? " you cry

And Fate with shrouded head murmurs, " Yes, for
you," and turns away, and you are alone with your
bitterness

The years go by and there comes the earnest suspicion
that all is good—even the wormwood and the gall.

HE intent of all art is to communicate your feelings and emotions to another. Art has its rise in the need of human companionship. You feel certain thoughts and you strive to express them. You may express by music, by chiseled shapes, by painted canvas or by written words. At the last all art is one. And as you work, over against you sits another, who says, " Yes, yes, I understand ! "

The person I write for is a Woman.

At times she sits and looks at me, leaning forward, resting her chin on her hand. She smiles indulgently, and sometimes a little sadly, as my pen runs on. She knows me so perfectly that she often anticipates what I would say and thus saves me the trouble of writing. She guesses my every mood. This woman has suffered and known and felt, and that is why she understands. Her heart has been purified in the white fires of experience. She knows more than I, for she sees all around me, and any little effort to palm off a white lie, or the smallest attempt at insincerity or affectation brings only a wondering look, that stings me for a week and a day. I can say anything to her I choose : no topic is forbidden—she only asks that I be honest and frank. I always know when I have pleased this woman with the wistful eyes, for then she holds out her arms in a slow, sweeping gesture. She is the sister of my soul, and for her I write—because she understands

God will not look you over for medals, degrees and diplomas, but for scars

The man who acts his thought and thinks little of his act is the man who scores

Sincerity without sympathy is devilish ; learning without pity is to be avoided ; education without humor is preposterous

CHRISTIANITY is one thing; the religion of the Christ is another. Christianity is a river into which has flowed thousands upon thousands of streams, springs, brooks and rills, as well as the sewage of the cities. In the main it traces to Pagan Rome, united with the cool, rapid-running Rhone of Classic Greece. But the waters of placid-flowing Judaism, paralleling it, have always seeped through, and the fact that more than half of all Christianity prays to a Jewess, and that both Jesus and Paul were Jews, should not be forgotten.

The blood of all martyrs, rebels and revolters who have attempted to turn the current of this river has tinted its waters, and that its ultimate end is irrigation and not transportation is everywhere evident.

To keep religion a muddy, polluted, pestilential river, instead of allowing it to resolve itself into a million irrigating-ditches, has been the fight of the centuries. The trouble is that irrigation is not an end —it is just a beginning. Irrigation means constant and increasing effort, and priests and preachers have never prayed, "Give us this day our daily work." Their desire has been to be carried—to float with the tide, and he who floats is being carried downstream. Men who have tried to tap the stream and divert its waters to parched pastures have usually been caught and drowned in its depths. And this is what you call history

All new religions have their beginning in exactly this way—they are streams diverted from the parent waters, and the quality and influence of the new religion depend upon the depth of the new channel, its current and the territory which it traverses

AS before stated, most of the rebels were quickly caught. Moses rebelled from the religion of Egypt; Jesus rebelled from the religion of Moses; Paul rebelled from Judaism, adopted the name and led the little following of the martyred Savior; Con-

stantine seized the name and good-will, and destroyed
rebellion and competition by a master stroke of
fusion—when you can not successfully fight a thing,
all is not lost, you can still embrace it ; Savonarola was
an unsuccessful rebel from Constantine's composite
religion; Luther, Calvin and Knox successfully
rebelled; Henry the Eighth defied the Catholic
Church for reasons of his own and broke from it ;
Methodism and Congregationalism broke from both
the canal of John Knox and that of Queen Elizabeth
and her lamented father; Unitarianism in New
England was a revolt from the rule of the Congre-
gational Church, and Emerson and Theodore Parker
were rebels from Unitarianism

Emerson and Parker were irrigators. They gave
water to the land, instead of trying to keep it for a
fishpond. Neither one ever ordered the populace to
cut bait or fall in and drown. As a result we are
enriched with the flowers and fruit of their energies ;
they bequeathed to us something more than a threat
and a promise—they gave us the broad pastures, the
meadows, the fertile fields and the lofty trees with
their refreshing shade

Nature's methods are evolutionary, not revolutionary

Happy is the soldier who turns his battlefield over
to the poets

As a man grows in experience, his theories of conduct
become fewer

To know but one religion is not to know that one.

Calvinism has gone, but it had several advantages:
for one thing it gave you peace by supplying a Hell
for your rivals and enemies

I TRY to fix my thought on the good that is in every soul, and make my appeal to that. And the plan is a wise one, judged by results. It secures for you loyal helpers, worthy friends, gets the work done, aids digestion and tends to sleep o' nights. And I say to you that if you have never known the love, loyalty and integrity of a proscribed person, you have never known what love, loyalty and integrity are. I do not believe in governing by force, or threat, or any other form of coercion. I would not arouse in the heart of any of God's creatures a thought of fear, or discord, or hate, or revenge. I will influence men, if I can, but only by aiding them ☞ ☞

Mental dissolution: that condition where you are perfectly satisfied with your religion, education and government ☞ ☞

M AKING men live in three worlds at once—past, present and future—has been the chief harm organized religion has done. To drag your past behind you, and look forward to sweet rest in Heaven, is to spread the present very thin.

❡ The man who lives in the present, forgetful of the past and indifferent to the future, is the man of wisdom ☞ ☞

The best preparation for tomorrow's work is to do your work as well as you can today.

❡ The best preparation for a life to come is to live now and here ☞ ☞

Live right up to your highest and best! If you have made mistakes in the past, reparation lies not in regrets, but in thankfulness that you now know better.

❡ It is true that we are punished by our sins and not for them; it is true also that we are blessed and benefited by our sins. Having tasted the bitterness of error, we can avoid it. If we have withheld the kind word and the look of sympathy in the past, we can today

give doubly, and thus, in degree, redeem the past.
And we best redeem the past by forgetting it and losing ourselves in useful work

It is a great privilege to live. Thank God! there is
one indisputable fact: We are here!

No man should dogmatize except on the subject of
theology. Here he can take his stand, and by throwing
the burden of proof on the opposition, he is invincible.
We have to die to find out whether he is right

Things are ridiculous just as they differ from our
things, and men are preposterous just in proportion
as they vary from us

Worry is futile and senseless, being born often of a
blindness that will not wait

WHEN a man tells you that the majority of
women do not want to vote, and therefore
Equal Suffrage should not be granted, set
him down as a Poll Parrot that has been
instructed by a Monkey

If Suffrage were compulsory it might be a hardship
to force it upon those who did not want it, simply
because there were others who did. But since the
women who do not want to vote, will, after the right
of Suffrage is granted, occupy exactly the same status
that they do now, they have no moral right to interpose their inertia as a reason why women who wish
to vote should be told they can't.

In other words, that some women do not want
to vote is no reason that no one should, any more
than that no male man should be allowed to vote
because others sell their votes

Voting is the act of recording your preferences.

All people who are not mental defectives are
interested in good government.

⟨ For a woman to exercise her sense of choice between political candidates is both natural and right. No one will dispute this, save those strange male men who imagine that through the accident of sex one-half of the race should be penalized; and those other male men, equally strange, who, without the sense of humor, maintain that brains is a monopoly of the male ⟨⟩ ⟨⟩
Education up to the time of Friedrich Froebel was the evolution of intellect ⟨⟩ ⟨⟩
Froebel held that education for character was the only education worth striving for.

⟨ Now comes Stanley Hall, who not only endorses Froebel's dictum, but declares that the first aim in the education of both boys and girls should be in the line of enabling the pupil to earn his own living.

⟨ And to earn your own living you must be able to serve humanity ⟨⟩ ⟨⟩
Society is a vast interchange of service through labor, ideas and commodities ⟨⟩ ⟨⟩
Now before you can wait on others you must be able to wait on yourself ⟨⟩ ⟨⟩
And before you wait on yourself, you have to decide upon what should be done, and what you want to do.

⟨ " The ability to make a decision—to think—then decide—is the very first element in pedagogy," said Froebel ⟨⟩ ⟨⟩
Again he says to mothers : " Do not decide everything for your children. You can not live their lives for them; and life consists in making decisions—clinging to the good and rejecting the wrong."

⟨ So if life consists, as Froebel says—and it seems to me that he is right—in making decisions, women should be encouraged to express their preferences.

LET me here say that women are the mothers of the race—the mothers of men. I hope that no dogmatist will arise and dispute the proposition ⟨⟩ ⟨⟩
So let us agree that women are the mothers of men.

⟨ Following this, I would also say that a woman's

children partake of her qualities; that a weak, irritable, idle and vain mother will be apt to produce a
brood that resembles her

On the other hand, the children of a wise, patient,
helpful and practical mother will be very apt to be
like her

If she has exercised her sense of choice, has made
decisions and come to conclusions, it will be easy
for her offspring to do likewise. When you decide,
you think. And no one can intelligently decide without
being better for the effort.

"The making of decisions leads to the habit of
self-reliance," says Froebel. And so I am led to believe
that the right of Suffrage is a movement toward the
higher mental development of woman.

The idea of the " kept woman," whether married
or not, is abhorrent to all good men and women. No
strong man wants a wife for whom he has to think.
Let her think, reason, decide—and by deciding she
will learn to decide

Women will never take a personal interest in the
Science of Government until they have a share in
its making

This is not a question of whether woman's vote will
give us a better government or not. My opinion is
that it will. But the real question is: Shall woman
be educated, or must she forever be kept a ward, a
doll and a plaything?

The welfare of the human race demands that
mothers should extend and widen their mental visions,
and that all which tends to enlarge woman's mentality
is good, and that which tends to limit, repress or suppress her is bad

THE Suffrage for woman means freedom—freedom
from her own limitations. It means a better education of women. And woman needs education for
three reasons:

First, for her own happiness and satisfaction

Second, so she may be a better mother, and add her influence to racial education.

Third, so that she may be a better companion for man, for all strong men are educated by women ⚹ ⚹

There may be good reasons why woman should be debarred from exercising her natural right to have her political preferences recorded, but I do not know what they are. All of the reasons which have been brought forward why women who wish to vote should not be allowed to vote have been exploded—try something new or read the " Essay on Silence " ! ⚹ ⚹

And yet one still hears how if women were allowed to vote, only the bad ones would avail themselves of the privilege. This is absolutely the reverse of truth. Equal Suffrage is now legalized in six States in the Union. The one report from these States is that the educated women vote, and the others do not. In Denver, the residence precincts, where the houses are largely owned by the occupants, gave the largest return of votes by women. The red-light districts and the tenements gave the smallest return ⚹ ⚹

Also fletcherize on this: Judge Ben B. Lindsey, the creator of the Juvenile Court in America, was opposed in Denver by the two big machine tickets.

�‖ He was elected on a very safe plurality by women. Why? ⚹ ⚹

Oh, I 'll tell you.

Women are mothers—actual, vicarious or potential. Ben Lindsey is the friend of the children. He stands between the child and the cold, cruel and often inhuman clutch of the Law. The Law threatened to strike the child. And lo! the great mother-heart throbbed with a divine indignation; and Ben Lindsey was endorsed with an emphasis that made the demagogues stand and stare. The women of Denver placed a hex on the rule of the boss, for once.

�‖ Do not say that woman has no sense of justice. Strike her child and see what happens to you ⚹ ⚹

Educate her, and in time all wrongs will go. Leave her forever a minor before the Law, and many wrongs will continue to flourish

Nature is the best guide of which we know, and the love of simple pleasures is next, if not superior to religion

The big reward is not for the man who will lighten our burdens, but for him who will give us strength to carry them

Insomnia never comes to a man who has to get up at six o'clock. Insomnia troubles only those who can sleep at any time

HE success of every great man hinges on one thing—to pick your men to do the work. The efforts of any one man count for so very little! It all depends on the selection and management of men to carry out your plans. In every successful concern, whether it be bank, school, factory, steamship company or railroad, the spirit of one man runs through and animates the entire institution. The success or failure of the enterprise turns on the mental, moral and spiritual qualities of this one man. And the leader who can imbue an army of workers with a spirit of earnest fidelity to duty, an unswerving desire to do the thing that should be done, and always with animation, kindness and good-cheer, should be ranked with the great of the earth

There is no prophylactic equal to equanimity

To supply a thought is mental massage; but to evolve a thought of your own is an achievement. Thinking is a brain exercise—and no faculty grows save as it is exercised

LIFE, now, is human service.

¶ To deceive is to beckon for the Commissioner in Bankruptcy.

¶ Nothing goes but truth

We know this—because for over two thousand years we have been trying everything else.

¶ Academic education is the act of memorizing things read in books, and things told by college professors who got their education mostly by memorizing things read in books and told by college professors

It is easier to be taught than to attain.

¶ It is easier to accept than to investigate. It is easier to follow than to lead—usually

Yet we are all heir to peculiar, unique and individual talents, and a few men are not content to follow. These have usually been killed, and suddenly

Now, our cry is, " Make room for individuality!'

TRUTH," says Doctor Charles W. Eliot, " is the new virtue."

Let the truth be known about your business

The only man who should not advertise is the one who has nothing to offer in way of service, or one who can not make good.

¶ All such should seek the friendly shelter of oblivion where dwell those who, shrouded in Stygian shades foregather gloom, and are out of the game.

¶ Not to advertise is to be nominated for membership in the Down-and-Out Club

About the best we can say of the days that are gone is that they are gone

The Adscripts and the Adcrafts look to the East They worship the rising sun. The oleo of authority does not much interest them. They want the Cosmic Kerosene that supplies the caloric.

¶ A good Adcraftscripter is never either a philophraster or a theologaster—he is a pragmatist. He seeks the good for himself, for his clients, and for the whole human race

The science of advertising is the science of psychology.
And psychology is the science of the human heart.

❦ The advertiser works to supply a human want;
and often he has to arouse the desire for his goods.
He educates the public as to what it needs, and what
it wants, and shows where and how to get it ❦ ❦
The idea of the " ethical dentist " who refrains from
advertising was originally founded on the proposition
derived from the medicos that advertising was fakery.
This view once had a certain basis in fact, when the
only people who advertised were transients. The merchant who lived in a town assumed that every one
knew where he was and what he had to offer. The
doctor the same ❦ ❦
This no longer applies. We are living so fast, and
inventing so fast, and changing so fast, and there are
so many of us, that he who does not advertise is left
to the spiders, the cockroaches and the microbes.

❦ The fact that you have all the business you can well
manage is no excuse now for not advertising ❦ ❦

O stand still is to retreat. To worship the god
Terminus is to have the Goths and Vandals that
skirt the borders of every successful venture pick up
your Terminii and carry them inland, long miles,
between the setting of the sun and his rising.

❦ To hold the old customers, you must get out after
the new ❦ ❦
When you think you are big enough, there is lime in
the bones of the boss, and a noise like a buccaneer is
heard in the offing.

❦ The reputation that endures, or the institution
that lasts, is the one that is properly advertised ❦ ❦
The only names in Greek History that we know are
those which Herodotus and Thucydides graved with
deathless styli ❦ ❦
The men of Rome who live and tread the boardwalk
are those Plutarch took up and writ their names large
on human hearts ❦ ❦

All that Plutarch knew of Greek heroes was what he read in Herodotus 〰 〰

All that Shakespeare knew of Classic Greece and Rome and the heroes of that far-off time is what he dug out of Plutarch's Lives. And about all that most people now know of Greece and Rome they got from Shakespeare 〰 〰

Plutarch boomed his Roman friends and matched each favorite with some Greek, written of by Herodotus. Plutarch wrote of the men he liked, some of whom we know put up good mazuma to cover expenses 〰 〰

ᗷUT of all the Plenipotentiaries of Publicity, Ambassadors of Advertising, and Bosses of Press Bureaus, none equals Moses, who lived fifteen centuries before Christ. Moses appointed himself adwriter for Deity, and gave us an account of Creation, from the personal interviews. And although some say these interviews were faked, this account has been accepted for thirty-five centuries.

❧ Moses wrote the first five books of the Bible, and this account includes a record of the author's romantic birth and of his serene and dignified death. Moses is the central figure, after Yahweh, in the whole write-up.

❧ Egyptian history makes not a single mention of Moses or the Exodus, and no record is found of the flight from Egypt save what Moses wrote 〰 〰

At best it was only a few hundred people who hiked, but the account makes the whole thing seem colossal and magnificent. And best of all, the high standard set has been an inspiration to millions to live up to the dope 〰 〰

The phrase, " The Chosen People of God," was a catch-phrase unrivaled. Slogans abound in Moses that have been taken up by millions on millions.

❧ When Moses took over the Judaic account, Jehovah was only a tutelary or tribal god. He was simply one of the many. He had at least forty strong com-

petitors. The Egyptians had various gods; the Midianites, Hittites, Philistines, Amorites, Ammonites had at least one god each
Moses made his god supreme, and all other gods were driven from the skies.

❧ What turned the trick?
I'll tell you—the writings of Moses, and nothing else. So able, convincing, direct and inclusive were the claims of Moses that the world was absolutely won by them
In the Mosaic Code was enough of the saving salt of commonsense to keep it alive. It was a religion for the now and here. The Mosaic laws are sanitary laws, and work for the positive, present good of those who abide by them
It is not deeds or acts that last—it is the written record of those deeds and acts.

❧ It was not the life and death of Jesus that fixed His place as the central figure of His time—and perhaps of all time—it was what Paul and certain unknown writers who never even saw Him claimed and had to say in written words
HORATIUS still stands at the bridge, because a poet placed him there
And Paul Revere still rides a-down the night giving his warning cry, because Longfellow set the meters in a gallop.

❧ Across the waste of waters the enemy calls upon Paul Jones to surrender, and the voice of Paul Jones echoes back, " Goddam your souls to Hell—we have not yet begun to fight! " And the sound of the fearless voice has given courage to countless thousands to snatch victory from the jaws of defeat
In Brussels there is yet to be heard a sound of revelry by night, only because Byron told of it.

❧ Commodore Perry, that rash and impulsive youth of twenty-six, never sent that message, " We have met the enemy and they are ours," but a good

reporter did, and the reporter's words live, while
Perry's died on the empty air 🙢 🙢
Lord Douglas never said,

> " The hand of Douglas is his own,
> And never shall in friendship grasp,
> The hand of such as Marmion clasp."

❡ Sir Walter Scott made that remark on white paper
with an eagle's quill, and schoolboys' hearts will beat
high as they scorn the offered hand on Friday after-
noons, for centuries to come 🙢 🙢
Virginius lives in heroic mold, not for what he said
or did, but for the words put into his mouth by a man
who pushed what you call a virile pen and wrote such
an ad for Virginius as he could never have written for
himself 🙢 🙢
Andrew J. Rowan carried the Message to Garcia,
all right, but the deed would have been lost in the
dustbin of Time, and quickly, too, were it not for
George H. Daniels, who etched the act into the
memory of the race, and fixed the deed in history, sending it down the corridors of Time with the rumble of
the Empire State Express, so that today it is a part of
the current coin of the mental realm, a legal tender
wherever English she is spoke 🙢 🙢
ALL literature is advertising. And all genuine
advertisements are literature 🙢 🙢
The author advertises men, times, places, deeds,
events and things. His appeal is to the universal
human soul. If he does not know the heart-throbs of
men and women, their hopes, joys, ambitions, tastes,
needs and desires, his work will interest no one but
himself and his admiring friends 🙢 🙢
Advertising is fast becoming a fine art. Its theme is
Human Wants, and where, when and how they may
be gratified. It interests, inspires, educates—sometimes amuses—informs and thereby uplifts and benefits, lubricating existence and helping the old world
on its way to the Celestial City of Fine Minds 🙢 🙢

Swollen fortunes are not nearly so dangerous as a
swollen navy. A nation which thinks it can lick the
world is getting ready to get licked

A man who can't forget is quite as bad as the one
who can't remember. Everybody should remember
to forget

Be natural and be proper, but not too proper

A degenerate is a man who renders the world no
service—who receives, but does not bestow, and who
has no disposition to carry his share of life's burdens.

To benefit others, you must be reasonably happy:
there must be animation through useful activity,
good-cheer, kindness and health—health of mind
and health of body

Metaphysics is the explanation of a thing by a person
who does not understand it

O this, then, is an essay on The American
Philosophy
The American Philosophy is founded on the
Science of Economics.

Just here, in order that we may speak a common
language, a few definitions are in order
Economics is the Science of the production, distribution and use of wealth
Science is accurate, organized knowledge founded on
fact—or, as Herbert Spencer expressed it, "Science
is the classified knowledge of the common people."

All that which is simply assumed, believed, con-
jectured, taken on dogmatic statement, or read out
of printed books, is unscientific, no matter how plausi-
ble

All practical businessmen are scientists.

⁋ Business is a vocation. Philosophy is—or should be—an avocation

To make a business of philosophy is to institutionalize and dilute it, just as to institutionalize love and religion is to degrade and lose them.

⁋ Religion is philosophy touched with emotion

Philosophy is your highest conception of life, its duties and its destiny

A religious organization is a different thing from religion. A religious organization is built on a feeling made static, or fear frozen stiff. It then becomes a superstition, and is employed as a police system, and is taxed all the traffic will bear

ⓈCIENCE is definite, accurate, organized knowledge concerning the things that make up our environment

Modern philosophy is the distilled essence of wisdom that eventually flows from science. Or, if you please, philosophy is the explanation of science—a projection from science

Transportation, manufacturing, distribution, advertising, salesmanship, all are variants of business. Each and all are scientific, that is, capable of analyzation and demonstration. Weight, size, color, number, qualities and time are all elements of science. Theology is antique and obsolete philosophy. It never is nor ever was scientific, not being derived from knowledge. Faith is the first item in its formula. Theology comes to us from the dogmatic statements gotten from books or the hearsay words of men long dead.

⁋ Theology is voodooism; in matters of importance it is in the class with alchemy, astrology, palmistry, augury and allopath medicine.

⁋ Science is understood, theology believed

Psychology is the science of human minds and their relationship one to another

Superstition is scrambled science, or religious omelet, flavored with fear

Organized religion, being founded on superstition, is, perforce, not scientific. And all that which is not scientific—that is, truthful—must be bolstered by force, fear and falsehood. Thus we always find slavery and organized religion going hand in hand ⚘ ⚘

BUSINESS, to be successful, must be based on science, for demand and supply are matters of mathematics, not guesswork. Civilization turns on organization. And organization, in order to be of any value, must be scientific ⚘ ⚘

Economics is a new science. History does not show a single instance of its existence in the days of Greece and Rome. They had simple mathematics, but not complex. Fractions, percentages, statistics, averages were beyond them. The blueprint, even for humorists, was unguessed. Philosophy was speculation; business was barter. Since then, up to within ten years ago, the problem of how man could save his soul has been uppermost. This world has been neglected in the endeavor to gain another ⚘ ⚘

When the Science of Economics is finally formulated, it will be expressed first in America. In America all the nations meet and blend. Here the factors, elements and categories of Economics are to be found. Here we have one language, and no more, and this is necessary for the expression of a new science ⚘ ⚘

The first endeavor to found Economics as a science was the work of Adam Smith.

⟨ And when Thomas Henry Buckle said that Adam Smith's " Wealth of Nations " had influenced the world for good more than any other book ever written, save none, he stated truth ⚘ ⚘

Economics changes man's activities. As you change a man's activities you change his way of living, and as you change his environment you change his state of mind. Precept and injunction do not perceptibly affect men; but food, water, air, clothing, shelter, pictures, books, music, will and do.

⁋ An Indian baby taken to New England and adopted into a Massachusetts family will grow up the proud possessor of all the Yankee prejudices and peccadillos.

⁋ Adam Smith, John Stuart Mill and Karl Marx all wrote on Economics, but none was an Economist. Each based his logic largely on presumption, assumption and hypothesis. If this happens, then that will occur

They were Political Economists—they pursued Economics as a policy, not as truth. They loved love, not the lady. They were students of Economics, and their work was not grounded in Science

Since the days of Smith, Mill and Marx we have had many students of Economics.

⁋ But the world has not yet produced an Economist. To be an Economist, a man must first be a Scientist. He must be both a man of action and one who knows why he acts. He must work and he must contemplate his work. He must act and he must think.

⁋ A Scientist is the man who has done the thing— who has seen and knows. Then from his positive knowledge springs his Philosophy. And the Philosophy of a businessman, analyzed, explained and formulated, would constitute a Science of Economics

THE American Philosophy will be formulated by Scientists—by Businessmen who have succeeded. Thackeray's lawyer in the Debtor's Prison, who was working out a new financial policy for the Nation, was not a Scientist. His knowledge was academic and his scheme conjectural. Science was outside of his orbit. He lacked experience. He had feelings, but not facts. He did not have enough cosmic mortar to construct an arch

Emotionalism, charity, altruism, optimism are not science, and they may be hysteria.

⁋ When I speak of success I do not mean it in the sordid sense

A successful man is one who has tried, not cried; who has worked, not dodged; who has shouldered responsibility, not evaded it; who has gotten under the burden, not merely stood off, looking on, giving advice and philosophizing on the situation The result of a man's work is not the measure of success. To go down with the ship in storm and tempest is better than to paddle away to Paradise in an Orthodox canoe

To have worked is to have succeeded—we leave the results to time. Life is too short to gather the Harvest —we can only sow

UP to the year Eighteen Hundred Seventy-six the business world was tainted by trickery in trade. The methods of booth and bazaar were everywhere practised. Business was barter, and he who could cheat and not get caught was accounted clever. On the customs of the time there was no copyright. They were a take-over from monarchial days.

But a new ethic has arrived. Within ten years' time the thought has gone through the entire business fabric that to cheat and not get caught is really a worse calamity than to get caught.

To be caught means that some one has applied the brake and you are given pause

Not to get caught means that you are headed for the precipice on the high clutch and down grade.

To cheat another is to cheat yourself

Theology did not teach us this, for precept and preaching never touch our lives. We shed them.

We are moved in only one way, and that is by self-interest. Cut off our food-supply and we are no longer apathetic

And self-interest is a form of selfishness; it is the desire for life. It is the instinct of self-preservation in action

It was all a matter of mental growth, evolution

The discovery of truth as our most valuable business

asset is the one great achievement of the age in which
we live. For truth there is no substitute, and this
discovery was made by businessmen.

❡ Honesty as a working policy was first put forth
by Benjamin Franklin; and his remark was regarded
as a pleasantry until yesterday.

❡ The clergy have not yet adopted it; the doctors
are considering it, and the lawyers have n't heard of
it ⸰⸰ ⸰⸰

However, all these will finally adopt it, as a last resort,
as a means of self-preservation ⸰⸰ ⸰⸰

ℭONOMICS based on falsehood leads to dissolution. Falsehood is a polite form of conquest.
The lie is exploitation ⸰⸰ ⸰⸰

The preacher has diverted us while the lawyer picked
our pocket; the doctor gives you ether and accomplishes the same result ⸰⸰ ⸰⸰

Egypt, Rome and Greece lived on their slaves and
outlying colonies. Slave labor is the most expensive
kind. In time the land is exhausted, and the slaves die.

❡ But before this happened to the capitals that were,
the aristocrats who wasted, destroyed and consumed
had gotten nervous debility, and were impotent, also
impudent ⸰⸰ ⸰⸰

Then they died and the barbarian overran the land.

❡ A wise Economist—and America has many—could
have figured out exactly how long Babylon and Nine-
veh would have lasted ⸰⸰ ⸰⸰

None of these ancient civilizations produced economists. They had soothsayers, priests, lawyers, poets,
artists, clowns, dramatists, orators, rhetoricians,
singers, philosophers. And most of all they had
guzzlers and gourmands ⸰⸰ ⸰⸰

But they had no scientists, and their philosophy,
being based on augury, dreams, theology and fear,
was futile and fallacious.

❡ A philosophy that is not founded on science is
false in theory and base in practise ⸰⸰ ⸰⸰

ODERN business betters human environment. It means gardens, flowers, fruits, vegetables; it means quick, safe and cheap transportation of people, commodities and messages; it means books, maps, furniture, pictures, playgrounds, pure water, perfect sewerage, fresh air, sunshine, health, happiness, hope, light and love—because business gives opportunities for all to work, earn, grow and become.

Business consists in the production, transportation and distribution of the things that are necessary to human life. Through this exercise of our faculties we educe the best that is in us; in other words, we get an education. Inasmuch as business supplies the necessities of life, it is impossible to have a highly evolved and noble race except where there is a science of business.

Business is human service. Therefore, business is essentially a divine calling

Once men believed religion to be the chief concern of mortals here below

Other men have thought that killing is the chief concern of mortals here below.

Gladstone once said, " Only two avenues of honor are open to young men in England—the army and the church."

This has been the prevailing opinion of the world for nearly two thousand years, and is the one reason why the Dark Ages were dark. During those years of night the fighting man was supreme. It was a long panic, and human evolution was blocked through fear. The race crawled, crept, hid, dodged, secreted, lied, and nearly died

We now say that the Science of Economics, or Business, is the chief concern of humanity. Business is intelligent, useful activity. The word " busy-ness " was coined during the time of Chaucer by certain soldier-aristocrats, men of the leisure class, who prided themselves upon the fact that they did no useful thing. Men of power proved their prowess by holding slaves,

and these slaves did all the work. To be idle showed
that one was not a slave.

¶ But this word " business," first flung in contempt,
like Puritan, Methodist and Quaker, has now become
a thing of which to be proud. Idleness is the disgrace,
not busy-ness

The world can be redeemed through business only;
for business means betterment, and no business can
now succeed that does not add to human happiness.

W̱E believe that only the busy person is happy,
and that systematic, daily, useful work is man's
greatest blessing.

¶ We are a nation of workers, builders, inventors,
creators, producers

We are the richest country, per capita, in the world;
and our wealth has come from the farm, the forest,
the factory, the mine, the sea.

¶ We have dug, plowed, pumped, smelted, refined,
transported and manufactured. We did not inherit
our wealth, neither have we laid tribute on other
countries as did those earlier civilizations

Any individual who uses the word " commercial "
as an epithet, who regards business enterprise as
synonymous with graft and greed, who speaks of
certain men as " self-made " and others as " educated," who gives more attention to war than to
peace, who seeks to destroy rather than to create
and build up, is essentially un-American.

¶ The word " education " sometimes stands for
idleness, but The American Philosophy symbols
work, effort, industry. It means intelligent, thoughtful, reasonable and wise busy-ness—helping yourself
by helping others

The world's greatest prizes in the future will go to
the businessman. The businessman is our only scientist,
and to him we must look for a Science of Economics
that will eradicate poverty, disease, superstition—
all that dissipates and destroys. The day is dawning!

So here, then, endeth *AN AMERICAN BIBLE*, and the same is submitted to the people, young and old, in the hope that it will help them to live, and mayhap, inspire them to write or compile other Bibles and better Bibles. Done into print by The Roycrofters, at their Shop, which is in East Aurora, Erie County, New York, Anno Domini, Nineteen Hundred Eleven.

www.ingramcontent.com/pod-product-compliance
Lightning Source LLC
Chambersburg PA
CBHW021210090426
42740CB00006B/177